CANADIAN POLITICAL PARTIES IN THE CONSTITUENCIES

*This is Volume 23 in a series of studies
commissioned as part of the research program
of the Royal Commission on Electoral Reform
and Party Financing*

CANADIAN POLITICAL PARTIES IN THE CONSTITUENCIES

R.K. Carty

Volume 23 of the Research Studies

ROYAL COMMISSION ON ELECTORAL REFORM
AND PARTY FINANCING
AND CANADA COMMUNICATION GROUP –
PUBLISHING, SUPPLY AND SERVICES CANADA

DUNDURN PRESS
TORONTO AND OXFORD

© Minister of Supply and Services Canada, 1991
Printed and bound in Canada
ISBN 1-55002-119-2
ISSN 1188-2743
Catalogue No. Z1-1989/2-41-23E

Published by Dundurn Press Limited in cooperation with the Royal
Commission on Electoral Reform and Party Financing and Canada
Communication Group – Publishing, Supply and Services Canada.

Canadian Cataloguing in Publication Data

Carty, R. Kenneth, 1944–
Canadian political parties in the constituencies

(Research studies ; 23)
Issued also in French under title: L'action des partis politiques dans les
  circonscriptions au Canada.
ISBN 1-55002-119-2

  1. Politics, Practical – Canada. 2. Canada. Parliament – Election districts.
3. Political parties – Canada. I. Canada. Royal Commission on Electoral
Reform and Party Financing. II. Title. III. Series: Research studies (Canada.
Royal Commission on Electoral Reform and Party Financing) ; 23.

JL195.C37 1991   324.7′0971   C91-090535-5

$24.95

Dundurn Press Limited   Dundurn Distribution
2181 Queen Street East   73 Lime Walk
Suite 301   Headington
Toronto, Canada   Oxford, England
M4E 1E5   OX3 7AD

CONTENTS

FIGURES

TABLES

FOREWORD

THE ROYAL COMMISSION on Electoral Reform and Party Financing was established in November 1989. Our mandate was to inquire into and report on the appropriate principles and process that should govern the election of members of the House of Commons and the financing of political parties and candidates' campaigns. To conduct such a comprehensive examination of Canada's electoral system, we held extensive public consultations and developed a research program designed to ensure that our recommendations would be guided by an independent foundation of empirical inquiry and analysis.

The Commission's in-depth review of the electoral system was the first of its kind in Canada's history of electoral democracy. It was dictated largely by the major constitutional, social and technological changes of the past several decades, which have transformed Canadian society, and their concomitant influence on Canadians' expectations of the political process itself. In particular, the adoption in 1982 of the *Canadian Charter of Rights and Freedoms* has heightened Canadians' awareness of their democratic and political rights and of the way they are served by the electoral system.

The importance of electoral reform cannot be overemphasized. As the Commission's work proceeded, Canadians became increasingly preoccupied with constitutional issues that have the potential to change the nature of Confederation. No matter what their beliefs or political allegiances in this continuing debate, Canadians agree that constitutional change must be achieved in the context of fair and democratic processes. We cannot complacently assume that our current electoral process will always meet this standard or that it leaves no room for improvement. Parliament and the national government must be seen as legitimate; electoral reform can both enhance the stature of national political institutions and reinforce their ability to define the future of our country in ways that command Canadians' respect and confidence and promote the national interest.

In carrying out our mandate, we remained mindful of the importance of protecting our democratic heritage, while at the same time balancing it against the emerging values that are injecting a new dynamic into the electoral system. If our system is to reflect the realities of Canadian political life, then reform requires more than mere tinkering with electoral laws and practices.

Our broad mandate challenged us to explore a full range of options. We commissioned more than 100 research studies, to be published in a 23-volume collection. In the belief that our electoral laws must measure up to the very best contemporary practice, we examined election-related laws and processes in all of our provinces and territories and studied comparable legislation and processes in established democracies around the world. This unprecedented array of empirical study and expert opinion made a vital contribution to our deliberations. We made every effort to ensure that the research was both intellectually rigorous and of practical value. All studies were subjected to peer review, and many of the authors discussed their preliminary findings with members of the political and academic communities at national symposiums on major aspects of the electoral system.

The Commission placed the research program under the able and inspired direction of Dr. Peter Aucoin, Professor of Political Science and Public Administration at Dalhousie University. We are confident that the efforts of Dr. Aucoin, together with those of the research coordinators and scholars whose work appears in this and other volumes, will continue to be of value to historians, political scientists, parliamentarians and policy makers, as well as to thoughtful Canadians and the international community.

Along with the other Commissioners, I extend my sincere gratitude to the entire Commission staff for their dedication and commitment. I also wish to thank the many people who participated in our symposiums for their valuable contributions, as well as the members of the research and practitioners' advisory groups whose counsel significantly aided our undertaking.

Pierre Lortie
Chairman

INTRODUCTION

The Royal Commission's research program constituted a comprehensive and detailed examination of the Canadian electoral process. The scope of the research, undertaken to assist Commissioners in their deliberations, was dictated by the broad mandate given to the Commission.

The objective of the research program was to provide Commissioners with a full account of the factors that have shaped our electoral democracy. This dictated, first and foremost, a focus on federal electoral law, but our inquiries also extended to the Canadian constitution, including the institutions of parliamentary government, the practices of political parties, the mass media and nonpartisan political organizations, as well as the decision-making role of the courts with respect to the constitutional rights of citizens. Throughout, our research sought to introduce a historical perspective in order to place the contemporary experience within the Canadian political tradition.

We recognized that neither our consideration of the factors shaping Canadian electoral democracy nor our assessment of reform proposals would be as complete as necessary if we failed to examine the experiences of Canadian provinces and territories and of other democracies. Our research program thus emphasized comparative dimensions in relation to the major subjects of inquiry.

Our research program involved, in addition to the work of the Commission's research coordinators, analysts and support staff, over 200 specialists from 28 universities in Canada, from the private sector and, in a number of cases, from abroad. Specialists in political science constituted the majority of our researchers, but specialists in law, economics, management, computer sciences, ethics, sociology and communications, among other disciplines, were also involved.

In addition to the preparation of research studies for the Commission, our research program included a series of research seminars, symposiums and workshops. These meetings brought together the Commissioners, researchers, representatives from the political parties, media personnel and others with practical experience in political parties, electoral politics and public affairs. These meetings provided not only a forum for discussion of the various subjects of the Commission's mandate, but also an opportunity for our research to be assessed by those with an intimate knowledge of the world of political practice.

These public reviews of our research were complemented by internal and external assessments of each research report by persons qualified in the area; such assessments were completed prior to our decision to publish any study in the series of research volumes.

The Research Branch of the Commission was divided into several areas, with the individual research projects in each area assigned to the research coordinators as follows:

F. Leslie Seidle	Political Party and Election Finance
Herman Bakvis	Political Parties
Kathy Megyery	Women, Ethno-cultural Groups and Youth
David Small	Redistribution; Electoral Boundaries; Voter Registration
Janet Hiebert	Party Ethics
Michael Cassidy	Democratic Rights; Election Administration
Robert A. Milen	Aboriginal Electoral Participation and Representation
Frederick J. Fletcher	Mass Media and Broadcasting in Elections
David Mac Donald (Assistant Research Coordinator)	Direct Democracy

These coordinators identified appropriate specialists to undertake research, managed the projects and prepared them for publication. They also organized the seminars, symposiums and workshops in their research areas and were responsible for preparing presentations and briefings to help the Commission in its deliberations and decision making. Finally, they participated in drafting the Final Report of the Commission.

On behalf of the Commission, I welcome the opportunity to thank the following for their generous assistance in producing these research studies – a project that required the talents of many individuals.

In performing their duties, the research coordinators made a notable contribution to the work of the Commission. Despite the pressures of tight deadlines, they worked with unfailing good humour and the utmost congeniality. I thank all of them for their consistent support and cooperation.

In particular, I wish to express my gratitude to Leslie Seidle, senior research coordinator, who supervised our research analysts and support staff in Ottawa. His diligence, commitment and professionalism not only set high standards, but also proved contagious. I am grateful to Kathy Megyery, who performed a similar function in Montreal with equal aplomb and skill. Her enthusiasm and dedication inspired us all.

On behalf of the research coordinators and myself, I wish to thank our research analysts: Daniel Arsenault, Eric Bertram, Cécile Boucher, Peter Constantinou, Yves Denoncourt, David Docherty, Luc Dumont, Jane Dunlop, Scott Evans, Véronique Garneau, Keith Heintzman, Paul Holmes, Hugh Mellon, Cheryl D. Mitchell, Donald Padget, Alain Pelletier, Dominique Tremblay and Lisa Young. The Research Branch was strengthened by their ability to carry out research in a wide variety of areas, their intellectual curiosity and their team spirit.

The work of the research coordinators and analysts was greatly facilitated by the professional skills and invaluable cooperation of Research Branch staff members: Paulette LeBlanc, who, as administrative assistant, managed the flow of research projects; Hélène Leroux, secretary to the research coordinators, who produced briefing material for the Commissioners and who, with Lori Nazar, assumed responsibility for monitoring the progress of research projects in the latter stages of our work; Kathleen McBride and her assistant Natalie Brose, who created and maintained the database of briefs and hearings transcripts; and Richard Herold and his assistant Susan Dancause, who were responsible for our research library. Jacinthe Séguin and Cathy Tucker also deserve thanks – in addition to their duties as receptionists, they assisted in a variety of ways to help us meet deadlines.

We were extremely fortunate to obtain the research services of first-class specialists from the academic and private sectors. Their contributions are found in this and the other 22 published research volumes. We thank them for the quality of their work and for their willingness to contribute and to meet our tight deadlines.

Our research program also benefited from the counsel of Jean-Marc Hamel, Special Adviser to the Chairman of the Commission and former

Chief Electoral Officer of Canada, whose knowledge and experience proved invaluable.

In addition, numerous specialists assessed our research studies. Their assessments not only improved the quality of our published studies, but also provided us with much-needed advice on many issues. In particular, we wish to single out professors Donald Blake, Janine Brodie, Alan Cairns, Kenneth Carty, John Courtney, Peter Desbarats, Jane Jenson, Richard Johnston, Vincent Lemieux, Terry Morley and Joseph Wearing, as well as Ms. Beth Symes.

Producing such a large number of studies in less than a year requires a mastery of the skills and logistics of publishing. We were fortunate to be able to count on the Commission's Director of Communications, Richard Rochefort, and Assistant Director, Hélène Papineau. They were ably supported by the Communications staff: Patricia Burden, Louise Dagenais, Caroline Field, Claudine Labelle, France Langlois, Lorraine Maheux, Ruth McVeigh, Chantal Morissette, Sylvie Patry, Jacques Poitras and Claudette Rouleau-O'Toole.

To bring the project to fruition, the Commission also called on specialized contractors. We are deeply grateful for the services of Ann McCoomb (references and fact checking); Marthe Lemery, Pierre Chagnon and the staff of Communications Com'ça (French quality control); Norman Bloom, Pamela Riseborough and associates of B&B Editorial Consulting (English adaptation and quality control); and Mado Reid (French production). Al Albania and his staff at Acart Graphics designed the studies and produced some 2 400 tables and figures.

The Commission's research reports constitute Canada's largest publishing project of 1991. Successful completion of the project required close cooperation between the public and private sectors. In the public sector, we especially acknowledge the excellent service of the Privy Council unit of the Translation Bureau, Department of the Secretary of State of Canada, under the direction of Michel Parent, and our contacts Ruth Steele and Terry Denovan of the Canada Communication Group, Department of Supply and Services.

The Commission's co-publisher for the research studies was Dundurn Press of Toronto, whose exceptional service is gratefully acknowledged. Wilson & Lafleur of Montreal, working with the Centre de Documentation Juridique du Québec, did equally admirable work in preparing the French version of the studies.

Teams of editors, copy editors and proofreaders worked diligently under stringent deadlines with the Commission and the publishers to prepare some 20 000 pages of manuscript for design, typesetting and printing. The work of these individuals, whose names are listed elsewhere in this volume, was greatly appreciated.

Our acknowledgements extend to the contributions of the Commission's Executive Director, Guy Goulard, and the administration and executive support teams: Maurice Lacasse, Denis Lafrance and Steve Tremblay (finance); Thérèse Lacasse and Mary Guy-Shea (personnel); Cécile Desforges (assistant to the Executive Director); Marie Dionne (administration); Anna Bevilacqua (records); and support staff members Michelle Bélanger, Roch Langlois, Michel Lauzon, Jean Mathieu, David McKay and Pierrette McMurtie, as well as Denise Miquelon and Christiane Séguin of the Montreal office.

A special debt of gratitude is owed to Marlène Girard, assistant to the Chairman. Her ability to supervise the logistics of the Commission's work amid the tight schedules of the Chairman and Commissioners contributed greatly to the completion of our task.

I also wish to express my deep gratitude to my own secretary, Liette Simard. Her superb administrative skills and great patience brought much-appreciated order to my penchant for the chaotic workstyle of academe. She also assumed responsibility for the administrative coordination of revisions to the final drafts of volumes 1 and 2 of the Commission's Final Report. I owe much to her efforts and assistance.

Finally, on behalf of the research coordinators and myself, I wish to thank the Chairman, Pierre Lortie, the members of the Commission, Pierre Fortier, Robert Gabor, William Knight and Lucie Pépin, and former members Elwood Cowley and Senator Donald Oliver. We are honoured to have worked with such an eminent and thoughtful group of Canadians, and we have benefited immensely from their knowledge and experience. In particular, we wish to acknowledge the creativity, intellectual rigour and energy our Chairman brought to our task. His unparalleled capacity to challenge, to bring out the best in us, was indeed inspiring.

Peter Aucoin
Director of Research

PREFACE

During the course of its hearings and through written submissions, the Royal Commission on Electoral Reform and Party Financing heard a variety of proposals for improving the electoral process, extending the scope of public funding for political parties, enhancing the capacity of political parties to select more women and members of visible minorities as candidates for political office, ensuring greater financial disclosure at the constituency level and requiring more democratic selection processes at the local level.

The Commission soon realized, however, that the feasibility of and means for implementing these proposals could only be assessed in light of the capacity of party officials and members at the local constituency association level to handle these changes. Two of the more striking features of Canadian political parties are that they are territorially based organizations and that the local associations of the national parties have significant responsibilities for candidate selection and the conduct of election campaigns. To obtain a better sense of the problems facing local associations and candidates the Commission organized, in the fall of 1990, a series of seminars with official agents for candidates and local officials from Elections Canada. It was felt, however, that the Commission needed to cast its net wider and obtain the views of as many local party officials as possible on all issues of electoral reform likely to affect the local associations.

For these reasons R. Kenneth Carty was asked to carry out a comprehensive survey of the local associations of the three traditional parties and of two of the newer parties – the Liberal Party of Canada, the Progressive Conservative Party of Canada, the New Democratic Party, the Reform Party of Canada and the Christian Heritage Party. The aim was to elicit the views of local officials and to assess the capacity of local associations to absorb the changes in candidate selection, party finance and other areas that were being proposed by a variety of groups and interveners at Commission hearings. In brief, the survey was designed to capture the growing complexity and diversity of the Canadian party system.

The survey was conducted over the winter and summer of 1991, using a mailed questionnaire addressed to the presidents of each local association. The survey asked questions in seven main areas: the organization of the electoral process; constituency organization and activity, during and between elections; the nomination and leadership selection process; campaign activities; finance and fund-raising; election expenses; and the level of participation in association affairs of different groups and individuals. The return rate was well over 50 percent, indicating a high level of interest and cooperation and ensuring the pool of respondents was representative of the target population. The use of different questions to probe specific issues proved to be invaluable. The responses conveyed a sense of the complexity of the many problems faced by those in local associations, suggesting how recommendations for change ought to be framed in order to make them feasible and how progress made so far in efforts by local associations to recruit women and members of visible minorities as candidates could be assessed.

In this monograph, Professor Carty provides an interpretative analysis of these data, focusing on relative differences between the parties with respect to the seven main areas. Equally important, he identifies patterns common to all parties, arguing that, in many ways, the crucial differences in the structure, behaviour and attitudes of local associations are to be found not so much between the parties as between differing circumstances in which associations find themselves – for example, whether the association has an incumbent in the House of Commons, whether the association is in a competitive or uncompetitive constituency, or whether it is found east or west of the Ontario–Quebec border. He seeks to account for these commonalities and differences by placing them in the context of Canadian political geography and the historical development of party organization at the local level.

Overall, he notes that local associations are a source of both the strength and the weakness of Canadian political parties, that Canadian parties remain highly decentralized in important respects and that proposed changes need to take into account the dynamics of local association activities and the nature of the resources associations can bring to bear on improving those aspects of their activities that many Canadians find wanting.

Systematic studies of Canadian political parties at the local level are extremely rare. Professor Carty is to be congratulated for the care and finesse with which the original research design was executed and for producing a superb analysis of the dynamics underpinning the organization and collective behaviour of the local associations of all political parties. This monograph not only fills a significant gap in the literature but will stand as a landmark study for many years to come.

Herman Bakvis
Research Coordinator

ACKNOWLEDGEMENTS

THIS STUDY is the last in the research program sponsored by the Royal Commission on Electoral Reform and Party Financing. It was deliberately left until last so that its design and execution might benefit from the early work of the Commission. The results of the study were first reported to the Commissioners, their staff and their research team in the form of raw data, preliminary analyses and working memos. Some of that material has made its way into other research reports, and the Final Report of the Commission (where specific findings are cited in seven different chapters). Those references are to the data gathered in the survey on which this study is based, and some of the particular individual findings may not appear in this volume. The data has been deposited in the Commission's archives where it will be made available in due course and with appropriate measures to protect the respondents' privacy.

I have a large number of people to thank for all their help in making this study possible:

- The members of the Royal Commission on Electoral Reform and Party Financing, for asking me to do the study. I appreciated their confidence and support, and I learned something every time we met. It was a delight for a political scientist to have the opportunity to work for such stimulating and thoughtful public figures, who themselves had answers to so many of the questions I was asking.
- The senior research staff at the Commission, for their support at all stages of the project. Peter Aucoin, the Commission's director of research, and Leslie Seidle, the senior research coordinator, provided encouragement (as well as giving me other

tasks), while Herman Bakvis kept me on course and ran interference whenever I asked for his help. Herman constituted my key link to the Commission's machinery on this project, and his thoughtful comments helped push the final study into shape.

- The staff at the Commission's office in Ottawa, for help at several critical moments when time was at a premium. They provided an important link to the parties' offices when we were finalizing up-to-date mailing lists, they translated the questionnaire on short notice and they assisted with innumerable smaller bureaucratic tasks. I appreciate all their help and, at the risk of singling out two, especially thank Guy Goulard and Richard Rochefort.

- Avivah Wargon at Dundurn Press, whose editorial finesse improved a hastily written manuscript and whose tact kept its author looking forward to more of her careful reading and her discerning "queries."

- Roseanne Sovka, who ran the project's Vancouver office. Without her creativity, energy and work – analytical, administrative, secretarial and personnel services – the project could not have been completed on time, and if it had got finished at all would not have been as good.

- The Department of Political Science at the Unversity of British Columbia, including its Head, Don Blake, and all my students. They have been very tolerant of my preoccupation with this study. In retrospect I probably should not have tried to squeeze the work in around all my regular obligations, and it was possible only because of the goodwill of those I work with.

- My wife and children, who have almost certainly had to pay a real cost for this study. I know I "owe them big."

- Finally, the respondents. It was only possible to do this study because of the cooperation of the political parties, and nothing would have come of it without over 500 constituency association presidents, and their colleagues, taking their time to answer what must have seemed to them an awfully long questionnaire about their local party's normally private business. I thank them all very much – even those we had to ask three times – and hope they recognize something of their world in this book.

R.K. Carty
Department of Political Science
University of British Columbia

CANADIAN
POLITICAL
PARTIES IN THE
CONSTITUENCIES

1

THE PLACE OF CONSTITUENCY ASSOCIATIONS IN CANADIAN PARTIES

CANADIAN POLITICAL PARTIES are at once both simple and complex organizations. Simple, because they exist to nominate candidates for elected office and then mount campaigns on those candidates' behalf. Their basic structures, and the rhythms of their activities, are largely governed by the electoral system, while their successes and failures are clear for all to see. Complex, because to do this successfully they must bind individuals together in a curious mix of informal networks that operate within multilevel formal organizations whose interests and resources are fragmented by the federal character of the nation's politics. Of course the very reasons why parties engage in electoral competition, and the range of other activities they take on to supplement it, vary widely and over time, which only adds to the layers of meaning that define the essence of their part in Canadian politics.

Parties tie Canadians together in a way that shapes the most fundamental political relationships of our system of representative democracy and responsible government. In that sense they are the simple, immediate links between the electors and the elected. But that makes parties complex organizations, for they become the common instruments of individuals with very different interests, stakes and roles in the governing of the country. At one end of the party chain are the professional politicians: their political life depends upon a party to elect, support and sustain them. At the other end are the parties' members and volunteer supporters: they take up and abandon party activity as it meets their needs. Democratic theory suggests they do so as citizens concerned to use parties as an instrument of popular control of government, but there is also a long tradition in Canada of doing so for material or social reasons. In between these two groups is a swelling band of party functionaries and political employees: they live off the parties. And surrounding all of these active partisans are a growing number of Canadians whose individual contributions constitute the parties' principal means of financial support: they bankroll the parties but often do not belong to them or take an active part in their affairs.

The parties are structured by a complex array of organizational units, some defined by their territorial reach – local, regional (provincial) or national – others by the interests of their particular constituents – e.g., youth, women, Aboriginals or trade unionists. Most party membership, on the other hand, is based on individuals' simple and direct participation in a local party association, whose purview is ordered by the boundaries of the electoral district – commonly called a constituency or riding in Canadian politics. That reality points to the geographic cast that the electoral system imposes on Canadian political parties.

The single-member constituency electoral system used in Canadian elections (the last of the few double-member ridings was abolished in the mid-1960s) accepts as one of its fundamental touchstones the notion that electoral competition, and the parties that manage it, are matters for citizens in their local communities to organize and animate. Elections are fought out in a series (currently 295) of constituency contests, and voters choose a local, party candidate to represent them in Parliament. However much contemporary politics takes on a national colour, or a centralizing dynamic, healthy, active local constituency party associations are thus vital to the working practices of Canadian democracy. The nature and character of the parties as national organizations has changed substantially over time as successive party systems have evolved to meet the needs of a changing Canadian state (Carty 1992). However one of the few things about Canadian parties that has not changed is their roots in, and dependence upon, strong constituency-level organization.

THE CREATION OF CANADIAN POLITICAL PARTIES

Sir John A. Macdonald and those who later sought to emulate him always saw their primary task as the building of great national political parties, which could be depended upon to provide the political support necessary to sustain their work (Stewart 1982). In the years after Confederation this meant establishing a disciplined caucus that bound together locally oriented constituency politicians. These men's survival depended on winning a struggle for electoral supremacy in small, often highly competitive electoral districts where the margin of victory might be only a few dozen votes. As English (1977, 14) notes, those early "parties lacked both mass organization as well as a cadre of permanent officials who [could provide] experience and discipline." What ultimately held them together was the patronage that a party leader could deliver, often through his constituency politicians, to the local electoral machine (Noel 1987).

This made the early parties essentially very simple organizations. At the top were leaders who had control of, or access to, (largely) government patronage; at the bottom were voters, clustered in the constituencies; and in between were MPs and candidates dependent upon a partisan organization whose key figures were supported by patronage positions at all levels of the public service (Noel 1987; Stewart 1980; Reid 1936). As Siegfried (1906, 118) remarked in describing turn-of-the-century Canadian parties, "there is, properly speaking, no organizing body dealing with the whole of the Dominion" and "The central organization of each party is reduced to a minimum. It may be said to consist in the one case of the prime minister, in the other of the leader of the opposition." Electoral battles were fought in the constituencies where the high patronage stakes involved induced a "fury and enthusiasm" Siegfried had rarely seen elsewhere (ibid., 117).

Despite the absence of formal party memberships and complex intervening structures linking the centre to the ridings, at their best the informal networks that defined the party machinery in the constituencies were effective and efficient, their operation well understood by all those involved, and their capacity to engender participation quite remarkable and the equal of many contemporary party organizations. Their central task was to find and nominate a candidate, and then run a campaign that would get him (in that era before female enfranchisement) elected. Though regional party managers watched over the process, and sometimes provided a conduit for election funds, in the absence of a significant national party campaign local organizations operated largely on their own. Of course not every riding party worked perfectly, and periods of one-party rule could lead to unequal competition, but as Johnston (1980) has demonstrated, the system was remarkably homogeneous by later Canadian standards.

It was in this period that the practice of party supporters in each constituency gathering together before every election to nominate their candidate became deeply entrenched. The newspapers of the period are full of accounts of the process and though it varied considerably from riding to riding, and often over time in the same riding, several features stand out. First, despite the absence of any formal notion of membership, or lists of paid-up party members, local partisans had no trouble setting up sophisticated and representative conventions to choose a candidate. In larger ridings, delegates would often be elected from each polling area and sent to a constituency-wide gathering to represent local opinion. Some contemporary reports describe a carefully defined process in which official "credential tickets" were issued to approved delegates entitling them to vote at the meeting. Second, it was not uncommon for nomination conventions (as they were customarily called) to draw hundreds of participants. Given that the average constituency (in 1896, for example) averaged only 4 220 voters, this suggests that the party organizations of the period were able to mobilize and involve a far larger proportion of the voting population than they do today. Finally, while there was a considerable degree of ritual to some of this activity, real contests stretching over several ballots were not at all unknown, and MPs who had dissatisfied their party supporters or constituents were occasionally denied a renomination.

Election campaigns in this period were hard-fought, in part because of the very small electorates, and "victory [could] only go to a party which [was] perfectly organized" (Siegfried 1906, 123). The organizations that managed these campaigns were sophisticated, and their basic approach has yet to be improved on. Essentially they set themselves the task of identifying the vote, focusing their campaign efforts on persuading the undecided and then turning out their vote on election day (Ames 1905). Their party politics were far more expensive than Canada has ever seen since. English (1977, 21) estimates that, at the turn of the century, votes were costing candidates between one and six dollars each at a time when one dollar was the equivalent of a full day's wages. Without public funding, a mass membership or tax-induced giving, this put enormous financial pressure on the local constituency election managers and their candidates.

Throughout this period the party leader was the critical figure as far as the national organization was concerned. He was at the centre of the vast informal patronage network that bound all the party's constituency organizations together. Yet those party organizations had no direct say in the selection or removal of a leader. That decision was the business of the caucus, from which he was chosen in private. Thus partisans in ridings with an MP in the caucus had a very indirect input into the process, while those without one were effectively shut out. (See figure 1.1 for a simplified schematic representation of the basic relationships.)

This is an image of a very decentralized party structure in which constituency associations had considerable autonomy, both from the centre and from one another, in the organization and management of

Figure 1.1
Early Canadian party structure

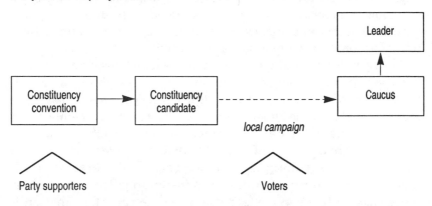

their affairs. It gave way under the pressures for increased democrati-
zation and regional politics in the aftermath of the First World War. But
the changes to the parties did not upset their reliance on constituency-
level organizations as their fundamental units: they added new structures and in doing so perhaps even strengthened the place of the riding
association in the life of the party.

THE EMERGENCE OF NATIONAL PARTY ORGANIZATIONS

The great Liberal convention of 1919 marks the emergence of national
extraparliamentary party organization in Canada. The convention was
designed to reunite the Liberal party in the aftermath of its split over
conscription during World War I, but it worked a series of changes on
the party that subsequently set the standard for national party organization (Wearing 1981, 7). The convention did three important things: it
chose a party leader; it asserted the right to set the party's policy agenda;
and it put an ongoing national extraparliamentary organization, with
its own executive and apparatus, in place.

Strong party discipline means that Canadian general elections
revolve around the choice of a government. Therefore, in choosing its
leader a Canadian party is essentially nominating its candidate for the
prime ministership. By selecting the national party leader, and usurp-
ing a role long the undisputed prerogative of the caucus, the Liberal
convention was taking to itself one of a party's primary tasks. It did so
not only because the caucus was seen as regionally unrepresentative,
and thus unsuited to choose a national leader, but also in response to
the growing demands for a more democratic party politics (Perlin 1991,
58). The result was to involve the constituency associations, through
their representative delegates, in the selection of the party leader

(nomination of a prime minister) in much the same way that poll delegates had traditionally participated in their constituency party's selection of its local parliamentary nominee. In so doing the party ensured that the constituency association would be the fundamental unit of national party organization and activity.

In assuming the right to set basic policy directions, and establishing a permanent party organization which drew its authority and legitimacy from the convention, the constituency delegates were asserting that they spoke for the wider national party interest and membership. By adopting similar national processes and structures in 1927 the Conservative party confirmed that this new pattern had become the Canadian party norm. The real weakness in this organizational model was that it proved difficult to institutionalize: conventions were called only when the leadership became vacant, so that ordinary constituency party members had but very intermittent opportunities to participate in this new wider party they had called into being.

For all the organizational innovation, the new structures made only a modest impact. Power (1966, 371) and Williams (1956, 110) both suggest that the new forms largely obscured the persistence of traditional practice, because Liberal and Conservative politicians continued to operate as they always had out of their constituency bailiwicks. Wearing (1981, 7) contends that, once in power, most working politicians simply lost any interest they had ever had in their party's national organizational bodies. But this is also to say that the new structures brought little real centralization to the parties' national organizations. Autonomous constituency associations, with their place in the national party explicitly recognized, remained the basic unit of party life.

Yet, while constituency autonomy remained the nominal order of the day, this was also the period when the Liberal ministers, operating as regional party bosses, played an increasingly important role in overseeing nomination and campaign activity in their territories (Whitaker 1977). That system, which provided for greater central control of party activity, depended upon the long period of Liberal electoral dominance so that "when ministers went down like ninepins before the Conservative onslaughts of 1957 and 1958, not much of the party was left" (Wearing 1981, 13). In fact what was left were the constituency associations, and it was on and through them that the party slowly rebuilt. Conservative associations themselves had varied considerably during those long years of Liberal government: across much of Quebec they "had ceased being very active," as John Meisel rather delicately puts it, but in areas of continuing strength old-style nominating conventions provided the local members with an opportunity to participate in party decision making (Meisel 1962, 121–23).

This second party system was also the era that saw the electoral rise (and sometimes fall) of a number of protest movements that turned to party politics: the Progressive party (a label encompassing various farmers' movements), Social Credit and the Co-operative Commonwealth Federation (CCF) being the best known and most successful of them. Though these groups each brought a distinctive ideological perspective to Canadian politics, they did share a commitment to democratic organization and an independent constituency politics. Thus, at various times, some of their members could be found arguing for freeing MPs from the tyranny of party discipline, supporting a local nomination process free from outside influence or advocating the use of the recall to tie MPs more closely to the wishes of their electors. In all this they reinforced the norms and traditions that had strong constituency associations at the heart of Canadian party organization.

THE RISE OF MODERN CANADIAN POLITICAL PARTIES

The contemporary period of Canadian party politics is widely perceived to have begun with the Diefenbaker realignment of the early 1960s that ended the long King–St. Laurent era of easy Liberal dominance. In the aftermath, none of the large political parties was left with a genuinely nationwide electoral base. Ironically, then, it became a period in which nationalizing and centralizing forces transformed party organizations and threatened to overwhelm the traditional constituency focus of much Canadian party activity and electoral life.

A series of reforms in the 1970s finally brought the national political parties into the legal framework governing the operation of democratic electoral competition. Parties were recognized and registered as principal actors in the process, and for the first time party labels appeared on the ballot. In an attempt to promote more equal competition, the state provided financial assistance to parties to help meet their election expenses, and it put limits on their election expenditures. To strengthen and broaden the base of the parties, the state gave them access to a system of income tax credits designed to entice large numbers of individual Canadians to support them financially.

These changes fuelled the growth of national party machinery and nationalized electoral campaign activity. The parties soon had far more ready money than they had ever had before, and were typically able to raise more in nonelection years than they were legally entitled to spend on a full general election campaign. Predictably, they spent it building central bureaucracies dedicated to raising yet more money, to increasing the reach of the national party leadership and to developing and implementing standardized national campaign plans. The latter became imperative when the advent of television and air travel made the national campaign central to the party's electoral appeal. The consequence was to produce a far more centralized and disciplined campaign organization and electoral politics (Wearing 1981).

Changes to the financial regime governing Canadian elections largely ignored the constituency party associations. Local election expenses were subsidized, but it was to the candidates and their agents, and not the local riding parties, that the money was directed. The law recognizing the party character of elections overlooked constituency parties, leaving the party leader to certify local associations' nominees for ballot-label purposes. That provision gave party leaders the capacity to veto candidates chosen by constituency associations and immediately changed the relationship between the national campaign planners and the riding activists. Using this tool the national parties were able to reject locally popular constituency politicians they disapproved of, and to impose heavy taxes on their riding parties. Both developments obviously threatened the autonomy of constituency associations.

Important recent changes in modern communications technologies represent a potentially powerful centralizing force in Canadian parties. The combination of sophisticated tracking polls, geodemographic targeting and computer-driven direct mail give the parties' central offices the ability to bypass their local constituency associations and speak directly to individual voters (Axworthy 1991). How this brave new world with its private mass media of personalized communication, as opposed to the public mass media of print or electronic journalism, will be married to open democratic politics is a large and fundamental issue now facing the political system. For the political parties, as organizations, one of the major problems this poses is the prospect of disrupting long-standing balances between the central headquarters machinery and the constituency associations.

Yet, while all these centralizing impulses were working themselves out within the parties, leadership conflicts were leading party members, working through their constituency association representatives, to assert a greater role in party decision making. The initial battle was fought out in the Conservative party over the extraparliamentary party's right to fire a leader (called, euphemistically, a "leadership review"): a right held to be the natural concomitant of the party convention's power to select leaders. The victory of party activists on this question institutionalized the power of the convention and made it a permanent focus of internal party authority – among other things, it guaranteed party conventions would become part of the regular life of the party.

Given that the constituency associations were the conventions' most important organizational base, it was perhaps inevitable that they quickly became one of the most important sites for mobilizing support in internal party disputes, over leadership or over policy. This development did two things: it led to the revitalization of many local riding parties and it legitimated the right of individuals to move into a constituency association and take it over through rather crass internal party faction fights. And what was acceptable in leadership contests soon became acceptable in nomination contests, opening up that process to more and different interests and exposing it to the wider public.

Thus, the development of a factionalized national leadership politics in the two major parties, which was forced to play itself out through the constituency associations, contributed to enhancing and solidifying the place of riding parties in Canadian parties. The New Democratic Party (as successor to the CCF) managed to escape many of these ferocious internal battles, in part because its traditions of internal organizational democracy already allowed for a much greater representation of members' views in party decision making, but also because the trade-union norm of solidarity was an important strand in its party culture.

Though each of the three large national political parties has a rather different organization and structure (Dyck 1991; Pelletier 1991), we can recognize a basic common pattern underlying them all (figure 1.2 provides a simple schematic portrait). When we recall that political parties'

Figure 1.2
Modern Canadian party structure

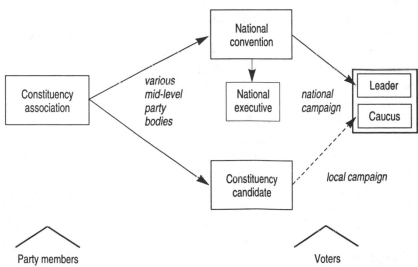

principal distinctive task in our system of democratic electoral competition is to nominate candidates and run campaigns, then we can see that the constituency association remains at the core of Canadian parties. It nominates the local candidate, and it is the basic building block of the convention that nominates the party's candidate for prime minister: it organizes the constituency campaigns, and national elections can only be won by winning a majority of them. If we compare the modern party (figure 1.2) with its counterpart in the first system (figure 1.1), it appears that the constituency association is more firmly entrenched in the modern Canadian party than it was in the earlier period, long considered the golden age of constituency politics.

POLITICAL PARTIES IN THE CONSTITUENCIES

The Canadian state recognizes the importance of constituency-level party organizations. It depends on them to help manage its electoral processes: explicitly, by requiring them (through their candidates) to name enumerators, supply election scrutineers, issue tax receipts and keep records of expenditures; implicitly, by expecting them to provide input for electoral boundary redistribution commissions, nominate candidates, define the terms of local public debate and mobilize voters. The electoral system as we know it could not operate without these tasks being performed. That the parties conduct all these activities with an eye to their own advantage should not obscure this point. Indeed, in some areas, such as voter enumeration, the activity is organized precisely to exploit the local party associations' inherent interest in the task. Ultimately, any change in the role, status or capacities of constituency associations is of interest to the state.

Canadian political parties know that they must have a set of strong, vital riding associations if they are to be successful. But they also know how complex and fragile is the whole structure. From one perspective parties can be thought of as a kind of elaborate national franchise network. Like commercial franchise organizations they have a central office that establishes a common policy product, provides common management training and backup services, and plans, finances and implements national advertising campaigns. And, like other franchise systems, the centre leaves it to the individual outlet (the constituency association) to manage its own local service (from finding a candidate right through delivering supporters to the polls). But despite these parallels, the analogy to a commercial franchise system is not a perfect one: the differences are important and might well drive a private-sector franchise executive to despair. In political parties, the local franchise is in the hands of occasional volunteers, and the national office has only the most limited and blunt tools with which to discipline or direct them. Success often depends on the efforts and commitments of these local amateurs, but it is next to impossible for the national party to take a franchise away from underachievers and give it to some other group that might be more enterprising or able. Indeed unwanted outsiders sometimes invade and capture a local franchise and put it to their own use, and party dissidents regularly use them as a base to attack the national leadership. And national parties are dependent upon 295 such local operations.

This sketch of national parties as elaborate franchise-like networks of temporary volunteers suggests that both the state, and the country's national political leaders, inevitably depend on fluid and uneven structures to sustain Canadian electoral democracy. But this is conjecture: there are no systematic studies of local party associations in Canada. Thus this study is designed to discover just what these riding parties really do, and how they do it. In this sense it provides the first constituency-based portrait of the country's national political parties.

2

The Constituency Party Study

CANADA'S NATIONAL PARTIES have been studied from a number of
perspectives. Many books have been written about individual parties
though, curiously enough, more on minor and regional parties than on
either the Liberals or the Progressive Conservatives, the only two genuinely national parties with sufficient support to have ever formed a government. In recent years these studies have been supplemented by
analyses of the working of the party system (e.g., Meisel 1963, 1979,
1991; Smith 1985); party leadership and leadership selection (e.g.,
Courtney 1973; Carty, Erickson and Blake 1992); the opinions and
behaviour of élite activists (e.g., Perlin 1988; Blake, Carty and Erickson
1991); party organization, structure and financing (e.g., Whitaker 1977;
Wearing 1981); governing style (e.g., Meisel 1975; Simpson 1980); the
extent to which the parties represent distinctive ideological traditions
(e.g., Christian and Campbell 1990); the regionalization of Canadian
parties (e.g., Smith 1981); the role of women in party life (e.g., Bashevkin
1985); and, of course, the role and activities of political parties in national
general elections (e.g., Johnston et al. 1992). All of these studies, in various ways, acknowledge the geographic cast of Canadian political life
and the importance of constituency-level organization and activity.
However, despite that importance, most research on Canadian parties
does little more than genuflect in the direction of riding-level organization. There are no systematic studies of Canadian parties in terms of
their constituency associations.

In many ways parties are defined as serious national organizations
to the extent that they are able to organize and contest elections in a
significant number of constituencies. The *Canada Elections Act* sets 50 as
the minimum number of ridings an organization must normally contest if it is to be officially recognized as a party (section 24(3)); the allocation of election broadcasting time to the parties is partially determined

by the number of candidates they nominate (section 310(1)); and the media uses local organizational strength as one of the criteria by which they judge the amount and type of coverage an individual party merits. This makes it particularly surprising that we know so little about how the parties' constituency associations are organized, what resources (both human and financial) they have available, what they do between as well as during elections, how they contribute to the democratic life of the wider party they are a part of and how they contribute to the smooth operating of the electoral system. This amounts to a vast gap in our knowledge and understanding of the parties as central actors in Canadian democracy. Since we know so little, it also means that we are not able to assess how well they perform their roles, or to compare the viability and capacities of the individual parties with those of their competitors. It also makes it very difficult to evaluate the consequences of changes in the regulatory regime that governs parties and elections, either in terms of any impact on the parties themselves, or on the ability of parties as key actors in the democratic process to implement changes in the spirit intended.

To fill these gaps in our knowledge of Canadian parties, the Royal Commission on Electoral Reform and Party Financing sponsored this study of constituency-level party organization and activity. As well as seeking to measure the extent and capacity of constituency party organization, and learn how the electoral system operates on the ground, the Commission was anxious to assess the opinions of key riding activists on the current rules and processes governing Canadian elections and to obtain grassroots reaction to a number of suggested reforms to the system. They did so knowing that many of the system's weaknesses would require the active cooperation of the many thousands of party activists who voluntarily participate in Canadian political life if they were to be corrected successfully.

THE SURVEY

The political parties' national offices and staff have remarkably little information on their own constituency-level organizations. For instance, none of them have any systematic or reliable membership data, records of candidate nomination meetings or even basic local financial accounts. This meant that to describe and analyse local-level party organization and activity required collecting, for the first time ever, a large amount of data from the individual constituency associations themselves. The first question was which parties to include in a survey of riding party organizations.

The country's three major political parties, the Progressive

Conservatives, Liberals and New Democrats, all regularly contest every electoral district in national elections so each have, in principle, 295 ongoing constituency party associations. These local party organizations are at the heart of most constituency-level politics in Canada and all were included in the study.

Since the beginning of the second Canadian party system in the period after World War I (Carty 1988b), minor parties have played a dynamic part in Canadian electoral life, though they have varied considerably in their strength and persistence over the decades. By definition, minor parties have fewer local constituency associations than the major parties, and their ongoing existence is more problematic. In 1988 nine officially recognized minor parties contested the election. The two largest of them, defined both by the numbers of candidates they ran and the vote share they won, were included in the study. The two, one practising regional politics, the other a more ideological (though narrow, almost single-issue) politics, represent quite distinct faces of the country's minor-party tradition.

The Reform Party ran 72 candidates in 1988 under the banner: "The West Wants In." In many ways it appeared to be quite typical of the regional protest parties that have been a central feature of Canadian Prairie politics for much of this century. Reform was so preoccupied with traditional regional grievances that its constitution prohibited it from contesting constituencies in the six provinces east of the Manitoba–Ontario border. (After the survey was conducted in early 1991, Reform began to transform itself into a national protest party, promising to run candidates everywhere but Quebec in the next election.) By contrast, the Christian Heritage party (CHP) had not so much a regional base as a philosophical and perhaps ethnic (white northern-European) one. With 63 candidates in 1988, it appealed to Canadians who feared the passing of what the party characterized as traditional Christian family values. For many observers this appeal often translated into single-issue politics, with the CHP being perceived as especially concerned with the abortion issue.

The Questionnaire

Because so little is known about local riding parties, the constituency association organization and activity survey was designed to collect information that would allow us to draw a basic, benchmark portrait of Canadian constituency party life. It was, however, also directed to a number of particular concerns dictated by the mandate of the Royal Commission, and those issues had to be accommodated in the questionnaire's content and design. As a result, the final questionnaire (which is reprinted in the Appendix) reflected the diverse concerns of the Commission's research team, the interests of the Commissioners themselves and the work of the principal investigator. On balance all that input made for an interesting, albeit rather long and diverse, questionnaire.

Constituency associations were asked a series of questions on seven distinct topics:

- enumeration and voting practice;
- constituency association structure, organization and activity;
- candidate nomination and delegate selection for leadership conventions;
- constituency associations' electoral campaign organization and activity;
- local association finances in nonelection periods;
- constituency association election funding; and
- efforts to increase and broaden the base of participation in party life.

Each section included questions about formal local party structures and organization as well as the local associations' real practices and experience. Then, in specially labelled subsections, a number of "options for reform" followed. These were to measure local practitioners' support for, or opposition to, suggested changes to the structure and rules of the contemporary electoral system.

The basic questionnaire produced a set of 316 separate variables for each responding constituency association. From those variables it was possible to create many more by combining them in a variety of ways (e.g., a series of annual membership figures could be used to produce measures of association growth rates), and by adding other constituency-level data, such as election statistics, to supplement the questionnaire responses. As a consequence the study had a very rich database and most of the analysis reported here drew on a dataset that contained about 450 pieces of information for each constituency association.

Translation of the questionnaire from English into French was undertaken by the Royal Commission's staff in Ottawa. There were some minor differences in the response sets provided for a few questions in the two versions, though they do not appear to have affected the replies, or our analysis of them, in any significant fashion. (The Appendix includes an account of these differences.)

Distribution

As it was not practically possible to contact personally over 1 000 constituency associations, the survey had to be administered by mail. The questionnaire was sent to each party's local association presidents on the assumption that they were the individuals best placed to answer most of the questions, but the covering letter encouraged them to "consult others in your constituency association" on any and all questions about which they might be uncertain. For questions concerning association structure and activity this was straightforward enough. However, on those questions that sought to tap grassroots organizations' opinions about reform possibilities, a questionnaire sent to one individual was less satisfactory. Obviously, different individuals will have different attitudes toward change and there is likely to be a variety of opinion within a single association. Thus, responses to the attitudinal questions must be interpreted as the views of a select group of party activists – the constituency association presidents. These are the women and men who occupy central leadership roles in local party politics and would have to help direct and manage any reform process. Their attitudes can be taken as a critical barometer of local party opinion.

Prior to the survey mailing, Pierre Lortie, Chairman of the Royal Commission on Electoral Reform and Party Financing, wrote to all the constituency presidents describing the study, setting it in the context of the Commission's mandate and research program and urging them to respond. He also wrote to each member of Parliament with the same message, knowing that local associations with incumbents would often consult their MP about participating in such a survey. Then, a few days later, each riding party's local president was mailed a copy of the questionnaire (and a prepaid return envelope) with a covering letter from the research office at the University of British Columbia. That letter again described the project and provided a phone number that could be used by anyone with specific questions about the survey or the use of the data being collected. For ridings classified by the chief electoral officer as either bilingual or French-speaking, the package included all the material in both French and English, and individuals were asked to complete and return whichever version they preferred.

Over the spring a careful, bilingual follow-up program was used to maximize returns. Two waves of reminder cards were sent out and then, in a final effort, all association presidents still not responding were telephoned and encouraged to do so. Each of those efforts produced additional responses (and requests for replacements of lost or discarded questionnaires). As noted below, this finally produced a 54 percent return rate.

THE UNIVERSE OF CONSTITUENCY ASSOCIATIONS

Despite the important role local party associations play in nominating candidates, enumerating voters and contesting elections, there is no central registry of constituency associations. Thus it was necessary to obtain the names and addresses of the current (January 1991) local riding-association presidents from the political parties' national offices. In fact, not one of the three national parties was able to provide a full list of 295 constituency presidents. This was not a matter of obstruction, for the party offices were very accommodating in providing the most up-to-date mailing lists available. It simply reflected the reality that, at any given moment, Canadian parties generally do not have a full set of local constituency associations. Or to put it another way, the national offices of the parties do not always know (at least between elections) who, if anyone, is conducting local affairs in their name in every constituency. Table 2.1 reports the number of constituency associations for which each party was able to provide names and addresses of riding presidents.

Each of the three large parties came close to a full list of 295 names, though the electorally weaker NDP could not identify a current local president in a dozen ridings. The Reform Party identified 87 local associations at the beginning of 1991, up 15 from the number of candidates they ran in the 1988 general election; the CHP named 61, 2 fewer than the number of Christian Heritage nominees in 1988. However these numbers may exaggerate the total population of active constituency associations: a number of questionnaires were returned as undeliverable, indicating that the name and address that the national party believed connected it to its local associations no longer led to any real

Table 2.1
Canadian parties' constituency associations

Party	Constituency associations identified	Questionnaires undeliverable	Constituency associations in place	Proportion of all ridings
Progressive Conservative	290	4	286	.97
Liberal	294	5	289	.98
NDP	283	35	248	.84
Reform	87	2	85	.29 (.96*)
Christian Heritage	61	0	61	.21
Total	1 015	46	969	

*Proportion of all constituencies west of the Manitoba–Ontario border.

person. In another instance, an individual took the trouble to write and say that there really was no NDP association in his Quebec riding, there was just himself (and one friend), and so he was returning an uncompleted questionnaire. Removing all these cases provides a somewhat more realistic first estimate of the number of associations each party actually has. As table 2.1 indicates, the two large national parties have associations in all but 2 or 3 percent of the constituencies. The NDP, on the other hand, appears not to have even nominal associations in up to 16 percent of the country's constituencies.

Given the vagaries of constituency-level politics, and of the interests and commitment of volunteer local activists, it is not at all surprising that each federal party should have some riding associations that are moribund, or completely expired. That the national offices are not always sure at any given time which of them may have fallen into that condition indicates that, between elections, the parties maintain a rather loose and decentralized organizational style. The larger number of these cases in the NDP, as compared to its two national opponents, may partially reflect the clear primacy of provincial-level sections over the national organization in much of that party (Dyck 1991). But that is not the whole story, for there is also a strong and distinctive pattern to the absence of local NDP associations. Half of the ridings for which the party simply had no local president's name, and a third for which questionnaires were returned as undeliverable, were in Quebec. Over half (51 percent) of all the 47 ridings for which we could not identify or locate even a nominal NDP association were in the five eastern provinces (Atlantic Canada and Quebec) which together constitute just 33 percent of the nation's electoral districts. This suggests that the party has not yet been able to build a genuinely national organization able to penetrate all parts of the country, a point to be explored in more detail in later chapters. That would certainly be consistent with the NDP's long history of electoral failure in those regions.

There were Reform Party associations in only 29 percent of the nation's constituencies in early 1991, but that was to be expected given the party's constitutional limitation to ridings east of the Manitoba–Ontario border at the time. That meant the party actually had an organizational presence in 96 percent of the constituencies it had identified as its natural territory. In the spring and summer of 1991 the party, through a convention decision subsequently ratified by a referendum of its full membership, decided to spread into all the other provinces except Quebec. This suggests that our constituency association survey provides a snapshot of the Reform Party just as it was completing one early stage of its development as a national party. Though this limits the utility of the information we have on the Reform Party, in the sense that it has now grown well beyond the portrait here, the data does provide an important benchmark against which the future growth of the party can be measured.

The Christian Heritage party had constituency associations in about one-fifth of the nation's electoral districts in early 1991. However they were not evenly distributed across the country: fully half were spread across southern Ontario. There were no constituency associations in Quebec and few in Canada's urban core – just three in Metro Toronto and none in cities such as Calgary or Vancouver. This suggests that the CHP is principally a party of small-town and rural Protestant, English-speaking Canadians. The fact that the party was able to identify virtually the same number of associations as it had run candidates in 1988, and that not a single questionnaire was returned as undeliverable, hints at a very stable, if limited, organizational base.

The Survey Return

The five parties indicated that, together, they had 1 015 active constituency associations. However in terms of our ability to reach individual local associations, the experience of the survey project (table 2.1) indicates that the real number at the beginning of 1991 was just 969. Table 2.2 reports the return rates in terms of parties, provinces and 1988 electoral results. As it notes, 54 percent of the associations responded, and they are representative of the broad range of Canadian constituency party life. There are some constituencies for which we have data on five local party associations, and there was at least one return from fully 88 percent of the constituencies represented in the House of Commons.

There is a small difference in the return rates by party, with fewer Liberal associations (47 percent) responding than was the case for either the Conservatives (55 percent) or the NDP (53 percent). This despite the fact that more Liberal associations than NDP ones responded, a quirk which is explained by the smaller population of NDP associations actually in existence. The highest returns were from the CHP (79 percent), perhaps evidence of the desire of many in this small minor party that it be considered a serious player in Canadian party politics.

The table indicates that, though there is a good sample of local associations from all provinces, the return rates were lower in New Brunswick and Quebec. It is not clear whether this may reflect differing propensities of French and English speakers to respond, for with all of the ridings in both provinces classified as either French or bilingual it is not easy to disentangle language from province. Three-quarters of

Table 2.2
Constituency association survey return rates

	Constituency associations in place	Questionnaires returned	Return rate (%)
Party			
Progressive Conservative	286	157	57
Liberal	289	136	47
NDP	248	131	53
Reform	85	50	59
Christian Heritage	61	48	79
Province/Territory			
Newfoundland	19	12	63
Nova Scotia	33	20	61
Prince Edward Island	13	7	54
New Brunswick	28	12	43
Quebec	202	79	39
Ontario	315	188	60
Manitoba	55	33	60
Saskatchewan	53	30	57
Alberta	109	65	60
British Columbia	134	71	53
Yukon/NWT	8	5	63
Total	969	522	54
1988 election winner	295	139	47

the associations in all the bilingual constituencies, and 5 percent of them in the French-speaking ridings, chose to respond in English. (Eighty-seven percent of all responses came in English, 13 percent in French.) Whatever the reason for the lower returns in New Brunswick and Quebec, the difference did not have a partisan dimension, for all three national parties are appropriately represented in each province's sample.

There were five responses from constituency associations in the North (the Yukon and the Northwest Territories). Because they were spread over four different parties it was often impossible to break the North out in tables reporting regional differences. At those points in the discussion, data from the North has simply had to be excluded from the analysis.

As table 2.2 also indicates, 47 percent of the associations which won the election contest in their constituency in 1988 responded to the survey. The distribution of those cases, both within and across parties, reflected the election returns. This makes it possible to consider the

impact of incumbency on local party organization and activity throughout the analysis.

DESCRIBING THE PARTIES

The emphasis in the chapters to follow is on providing a benchmark
description and analysis of Canadian political parties in terms of their
constituency associations. This starts with examining the parties in the
periods between elections when they are largely engaged in the normal
routines of organization maintenance. There we are particularly concerned with seeing how local riding parties organize and just what they
do between elections, as well as identifying what differences, if any,
distinguish the parties from one another, so chapter 3 considers constituency parties' organization, membership and activity. Chapter 4
then takes up the question of their finances. In chapter 5 the analysis
shifts to focus on the issue of internal party democracy. Local constituency associations continue to be the organizational units that choose
election candidates and select the majority of delegates to national party
leadership selection conventions. The survey data allow us to explore
these two critical activities from the perspective of the local associations and to assess the impact of local contests on the associations themselves. Both the NDP and the Liberal party had leadership contests
during the period covered by the survey, and the evidence from their
respective constituency associations demonstrates just how different
the conceptions of party democracy, as manifest in their internal workings, are in those two parties.

The three chapters that follow shift the focus to the election period.
Since interested observers from the time of André Siegfried have characterized Canadian parties as little more than "agencies for the con-
quest of power ... a machine for winning elections" (1906, 112), one
would expect local associations to be much more active at that time.
Certainly the three major parties are quickly able to mount some minimal local organization in every constituency even though, as we discovered above, they do not always have a real local association in place
between elections. Chapter 6 begins with a specific institutional question. It considers the role played by riding parties in the enumeration
of voters as currently required by the *Canada Elections Act*. This analysis includes only a subset of the associations responding to the survey,
for the Act requires only the associations of the parties whose candidates
placed first or second in the previous election to name enumerators.

The election-period analyses of chapters 7 and 8 broadly parallel
those in chapters 3 and 4 which dealt with the interelection years.
Chapter 7 primarily concerns itself with the ways in which the local

party associations organize and mobilize to fight a constituency-level election. After dealing with structural and organizational questions it explores the extent to which local parties are now able to mobilize the armies of volunteers they need, and the communication links between campaign organizations and their electorates. Chapter 8 reports on the financial dimension of constituency association electoral activity. Since the Act requires that candidates appoint official agents to handle all their constituency campaign finances, much of this decision making and accounting is at one remove from the direct control of riding associations. Thus chapter 8 needs to be read in conjunction with William Stanbury's thorough analysis of candidate campaign finances (1991, chap. 12). Its goal is to help put constituency organizations' election financing into the context of other party activity.

Then the last chapter pulls the disparate threads of the analysis together. In doing so it provides a summary interpretation not only of constituency party organization and life in Canada but also a sketch of the individual parties and the distinctive contributions they make to the organizational mosaic of Canadian party politics.

However, it must be remembered that the constituency association survey provides us with a portrait of Canadian parties snapped at one moment in time. It was taken in the aftermath of the 1988 general election, which saw the return of a majority Conservative government for a second term. That had not happened in the century since 1896. Inevitably this electoral turnabout must have had major consequences for Conservative constituency party organizations, as well as for those of the other parties, but the survey can tell us little about the unfolding of those developments. What it will do is provide the basis from which we can measure subsequent changes in constituency party organization and activity.

Describing and analysing the typical Canadian party constituency association is no simple matter for, as the analysis will show, they vary enormously, and often a number of cases will be found at the end of whatever range exists. While extreme cases, for instance local associations with huge memberships or very expensive nomination fights, often attract wide media attention, and are necessarily of interest to those concerned with abuses of the system, they are often unrepresentative and misleading and so draw attention away from the more common and pervasive patterns of constituency party politics. Certainly that is one of the findings in Carty and Erickson's (1991) detailed study of the nomination process. A simple example here will illustrate the nature of the problem and indicate how it is dealt with in the chapters to follow.

One of the pieces of information the individual constituency associations reported in the survey was the size of their local membership in 1990. It ranged from 0, admitted by 2 Quebec NDP associations, to over 13 000, claimed by one Alberta Liberal association. (The latter is unusually high: the same association reported just 600 members the year before, and its startling growth was due to a membership drive stimulated by the 1990 Liberal leadership contest.) But with constituency parties ranging in size from 0 to 13 000, how are we to characterize the typical association? The average (measured by the arithmetic mean) 1990 constituency party membership was 655, a number inflated by a small number of very large associations. The median-sized association, with 326 members, was just half that size, and the most common membership size (cited by just 6 percent of the associations) was only 200. Of these three, the median figure of 326 members seems the most realistic measure of a "typical" association. After all, the median association is at the point where half the other associations are larger, half smaller. This line of reasoning leads me to prefer the median over the mean as a measure of central tendency for most of the descriptive analyses of the parties' constituency associations.

The principal concern throughout this study is with the national political parties as seen from the constituency level. While we are interested in the differences among associations across the provinces or regions, or in terms of the impact of incumbency, we look at these differences only in order to enrich our understanding of how the five parties organize and work. As a result no sophisticated statistical analysis is provided of the factors which effect variations in the associations themselves, though the data might well lend themselves to such a study of local parties.

We start, in the next chapter, by mapping the size and strength of the riding parties, and by exploring how they fluctuate with the electoral cycle. Having done that, we will be able to go on to ask just what these local associations do.

3

PARTY ORGANIZATION
AND ACTIVITY
ON THE GROUND

F OR THE VAST MAJORITY of individual Canadians, it is the local constituency association that provides them with their principal organizational tie to the nation's political parties. It is the local association
that they effectively join, contribute to, participate in, campaign for and
use as a base for involvement in province- and nationwide activities.
For the parties themselves, their local associations constitute the basic
units necessary to sustain a presence and fighting capacity in a single-
member electoral system. In this chapter we shall look at some of the
basic features of local party associations, to draw a portrait of their
resources, structures and activities.

Their constitutions suggest that Canada's national parties have
rather simple notions of membership. Individuals join through their
local constituency association: the principal test seems to be that they
(to take the Progressive Conservative wording as an example) "support the aims and principles of the Party." The NDP excludes members
of other parties, as the Liberal party does members of other federal
parties, but the Progressive Conservative party is silent on the issue
of its members' involvement in other parties. This is a practical recognition of the fact that many Conservatives are active in other provincial parties in provinces such as Quebec or British Columbia where
the Conservatives have no significant presence (Blake, Carty and
Erickson, 1991). Though the Reform Party restricts membership to
electors, the three established parties do not: all of them accept
Canadian residents, including noncitizens, and set a minimum age
below 18, the current franchise threshold. Thus some proportion of
Conservative, Liberal and NDP membership is likely to consist of non-
electors. In the NDP this can vary by province, for the national NDP's
constitution assigns responsibility for individual party membership
to the various provincial parties and their constitutions. In short, none

of this suggests that Canadian parties have adopted exclusive or restrictive membership patterns.

Despite the fact that the national parties are open and accessible, relatively modest numbers of Canadians choose to join or participate in them in even the most nominal fashion. Over the four-year period from 1987 through 1990, local party association memberships averaged 600; during 1988, an election year, the figure was 150 higher at 750. Assuming something in the order of three active local associations per constituency, this suggests that about 550 000 Canadians may be members of a political party at any time, with up to another 150 000 joining for general elections. As we shall see, the apparent volatility of membership figures suggests that many of these attachments must be rather shallow and minimal.

To put this in perspective, we can examine some comparative data from other Western liberal democracies (summarized in table 3.1). Given that reports of party membership figures are often imprecise, and membership is itself variable (Selle and Svasand 1991), these figures might best be interpreted as indicators rather than measures. But the general message is clear enough. Canadian parties are at the bottom of the table, enrolling a smaller proportion of their country's electorate than all but the Australian parties. At the top are parties in the smaller Western

Table 3.1
Comparative party membership rates
(percentages)

Country	Rate of membership*
Austria	21.8
Finland	12.9
Belgium	9.2
Denmark	6.5
Ireland	5.3
West Germany	4.2
United Kingdom	3.3
Netherlands	2.8
Canada	2.7
Australia	2.4

Sources: Katz and Mair (1992); Ward (1991).

*Percentage of the electorate members of a party circa late 1980s.

European democracies, where political parties have traditionally mobilized distinctive social constituencies, but even in larger countries like
Germany or the United Kingdom the rate of party membership is higher.
That being so, Canadian parties are not likely to be able to do all the
things that European parties do.

In Canada, over 17 1/2 million electors were enumerated for
the 1988 general election. Since not all party members are eligible
voters (for reasons of age or citizenship) it seems that the local party
associations do not manage to engage much more than 2 2/3 percent
of the total electorate. This becomes clear when we look at the membership figures for 1988. That year 40 percent of the parties' constituency associations had memberships of less than 1 percent of
their local electorate, and three-quarters of them enrolled less than
2 percent. Only a handful had a membership greater than 4 percent
of the local electorate. As one might expect, these bigger associations
were more common in the governing Progressive Conservative party and in instances where a party had an incumbent member of
Parliament.

The number of partisans who contribute financially to the local
associations is much lower than those who take out membership. In
1990, the typical (median) constituency party association received contributions from just 50 individual donors, equivalent to about a fifth of
its membership. However in election years, when the associations'
needs are greatest, individual donors are more forthcoming. For example, in 1988, the typical association received contributions from
120 individuals, equal to a third of its membership, though it is almost certain that not all contributors were themselves members. All
in all, the total number of contributors to local associations was likely
less than the 313 000 that Stanbury (1991, table 8.1) reports gave to parties or candidates that election year. It appears then that the typical
local party association has a very small base of financial supporters
and must compete with other levels of the party for the financial support of many of its nominal supporters.

But this simple portrait of the typical Canadian constituency party
association as a small company of partisans conceals more than it reveals.
Before we can explore the range and variety of party activity in the constituencies, it is necessary to examine the patterns of party membership in greater detail. Local associations vary enormously in size and
stability, and they provide evidence to support the proposition that the
different national parties are themselves quite different kinds of organizations.

CONSTITUENCY ASSOCIATION RESOURCES: MEMBERS AND MONEY

Parties and Their Members

In his classic discussion of party membership, Maurice Duverger (1954) argues that the very concept varies by party, and he makes this difference the basis for his famous distinction between *mass* and *cadre* parties. In the mass party "members are the very substance of the party, the stuff of its activity" (ibid., 63). Building a mass party involves recruiting members who continually support and participate in a wide variety of party activities. A successful mass party ultimately depends on a large membership to overcome its opponents. On the other hand, a cadre party is typically centred on a smaller, more narrowly focused band, what Duverger calls a "grouping of notabilities for the preparation of elections, conducting campaigns and maintaining contact with the candidates" (ibid., 64). This sort of party is little more than an electoral machine, so any concern to maintain formal memberships at a high level between elections has something of an artificial cast to it.

It follows then, that mass and cadre parties ought to differ in the size, stability and activity levels of their memberships. On all three criteria the mass party will have relatively higher values. However Duverger warns us that "this distinction, though clear in theory, is not always easy to make in practice" (1954, 64). Modern parties learn from one another and are now quick to emulate organizational features that they think will be to their advantage (Kirchheimer 1966). Thus, as a secondary guide to recognizing mass–cadre differences, Duverger notes that the distinction also generally corresponds to the parties of the left and right, and that mass parties typically grow out of radical political movements while cadre parties evolve out of parliamentary caucuses.

To the extent that Canadian parties can be readily classified, the Progressive Conservative and Liberal parties come closest to the cadre party model, the New Democrats and enduring minor parties to the mass party type. The Conservative and Liberal parties' early organizations consisted of extensive patronage networks tied to their great party chieftains (Stewart 1980). They did not develop national extra-parliamentary organizations until after the First World War, so that formal party membership was hardly an issue for them over the first half-century of their existence. In contrast, the CCF, the precursor of the NDP, was especially concerned to define and sustain a democratic member-based organization. This perspective leads us to expect that membership in Tory and Liberal constituency associations will be more open and volatile, and the members may be less active between elections, than is the case in the NDP.

We have, in effect, two models of party organization that may distinguish the parties, and the patterns of membership and involvement of Canadians in them. As cadre-style parties, the Liberals and Conservatives ought to have unstable memberships that follow the rhythms and outcomes of the electoral cycle. In the period immediately before and after an election their party memberships will be at their highest, but will decline over the next several years until another election reactivates partisans, who rejoin to participate in the candidate nomination and campaigning processes. This should result in a wavelike membership cycle with the peaks generally corresponding to election years (see figure 3.1).

Parties with a tradition of a mass organization like the NDP, and newer, programmatic parties such as the Christian Heritage party, are likely to have quite different membership patterns. Because these parties seek to involve their members in more than just electoral activity, the pattern of their memberships is likely to be relatively independent of the electoral cycle (figure 3.1). Thus their memberships should be much more stable and regular.

In the period since 1987 the Reform Party has burst into Canadian politics. Starting from nothing in Alberta, the party quickly spread across first that province, and then much of the rest of English-speaking Canada. Its development has been typical of the first stage

Figure 3.1
Party membership patterns

Membership

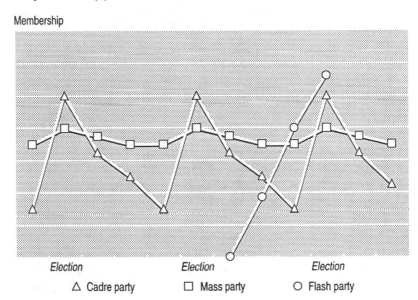

Election   Election   Election

△ Cadre party   □ Mass party   ○ Flash party

of what Converse and Depeux (1966) called a *flash* party. Such parties typically peak quickly, then decline. However it is equally possible that one will establish a permanent place in the party system as either a cadre or mass-based organization. At its current early stage of development it is difficult to predict whether the Reform Party will go into rapid decline or will institutionalize one of these two (electoral-cycle or stable) membership patterns.

The constituency survey data allow us to explore, for the first time, the extent to which these characterizations of the Canadian parties hold true. Each constituency party association was asked the size of its membership for each of the four years from 1987 through 1990. Given that there was a general election in 1988, this takes us from the year before an election through to the midpoint of the next electoral cycle and should allow us to discover what short-term rhythms underlie constituency party memberships.

Our theoretical expectations on these questions must be tempered by a sensitivity to the reality of Canadian politics. Large regional variations in the national parties' electoral support remain a central feature of the party system and these are likely to be mirrored in parties' membership strength. At the same time, a single-member electoral system means that individual parliamentarians can be key figures in building and nurturing strong constituency party organizations. Certainly they generally have the resources (in their constituency offices and staff) and incentives (an unchallenged renomination and an effective election machine) to do so. Thus it seems reasonable to expect that the existence of an incumbent MP can make a positive difference in the character, size and activities of local party organizations.

The typical constituency party association in Canada had 350 members over 1987–90 (table 3.2). The data indicate that the governing Conservatives did not generally have exceptionally large local memberships; their typical size (350) proved to be the norm among all five parties. Surprisingly, it was the Liberals, an opposition cadre party, who appear to have had the largest memberships (537), though the absolute size of their local associations varied more than those in the Conservative party. The median NDP association was smaller (285) than those in both its two older and successful opponents, but at the same time there was relatively more variation in NDP memberships than for either the Liberals or Conservatives. This suggests something of a feast-or-famine character about NDP local association strength. In contrast to the three national parties, the Christian Heritage party had the classic organizational base of a minor, ideological party: a small number of small (117) associations with comparatively limited variation among them.

Table 3.2
Constituency association membership, 1987–90

	Median size	Range
All parties	350	7–6 000
Progressive Conservative	350	31–2 325
Liberal	537	7–6 000
NDP	285	8–5 500
Reform	308	95–1 200
Christian Heritage	117	37– 775
Incumbent	644	45–5 500
No incumbent	281	7–6 000

Note: Includes only associations reporting membership data for all four years.

Having an incumbent member of Parliament appears to make a difference down in the constituencies. The typical local association with an MP was more than twice the size of those without one. It is, of course, not immediately obvious whether incumbents generate larger organizations or large organizations win and produce incumbents, but the overall difference does suggest that incumbents are likely to have a marked local organizational advantage as they prepare for an election. As we shall see there are some striking interparty differences in the extent of this incumbency effect.

Table 3.3 reports the extent of regional variation in the membership strength of constituency party associations. Riding parties were typically smallest in Atlantic Canada, largest on the Prairies, but the overall variation does not seem to be especially great. However the table also reveals that the regional medians conceal very significant differences between individual parties. As one might expect, these differences were smallest within the governing Progressive Conservative party, though even there the average Quebec PC association was three and a half times the size of its opposite number in Atlantic Canada. In the Liberal party an east–west gradient seemed to govern local association membership: constituency associations in Atlantic Canada were more than seven times the size of those in British Columbia. The Prairies seem to be the exception to this rule, though that may be partially explained by the temporary mobilization successes of leadership candidates. Of the three parties that claimed to be national in scope, the NDP suffered the greatest variation in its local membership. East of the Ottawa River average constituency party memberships were relatively feeble and in many instances must signal only a nominal presence,

Table 3.3
Constituency association membership by region, 1987–90
(median association)

	B.C.	Prairies	Ontario	Quebec	Atlantic
All parties	350	438	300	380	295
Progressive Conservative	404	439	291	775	215
Liberal	275	683	494	669	2 077
NDP	1 200	1 000	281	109	167
Reform	218	316	—	—	—
Christian Heritage	100	106	150	—	66

what mass parties in Europe often refer to as a "paper branch." On the other hand, the NDP associations west of the Ontario–Manitoba border are the largest for these regions reported in the table. The two small parties have obvious regional bases, though in the case of Reform it must be remembered that its own constitution limited it to areas west of Ontario at the time the data was collected. Since then it has moved aggressively to build local associations in all other provinces except Quebec.

These differences remind us that the parties have very different organizational presences, and organizational capacity, in the various regions of the country. This reality underlies many of the differences in their activities and electoral success. At the same time it suggests that local associations are not all going to be able to respond similarly to demands made on them by either their national organizations or the state. This seems inevitable as long as they remain essentially relatively informal voluntary organizations reflecting the enthusiasms (or lack of them) of local partisans.

Not only is there a very substantial variation among constituency association membership size within parties, the evidence also reveals that membership varies considerably within individual associations from year to year. The volatility of the typical constituency membership is summarized in table 3.4. The measure indicates how much the constituency changed, from its smallest to its largest membership, over the four-year period. This change need not have been regular or unidirectional, the indicator simply records how much of it there was during the four years. The median local association underwent a 224 percent change from its lowest to its highest membership point. And as we can see from the table there were some sharp, but not surprising, differences among the parties.

In the three national parties, local association membership was much more volatile in the Liberal party (the median change was

Table 3.4
Constituency association membership volatility, 1987–90
(percentages, median association)

	Volatility
All parties	224
Progressive Conservative	207
Liberal	340
NDP	67
Reform	1 500
Christian Heritage	237
Incumbent	171
No incumbent	250

Note: Based on membership size over period for associations reporting all four years. Calculated as: [(largest – smallest)/ smallest] x 100.

340 percent) and the Progressive Conservative party (207 percent), as one might expect in cadre-style organizations that are primarily electorally focused. Thus, in the governing Conservative party, 80 percent of the local associations reported that over the four years their membership was largest in the election year (1988). Constituency membership in Liberal associations was typically more volatile, in part because a party in opposition has fewer MPs who have incentives and opportunities to stabilize their local association's membership. However, as we shall see later, there were also other forces at work in the Liberal party over this period capable of driving local memberships on a rollercoaster.

By comparison, individual NDP local associations appear to have much more stable memberships: their volatility was only a third of the national norm, and a fifth of the Liberals'. This despite the fact that there was as much range in the absolute size of NDP associations as there was in the Liberal party. But this is what we might expect in a party with a tradition and organizational style typical of a mass-based party. It could be, of course, that even this aggregate stability masks a considerable turnover of individual members, as Selle and Svasand (1991, 463) report is the case in both Norwegian and Swedish socialist parties. Unfortunately our constituency-level data do not allow us to compare the length of individual memberships across the associations and the parties.

Though there are only a small number of Reform Party local associations for which we have four years of membership data, their story is one of enormous change (the median volatility rate was 1 500 percent), in this case the explosive growth that characterized the emergence of Reform as a new party in the Canadian system. At the time of this study the party was still aggressively adding new constituency associations as it expanded eastward. Until this stage of the party's development has been completed, and its immediate future charted by the outcome of the next general election (its first nationwide campaign), it is impossible to say a great deal more about its membership patterns.

The figures in table 3.4 also indicate that, on the whole, local party associations with a sitting MP have a more stable membership than do those without one. This, no doubt, reflects both the volatility of minor parties and the opportunities to expand membership in contested nomination battles that are more common in open seats (Carty and Erickson 1991). But it may also be that incumbent MPs, having built a winning team in their riding association, are able to hold their members, since members take pride in their association with the dominant local political organization. However, given the greater differences among the parties, one probably ought not to read too much into the effect of incumbency on membership volatility.

Party Membership and the Electoral Cycle

At the heart of Duverger's distinction between cadre and mass parties is the extent to which their organization and membership are driven by an electoral cycle. This leads us to expect sharp differences in the patterns of constituency association membership over time among the three large established national parties (figure 3.1). The evidence rather dramatically confirms this interpretation: the Conservatives and Liberals do have cadre-type memberships, the New Democrats those typical of a mass party (figure 3.2).

The typical Conservative association membership pattern is classic. In 1988, the election year, it doubled from what it had been the previous year and then went into decline, falling so much that by 1990 it was at its lowest point of the four-year cycle (table 3.5). This is precisely what one would have expected of a successful cadre party, though the extent of the decline also reflects some membership desertion to Reform: the typical Conservative constituency association membership in Alberta (Reform's base) fell from 725 in 1988 to 150 in 1990.

The Liberal pattern is much the same, though two aspects of it explain that party's generally larger and more volatile memberships, as well as revealing something about the character of membership in electorally focused Canadian party organizations. First, despite being the same size as the Tory one in 1987, the typical Liberal constituency association grew more in the election year. In large part this reflects the

Figure 3.2
Cycle of Canadian constituency association membership, 1987–90

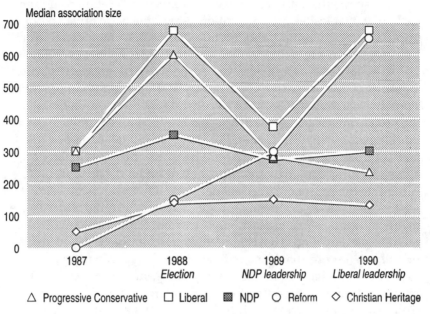

vigorous membership campaigns that went on in the larger number of contested nomination meetings held by the Liberals. It demonstrates how the electoral impulse may produce larger, but hence more volatile, memberships for a party in opposition. A second, more dramatic, Liberal–Conservative membership difference shows up clearly in figure 3.2. After the expected post-election-year membership decline, Liberal constituency association membership quickly peaked again in 1990 to election-year levels. The explanation, of course, is to be found in the hard-fought party leadership contest of that year. Supporters of

Table 3.5
Median constituency association membership

Party	1987	1988	1989	1990
Progressive Conservative	300	600	283	235
Liberal	300	675	375	675
NDP	250	350	275	300
Reform	—	150	300	650
Christian Heritage	50	140	150	132

Jean Chrétien and Paul Martin, and to a lesser extent of the other three candidates, recruited large numbers into local associations as they struggled to capture the delegates each constituency association could send to the national leadership convention. Again the basic organizational imperative was electoral, though in this case driven by the electoral dynamics of the party itself rather than the wider political system.

It seems that for large numbers of the two national cadre parties' supporters, formal party membership is at once limited but (occasionally) valuable. That so many readily take it up at election times, but then put it down equally quickly, suggests it has limited intrinsic meaning for Conservative and Liberal partisans in interelection periods. It has value precisely, and perhaps only, because it provides a party franchise. Thus when party elections are to be held – to nominate a candidate in an election, or select delegates for a leadership contest – membership takes on its meaning and worth, and individuals are mobilized for those contests with little concern for longer-term involvement or participation. This is not a membership that is easily institutionalized, nor one that is likely to lead the extraparliamentary party to play an effective part in political activities, such as policy development, that have only indirect electoral consequences. If Liberal or Conservative party membership simply confers a vote on those who hold it, then constituency association membership fees may, in terms of their significance for the wider political system, represent a kind of poll tax regulating participation in a specific set of electoral contests. We can return to the implications of this when we consider the internal electoral (nomination and leadership selection) activities of these associations in chapter 5.

Membership in the New Democratic Party is quite different. Though there is a modest increase in the size of the median constituency association in the election year, it is nowhere near as pronounced as in the Liberal or Progressive Conservative parties. By and large, NDP associations appear to have memberships that are stable and relatively independent of the electoral cycle. This different orientation toward membership held by the party comes into even sharper focus when we remember that the party held a national leadership contest (the first in 14 years) in 1989. Yet the median association had a smaller membership that year than for either 1988 (admittedly an election year) or 1990. Unlike that of the Liberals in 1990, the NDP leadership contest did not stimulate the mobilization of larger numbers of new members, it was simply part of the business of an ongoing well-established membership. To the extent that NDP membership also conveys a party franchise, it does so in a mass party organized on fundamentally different principles from those that characterize the Liberals and Conservatives.

Something of this difference was revealed by the constituency association presidents in their response to a question that asked them to account for any sudden changes in local membership over the 1987–90 period. To begin with, only half as many New Democrats as Liberals or Conservatives felt they had anything to explain, though in all three parties the federal election was then identified as the single most important stimulus to membership change: between 40 and 45 percent of those responding named it. Among Conservatives a scattering of other reasons were offered, but in the Liberal party a majority of all the riding presidents pointed directly to the leadership contest as an explanation for membership volatility. In contrast, not one of the NDP respondents indicated that the party's leadership contest was responsible for changes in local membership. However, unlike Liberals or Tories, New Democrats did identify provincial or municipal electoral activity as a significant factor. This testifies to the New Democrats' mission, as a mass party, to integrate party organization and activity across the full spectrum of Canadian political life.

The membership data also confirm our images of the two minor parties. The profile of the median Reform Party constituency association size demonstrates that party's extraordinary growth (figure 3.2). By 1990, only in the Liberal party was the median constituency association larger, and that was an atypical year for the Liberals. It is true that the Reform Party had associations in fewer constituencies over this period than the three national parties, but the number of Reform associations was increasing even as was their average size. There can be little doubt that the Reform Party was exciting growing numbers of Canadians to engage in a protest politics that aimed at recasting party competition and perhaps the very definition of Canada itself.

The membership profile of the Christian Heritage party's local associations is rather flat, not unlike that of the NDP. This reflects the same mass-party organizational style. The CHP has smaller constituency associations, and there are fewer of them; this reflects the narrower appeal of its attempt to build a political party focused on traditional Christian family values. On the other hand, the very stability of the CHP's mass membership pattern suggests that the party's ongoing activity and continuing existence may be somewhat independent of the vicissitudes of electoral outcomes.

MPs' Constituency Associations

Figure 3.3 demonstrates the impact of an incumbent MP on the size of constituency party associations. In both the Progressive Conservative

Figure 3.3
Incumbency and constituency association membership

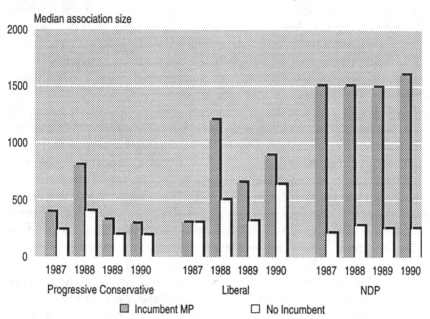

Median association size

| | Incumbent MP | | No Incumbent |

and Liberal parties membership fluctuated over the electoral cycle but the median constituency association was generally up to twice as large when there was an incumbent. This is a marked difference and can be taken as a measure of the impact of electoral success on a cadre-style local organization. In 1988 the difference was even greater in the Opposition Liberal party, which was struggling to recapture seats lost in the 1984 Conservative landslide. This leads us to infer that vigorous local memberships may have been part of the story in areas where Liberals did win. On the other hand, in the leadership-contest year of 1990, the difference between incumbent and nonincumbent Liberal constituency associations seems to have shrunk. This pattern is consistent with the tactics of leadership-campaign politics in which candidates' organizations make particular efforts to mobilize support in ridings where the absence of a sitting MP leaves the local association weaker and so more permeable (Carty 1988a).

New Democratic Party constituency membership was not affected by the electoral cycle, but the presence of an incumbent did make a much greater difference than in either of the two cadre parties. The median NDP association with a sitting MP was over six times larger than the association without one. In areas of electoral strength the party was obviously able to mobilize a substantial body of supporters and keep them participating at least to the extent of maintaining formal party membership. This is consistent with the New Democrats' mass-membership organizational style, though it raises the question whether the resources of elected office may be an important element in sustaining such an organization in a pluralistic society like Canada.

Though there were only a relatively small number of these large MP-led constituency associations in the NDP, this large difference may not be unimportant for internal party politics. This is because party democracy in the New Democratic Party is tied to members, not territory as in the Liberal and Progressive Conservative parties. While conventions in the two big parties have all constituency associations represented equally, New Democratic conventions give more representatives to larger associations in an attempt to equalize individual members' influence. In practice this must mean that, as a group, constituency delegations headed by MPs will have considerable influence in NDP decision making. In light of this, it is perhaps not too surprising that the candidate favoured by the party establishment and the majority of the caucus has rarely had much difficulty in winning the party's leadership (Morley 1992).

The typical NDP MP's constituency association is not only much larger than others in the party, it is much larger and more stable than those available to Liberal or Conservative members. To the extent that the membership of a local association is a valuable election asset, it seems that the NDP's MPs are better prepared to fight an election than are those in the electorally oriented Liberal and Progressive Conservative parties. Any irony in this is more apparent than real. As the inventor of modern mass-mobilization electoral politics Daniel O'Connell (who campaigned for Catholic emancipation and Irish Home Rule) demonstrated almost two hundred years ago, the point of a mass party is just that: to provide political outsiders with a vehicle to challenge the established political élites.

Those who wish to strengthen and expand the role of the extra-parliamentary parties in Canadian politics, particularly in terms of formulating and debating public policy and in holding politicians more responsible (however defined) to their constituents, may find this portrait of local membership discouraging. After all, that sort of activity requires a substantial membership with an ongoing commitment to party work, and only a few constituency associations (the NDP-held ridings) now have one. This pattern of low, fluctuating party membership is obviously an important part of the explanation of the failure of the "participatory democracy" experiment in the Liberal party during the early 1970s (Clarkson 1979). Of course one might argue that the opportunity for fuller and more meaningful participation would change membership patterns, though the differences among NDP associations, which seem related to electoral success, must cast some doubt on that as a general proposition. After considering the financial base that these members provide for the parties' constituency associations, and what other assets they possess, we can turn to the question of how these associations are organized and just how active they really are.

The Financial Base of Membership

Members constitute the core of the constituency associations' human resources. Through their membership fees they also provide local associations with a financial base. Most associations have financial resources other than their annual membership fees and the next chapter provides a fuller examination of local association finances. At this point we are concerned to estimate the potential financial contribution (in the form of local fees) that membership per se can make to the local associations. Many constituency party associations find that, in practice, their parent organizations insist on some form of fee-splitting arrangement so that fee income is shared with other party units. Thus a constituency association's total fee income represents what regular membership might contribute, and not necessarily what it does, to local coffers.

Membership fee income depends upon two variables: the number of members and the fees charged. The parties' membership profiles have been described above. Their constituency associations' fees vary, though the general picture is one of fairly modest amounts: 5 percent of them report that they have no fee at all, while none charge more than $35.00 per year. The typical (median) constituency association sets its annual membership fee at just $10.00, though there are some significant differences among the parties in terms of their local membership charge. The pattern of membership fees is not random. Parties that take membership more seriously, and depend more upon their members for financial support (perhaps because they have less easy access to those who control society's wealth), will almost inevitably have higher fees. Thus, of the three major parties, the Conservatives have the lowest fee at $5.00, while the median NDP charge is three times that at $15.00. The Liberals sit in between at $8.00. The two minor parties differ from one another as well: the median Reform Party association reported charging $9.00, while the Christian Heritage party was twice that (and the highest of any party) at $18.00.

Applying the annual fee to the size of the association provides a

Table 3.6
Constituency association membership fee income, 1987–90
(dollars, median association)

	1987	1988	1989	1990
All parties	1 550	3 250	2 500	3 000
Progressive Conservative	1 500	3 000	1 450	1 250
Liberal	2 000	4 000	3 000	5 000
NDP	2 450	3 920	3 350	3 200
Reform	—	1 500	3 000	6 500
Christian Heritage	1 000	2 600	2 810	2 400

measure of a constituency party's raw membership income. Table 3.6 summarizes this in the form of the median income of a constituency association in each party over all four years for which we have membership figures. The patterns are quite clear and obviously mimic those for association membership numbers. Membership income peaks in the Liberal and Progressive Conservative parties in electoral years, it is generally flatter in the NDP and CHP, and it has grown at quite dramatic rates in the Reform Party. But while both the old cadre parties typically had more members than the NDP, the higher membership fees in the latter meant that its associations often had a higher membership income. Only in the Liberal leadership contest year of 1990 did the typical Liberal association have a markedly higher membership-fee income than its NDP counterpart, and not once in the four-year period did the median membership income of Conservative associations (with their much lower fees) approach that of the NDP. Even in the election year of 1988, the governing Conservative party's typical association had a membership income ($3 000) that was only three-quarters that of one in the third-place NDP.

Association membership levels are influenced by the presence of a local MP, and the same is true for membership incomes (table 3.7). But here again the cross-party differences are quite striking. Thus, with the exception of 1988, nonincumbent NDP riding associations actually had larger membership incomes than did associations with an incumbent in the governing Progressive Conservative party. By far the most affluent associations, in terms of the base provided by their own membership, were those in the NDP that had an incumbent MP. If we take the 1987–90 period as an approximation of a normal four-year electoral cycle, then the total four-year membership income reported in table 3.7 indicates what formal party membership can be thought of as contributing to the local association's financial base.

Table 3.7
Constituency association membership income: the effect of incumbency, 1987–90
(dollars, median association)

	1987	1988	1989	1990	Total
All parties					
Incumbent	2 000	5 000	2 500	2 100	11 600
No incumbent	1 500	2 830	2 500	3 000	9 830
Progressive Conservative					
Incumbent	1 650	4 000	1 500	1 375	8 525
No incumbent	1 225	1 900	882	940	4 947
Liberal					
Incumbent	2 200	7 500	4 290	6 000	19 990
No incumbent	1 650	3 750	2 500	4 882	12 782
NDP					
Incumbent	22 000	22 000	23 000	24 000	91 000
No incumbent	2 250	3 800	3 125	3 025	12 200

It is quite clear that membership income is relatively unimportant to Conservative constituency associations. Even those with incumbents typically took in just $8 500 over a four-year cycle. At the other end of the spectrum are the limited number of associations headed by NDP MPs whose average membership income over the period was over $90 000. Only in these latter cases was the total membership income larger than the typical candidate is allowed to spend under the current electoral expenses regime. For those NDP MPs, it was twice the average allowable expense in 1988. (For an account of candidate expense regulation see Stanbury 1991, chap. 12.) Though membership fees in all parties go to a wide range of activities, only NDP MPs have local associations that are, in principle, self-sufficient. In all other cases local associations must depend upon other funding, in the form of transfer payments from other units in the party, voluntary giving by regular activists or the charity of people who are not party members, to accumulate the funds necessary for electoral or other activities. This financial dependence would seem to compromise the autonomy of local associations as independent organizations, making them uncertain instruments for party members and a questionable base for a healthy party democracy.

Local Association Assets
Individual constituency associations may have a number of other assets that help them support their membership. As we have already noted, the most important asset may well be an incumbent member of

Parliament. Yet when associations with incumbents were asked "If your party holds the riding, does the constituency association use the MP's office for association business?" two-thirds of the Conservatives, over half of the Liberals and nearly 40 percent of the New Democrats said they never did: the great majority of the rest reported using the office only occasionally. The distinction between an MP's activities and the partisan interests of the constituency organization may sometimes be difficult to draw (especially as an election approaches). However, these responses suggest that local associations generally do not see themselves as exploiting the facilities that are available to MPs in their role of representing and serving all their constituents.

Only a very few (1 percent) of the local parties regularly employed any paid staff. Rather more of them possessed a variety of the modern office equipment commonly used by organizations concerned with communicating with the public (table 3.8). Particularly notable is the absence of computers, generally thought vital to membership and financial record-keeping, desktop publishing, direct-mail activities, campaign planning and organizing, and detailed tracking of the electorate, all of which constitute vital tasks for effective local parties. Even among the Tories, who far outpaced their opponents in this regard, less than half of the associations had their own computer. While more might have had access to one through an individual member, that is hardly a desirable substitute for it leaves the local association dependent on volunteer resources and vulnerable to losing access to equipment and data at critical times. Certainly any change in the law that imposed significant new record-keeping and reporting burdens on local associations would require that they significantly increase their capacity in this regard. How realistic this is for the large number of small associations (17 percent had 100 or fewer members in 1990) is difficult to assess.

Table 3.8
Constituency association assets
(percentage owning asset)

Asset	Progressive Conservative	Liberal	NDP	Reform	Christian Heritage
Office furniture	31	16	38	11	19
Computer	46	19	12	14	14
Photocopier	10	3	2	18	—
Telephone/answering machine	14	10	15	39	—

Reform Party associations stand out as having quickly accumulated various kinds of hardware. In several instances they appeared, as a group, to be better equipped than the associations of the long-established national parties and, given the rapidity of Reform Party growth, this picture may underestimate their infrastructure development. Having to start from scratch does not appear to have hindered Reform association organization. In fact, the absence of local élites committed to "doing it the way we have always done it," may make it easier for the party to put modern technology in place and to work in its constituency parties.

THE POLITICAL FOCUS OF CONSTITUENCY PARTY ASSOCIATIONS

The organization of constituency parties is structured by the federal electoral maps in each province; the local associations exist to organize members and supporters in each federal electoral district. The parties, however, see the place of their members and constituency organizations in different ways. As Rand Dyck (1991) has shown, sharply contrasting models of party organization are used by Canadian parties. The *confederal* model has the federal and provincial wings of what is nominally the same political group quite distinct from one another, with little or no formal organizational linkages between them. That would appear to be the most efficient structure for an electorally oriented cadre party. The alternative model has the organization and activities of both federal and provincial wings of a party highly *integrated* and mutually supportive. That is a form that seems particularly appropriate for a mass party such as the NDP. These models are useful for identifying the various parties' dominant organizational forms though, as Dyck notes, the historical development of Canadian politics has ensured that none of the three national parties' organizations are completely homogeneous.

The Progressive Conservative and Reform parties have confederal organizations, with Reform, to date, refusing to lend its name to any provincial party. In these two cases individuals are members of the national party and articulate that membership through their local federal constituency association. Organizationally, party membership is quite independent of any provincial party structure. The New Democrats, who have an integrated organizational structure, are at the opposite end of Dyck's spectrum of party types. Their much more complex structure provides for both direct individual membership and the indirect affiliated membership of trade unionists. However, individual members can join the federal party only by joining their respective provincial NDP, so that the federal constituency associations have often played second fiddle to provincial constituency organizations in provinces where the NDP is strong. As well, in some localities NDP branches have been active in municipal government, which has traditionally been organized on a nonpartisan basis in Canada. The Liberal party has neither a confederal nor an integrated structure but is something of a hybrid. It is structured as a national federation, but members encounter two quite distinct patterns of membership. In four provinces (British Columbia, Alberta, Ontario and Quebec) individuals join the Liberal Party of Canada (province) independently of their membership in a provincial Liberal party. In the other six provinces (and two territories) the provincial and federal Liberal party are one and the same, so individuals join both simultaneously.

Whatever formal structures exist, Dyck suggests that party organizations and their activities are more integrated in the Atlantic provinces. That, he argues, is because of the more limited party resources available in these smaller provinces and the persistence of the traditional two-party system in the region. Quebec is just the opposite: in that province confederal arrangements dominate, and even the NDP has had to make an exception to its normal structure and separate its provincial and federal party organizations.

To explore the impact of these formal structural differences on the local associations, we asked about the exclusiveness of the associations' membership and the focus of local activity. Are the differences Dyck describes as characterizing the parties' constitutional forms reflected in their constituency organizations' memberships? Are associations with less exclusive memberships more likely than others to mix federal and provincial political activity? Answers to these questions reveal something of the gap between national constitutional forms and local association practice in the major parties.

In principle, confederal parties will have constituency associations whose membership is, as the questionnaire puts it, "exclusively federal," while integrated parties should have a membership that is "joint with the provincial party." A further possibility is that some riding associations will have no formal memberships, preferring to rely on more traditional understandings of just who is part of the local party. However the formalization of membership engendered by convention and leadership politics in recent years ought to have nearly eliminated all such local organizations. Table 3.9 summarizes the responses to a question that asked which of these three categories described the local association's membership. Fifty-nine percent reported an exclusively federal membership, 39 percent one that was joint. Only a handful of associations claimed they had no formal membership, though there were a few in each of the national parties.

Table 3.9
Constituency association membership status
(percentage)

	Exclusively federal	Joint with provincial party	No formal membership
All parties	59	39	2
Progressive Conservative	74	23	3
Liberal	48	50	2
NDP	25	73	2
Reform	100	—	—
Christian Heritage	98	2	—
Province			
Newfoundland	40	50	10
Nova Scotia	20	70	10
Prince Edward Island	—	83	17
New Brunswick	33	67	—
Quebec	57	43	—
Ontario	67	31	2
Manitoba	42	54	3
Saskatchewan	45	52	3
Alberta	81	19	—
British Columbia	61	37	1

The pattern of local membership is just what Dyck's analysis of the parties' structures would suggest. Three-quarters of the Conservatives' local associations claimed to have exclusively federal memberships while only one-quarter of the New Democrats' did. The Liberals sit firmly in the centre with half of their associations having an exclusive (confederal-model) membership and the other half a joint (integrated-model) membership. But this still leaves about a quarter of the Conservative and New Democratic associations operating in a fashion that is at least counter to the spirit of their constitutional/organizational norms.

Of the two, the New Democrats appeared the most consistent: only in three provinces (but the three biggest – Ontario, Quebec and British Columbia) did some associations report exclusively federal memberships, and two-thirds of them were in Quebec. By contrast, and despite a national constitution which eschews joint federal-provincial memberships, the Progressive Conservative party had associations in eight provinces which claimed to share members with a provincial party. This confirms the conventional wisdom that the NDP has a more homogeneous cast to its membership than does the Progressive Conservative party. The NDP's close approximation to the integrated party model probably reflects the greater seriousness the party attaches to membership, but it is also consistent with our portrait of the NDP as a mass party rooted in a dependable and involved membership.

As expected, local association membership also varied across the country (table 3.9). The vast majority of the constituency associations in the three Maritime provinces had local memberships that were jointly held with provincial parties. This is true, regardless of party, in a region that continues to be dominated by the Liberals and Conservatives and where NDP organizational forms have made little impression. Exclusive memberships were most common in the four largest provinces – Ontario, Quebec, British Columbia and Alberta. If we take the proportion of associations with exclusive memberships as an indicator of the degree to which federal and provincial party life is separate, then this data suggests that Alberta is the province whose federal and provincial party politics are most alienated from one another.

An association's membership structure is one thing, its focus of activity is quite another. In an attempt to get some idea of the latter, the survey asked respondents what their local association executive was concerned with, and provided four possible responses: (*a*) "federal politics exclusively," (*b*) "mainly federal politics but sometimes provincial affairs," (*c*) "federal and provincial politics equally" and (*d*) "mainly provincial politics but sometimes federal affairs." The responses by party and by region appear in table 3.10. The differences

Table 3.10
Activity focus of constituency association executives
(percentages)

	Only federal	Mainly federal	Federal and provincial equally	Mainly provincial
All parties	47	36	14	3
Progressive Conservative	52	35	13	—
Liberal	36	45	18	1
NDP	32	38	22	9
Reform	86	14	—	—
Christian Heritage	60	34	4	2
Region				
Atlantic	22	49	26	4
Quebec	70	24	6	—
Ontario	45	36	17	4
Prairies	45	42	12	1
British Columbia	49	36	13	3

were not as sharp as one might have inferred from those just considered on membership.

As Dyck's confederal-integrated party structure analysis suggests, Conservative constituency associations were more concerned with federal politics, those in the NDP with federal and provincial (or even mainly provincial) political activity. Reform associations were clearly focused on federal politics, though 14 percent of them admitted to some concern with provincial affairs, despite their party leader's oft-declared determination to keep them out of provincial politics.

These modest party differences were not nearly as striking as those among the regions. West of the Ottawa River there did not appear to be much variation, but associations in the two eastern regions were dramatically different. In Quebec, constituency associations were almost completely concerned with federal politics and claimed to be little concerned with provincial politics. In Atlantic Canada, however, a far smaller proportion reported that they were exclusively concerned with federal politics. This, of course, matches the pattern of far more integrated federal-provincial party memberships that we discovered in that part of the country.

There was a moderate relationship between the type of membership and the focus of an association's activity, though it was less compelling than one might have anticipated. A majority of the associations with an exclusively federal membership were solely concerned with federal politics but a third of them reported giving at least some attention to provincial politics. Among those with joint memberships only a quarter claimed to be exclusively concerned with federal politics and 27 percent reported giving equal attention to federal and provincial affairs (table 3.11). This is a pattern that held fairly consistently across all three national parties.

Table 3.11
Constituency association activity focus by membership type
(percentages)

	Membership type	
Activity focus	Exclusively federal	Joint with provincial party
Federal only	64	24
Mainly federal	32	43
Federal and provincial equally	4	27
Mainly provincial	—	6

Eleven percent of the national parties' constituency associations reported that they were involved (in an unspecified way) in municipal politics. There were sharp differences across the three large parties in this regard: 7 percent of the Conservative associations reported such activity while three times that many (22 percent) of the New Democrats did. The Liberals, with a 10-percent involvement rate, were between those two at close to the national average. This means that some parties are more likely than others to be diverting federally receipted (with the help of the tax credit provided by Parliament) funds into municipal politics. To the extent that this is seen as a public policy issue, these data remind us that the parties have quite different interests in it.

The general picture that emerges from this brief discussion of the membership and orientation of these federal constituency associations is that they are not just federal constituency associations pure and simple. All told, only 38 percent of them had an exclusively federal membership and were solely concerned with federal politics. The majority are more complex multifaceted organizations. Their members are shared and their activities are correspondingly oriented toward more than just national politics. Not surprisingly, this fluctuates with the electoral cycle and the demands parties are able to make on their local activists.

Dyck (1989, 213) has argued that the advent of federal and provincial election expense legislation was a significant factor in "increasing the separation between federal and provincial branches of the three parties." A detailed regulatory regime that went a step further, and provided for the registration of constituency party associations, might be expected to foster even more local organization specialization. This would probably take the form of either more confederally structured parties or more Byzantine overlap and obfuscation within parties committed to an integrated approach to political party life in Canada.

CONSTITUENCY ASSOCIATION ORGANIZATION

Canadian party constituency associations, with relatively small and often variable memberships, are multifaceted but not especially complex organizations. They are generally run by local volunteers and their level of activity depends upon the time and energy their leading activists are able to give them. Despite a growing interest among the national parties in having their associations adopt standard constituency association constitutions, there appears to be a wide range in local practice with respect to the structure and activities of individual associations.

At the centre of virtually all constituency association organizations is a local executive responsible to the membership. Though the size of these executives varies from 2 to 98 (a third reported 9 people or less,

10 percent reported more than 30), the median size is 12. Liberal and Conservative executives are a little larger (at 15), New Democratic executives a bit smaller (at 9). Reform associations, perhaps reflecting the enthusiasm of a new party, typically have larger executives (at 18) while those in the Christian Heritage party are the smallest with just 7. We shall see something of how active these executives are in the section on the associations' interelection activity.

Small executive committees could be a reflection of a local oligopoly. We have no direct measure of this, but the fairly frequent turnover of local presidents indicates that in most cases constituency-level party offices are not valuable assets vigorously defended by those who hold them. The portrait is more consistent with the position being seen as something of an honorific responsibility passed around among volunteers. The data on length of service in association presidencies indicates that about a third turn over in a given year. Only 15 percent of the associations indicated that their local president had been in office for four years or longer, that is to say, had a tenure that had clearly begun before the previous general election.

Members of Parliament do not seem to be unduly concerned about installing particularly trusted individuals in their local riding associations to manage the home front, for this general pattern of short local-association presidencies seems to hold irrespective of the presence of an MP. Long-term (four years or more) local presidents are twice as common among Liberal and New Democratic associations as among Conservative ones, but the biggest difference over the period covered by the survey is a regional one. Constituency associations in Quebec are three times as likely to have long-serving presidents as those in the rest of the country. But even there, only a third of the local presidents had been in office for more than three years. If there is little in these data to suggest that single individuals long dominate riding parties, the opposite side of the coin is that a substantial number of local associations are headed by individuals rather new to the job.

In any voluntary organization there may be a distinction between those who do most of the work and those who occupy the formal organization positions, though the overlap is often considerable. The same is obviously true in these local party associations. To the question "Would you say there is a 'core group' in your riding that does most of the work between elections?" 94 percent responded yes. When asked how large this core group was, fully half of the respondents indicated that it was larger than the executive, though typically the median size of this core group was only two or three larger than the formal executive. In neither case do we have a picture of a large number of activists regularly engaged in local party work.

Though constituency associations are simple organizations with limited memberships, half of them have branches attached that are designed to attract and involve specific groups, presumably on the assumption that this will increase partisan activity beyond what the association itself can accomplish. The proportions of associations with such specialized branches are reported in table 3.12. As the table reveals, they were found far more frequently in the two old cadre parties. Whether they represent historical anachronisms in the traditional parties that have been rejected by newer or mass parties, which seek to integrate all their local members into a common association, or are the product of a modern opportunistic mobilization strategy is not entirely clear. Given that within the Liberal and Progressive Conservative parties separate branches were more frequently found attached to constituency associations in the five eastern provinces, it may be the former. These patterns do suggest, however, that any attempt to regulate local party activity would have to recognize that, in some parties and in some regions, different amounts of it may go on in affiliated groups, outside the formal bounds of the constituency association proper. Unfortunately we do not have any data on the activities of these secondary groups, though some of them provide the organizational basis for special representation at party policy and leadership selection conventions.

Table 3.13 indicates what sorts of groups are attached to local party associations. By far the largest group in every party is youth: 71 percent of all associations with affiliated units reported that they had a branch devoted to young people. These branches allow the parties to recruit young people who can then be encouraged to do their own thing, without seriously interfering with the activities of the regular, senior party

Table 3.12
Constituency associations with attached group branches
(percentage)

	Number of separate attached branches				
	0	1	2	3	4
All parties	51	30	15	4	1
Progressive Conservative	35	38	26	2	—
Liberal	39	36	18	7	—
NDP	69	15	11	5	2
Reform	82	16	—	—	—
Christian Heritage	60	40	—	—	—

Table 3.13
Constituency associations: types of attached branches
(percentage associations reporting attached unit)

	Women	Youth	Ethnic groups	Other
All parties	36	71	8	6
Progressive Conservative	41	80	4	2
Liberal	45	71	13	6
NDP	35	59	16	17*
Reform	5	40	—	10
Christian Heritage	—	79	—	—

*In NDP, majority of "other" category consists of labour groups.

members. The New Democrats and Liberals stand out as the two parties that have used branches of ethnic groups to try and expand their reach into the multicultural community. Not surprisingly, such groups are far more common in Ontario and Quebec where large numbers of ethnic minorities provide the parties with target populations. Unlike those of the two smaller parties, substantial numbers of the associations in all three national parties continue to have women's branches, originally conceived of as auxiliaries. This despite the fact that the national parties have all argued that they are anxious to see greater numbers of women playing more active roles in the central organs of their parties.

THE ROLE OF WOMEN IN CONSTITUENCY ASSOCIATIONS

The place of women, or more particularly their lack of an equal place, has become an important issue in Canadian society, and institutions like political parties have not been immune from pressure to change the practices that have traditionally left women in secondary roles. In the section on associations' interelection activity we shall consider the extent to which local associations are doing something to increase participation by women; here we look at the place they currently hold in constituency parties.

Women are no less interested than men in joining constituency associations. The typical association reported that its current membership was split evenly, 50–50, between men and women. This was true irrespective of the presence of a special women's branch, or of an incumbent. Indeed, even the local leadership of a female MP did not appear to increase the proportion of women in a constituency party. This gender balance in local memberships held in the three national political parties all across the country. Only in the two smaller parties did we find

Table 3.14
Women holding constituency association office, 1991
(percentages)

	President	Treasurer	Secretary
All parties	20	32	69
Progressive Conservative	21	22	69
Liberal	23	35	74
NDP	26	42	63
Reform	5	27	65
Christian Heritage	2	27	72
Incumbent	23	28	75
No incumbent	18	33	66

associations with disproportionate numbers of male members: in the Reform Party the median was 60 percent, in the CHP 55 percent.

However, this apparently equal involvement of men and women as party members did not translate into equal participation in local office holding. As table 3.14 indicates, while constituency associations still recruit women in disproportionately high numbers to the traditionally female position of secretary, far fewer become presidents or treasurers of their local parties. There was not a great deal of difference among the parties in this regard, though both Reform and the CHP did seem to be singularly resistant to choosing a woman to head their local association. The evidence does not support the proposition that women are more likely to be given an opportunity to lead in weak ridings: table 3.14 indicates little difference in this regard between associations with an MP and those without one, and a more elaborate analysis based on the associations' finishing positions in 1988 confirms this basic pattern.

THE ASSOCIATIONS' INTERELECTION ACTIVITY

Our examination of the constituency associations' membership suggested that there were systematic differences in size that revealed something of the different character of the parties themselves. These differences might be expected to show up most clearly in the activities of the parties' riding associations in the period between elections. As electorally focused cadre parties, the Liberals and Conservatives suffer marked membership declines during the interelection period, and may well become semidormant until the next round of electoral activity revitalizes them. By comparison, as units in a mass party, we would expect NDP associations to exhibit higher levels of regular interelection activity, and would expect such activity to be more diverse than the limited routine organizational maintenance that might preoccupy the two large parties' associations. The very rapid growth of the Reform Party suggests that its associations might be the most active of all, and that they might, as a new force, be particularly concerned with prose-lytizing activities.

Whatever partisan differences exist, one would also expect associations with an incumbent MP to be more active than others. Given the high turnover rates that characterize Canadian electoral politics (Blake 1991), individual MPs have strong incentives to keep the team that helped elect them active and involved, and they have the prestige and resources of office to help them do so. In this situation of having a member to support and defend, rather than an organization to nourish and a challenger to find, the patterns of interelection activity are likely to be quite different.

Association Activity Levels

To obtain a measure of the general level of activity in constituency associations, the survey asked three questions. First, we asked respondents to rate "the level of activity of your association" on a scale from very active ("something happening every month"), through active ("at least several events a year"), or quiet (meeting "only for annual meetings, nominations, etc.") to inactive (meeting "very infrequently between elections"). Then we asked two questions about how often regular meetings, of the full membership and the executive, occurred. As one would expect, the general level of activity was strongly related to that of the association's executive: two-thirds of those who described their local association as inactive noted that its executive met only irregularly, and another 20 percent reported no more than an annual meeting. As table 3.15 reveals, there are party differences, but not all are those we predicted.

Overall, 81 percent of the associations rated themselves as being active (ie., "active" or "very active") and only 6 percent confessed to being inactive (though the survey may naturally underrepresent the latter). As befits a new and rapidly growing party, Reform associations are clearly the most active: not one reported itself as inactive. On the other hand, NDP associations reported the lowest amount of activity: just under half described themselves as generally active and one in five admitted they were inactive. This pattern is not what one expects in a mass party whose membership demonstrates the stability we have seen is characteristic of the NDP. It is all the more striking for, by comparison, many more Conservative and Liberal associations are active in their communities. However, this generally lower level of NDP

Table 3.15
Constituency association general activity levels
(percentages)

	General activity level		
	Active*	Quiet	Inactive
All parties	81	20	6
Progressive Conservative	80	16	3
Liberal	70	23	7
NDP	49	32	20
Reform	96	4	—
Christian Heritage	81	13	6
Incumbent	84	15	1
No incumbent	67	22	11

*Includes "active" and "very active."

constituency association activity masks considerable regional variation within the party. Eighty percent of its constituency associations in
British Columbia claimed to be active, while only about 21 percent of
those east of the Ottawa River, in the five eastern provinces, did so.
Fully 54 percent of the NDP's riding presidents in Quebec characterized their local associations as inactive. Though there are regional differences in the activity levels of local associations in the Conservative
and Liberal parties they are not nearly as sharply drawn as those in the
NDP. For instance, in the Liberals' weakest region of the Prairies, only
13 percent of their associations reported that they were essentially
inactive. Here then is strong evidence that the NDP is not a national
party in the same sense as the two large parties are, for, by the testimony of its own key local activists, its grassroots presence in large
parts of eastern Canada is more nominal than real. Most ridings there
may have a very small cadre of party enthusiasts who can be counted
on to carry the flag at election time, but they do little else.

Local associations that are inactive are typically also quite small. In
the Liberal party their membership was half that of the party's average
while it was just 29 percent and 21 percent of the typical constituency
membership in the Progressive Conservative and New Democratic parties respectively. This is not surprising for small memberships and inac-
tivity go together. It may, however, imply that before local party
associations could become more active, or be asked to take on more
responsibilities by either the central party organizations or the state,
they would have to recruit more members. At the other end of the spectrum, as expected, are the larger associations with incumbent MPs. As

table 3.15 indicates, they are generally more active: only 1 percent described themselves as inactive.

Virtually all associations reported holding an annual meeting, but the majority did not have their full membership meet more than once a year. The exception to this was the Reform Party in which, at the time of the survey, 70 percent of the constituency associations reported that their full membership was meeting more than once a year.

We have already noted that the typical local party association is run by a fairly small group. Table 3.16 reports the frequency with which local party executives met: about half reported meeting once a month, the other half less often. The pattern is much the same as that for the reported general levels of association activity: Reform Party local executives met much more frequently than the norm, those in the NDP less frequently. This appeared to be true for NDP associations irrespective of whether they were concerned with federal politics only or were focused on both federal and provincial affairs. It implies that the distinction between the NDP as a mass party with engaged activists, as opposed to the Progressive Conservatives and Liberals as cadre parties active only at election time, is over-drawn. Indeed, traditional assumptions about partisan involvement among Canadians may be wrong: perhaps the NDP is able to maintain a more stable, albeit smaller membership, in its local associations precisely because it makes fewer demands upon it.

These characterizations of local activity provide only a general overview of the extent to which the parties' associations maintain an active presence in their constituencies. We now have to ask, more specifically, just what it is these local party associations do.

Table 3.16
Constituency association executive activity levels
(percentages)

	Frequency of executive meetings		
	Monthly	1–4/year	Irregularly
All parties	47	39	14
Progressive Conservative	49	40	11
Liberal	47	41	12
NDP	23	52	25
Reform	84	12	4
Christian Heritage	63	29	8
Incumbent	50	45	5
No incumbent	45	38	17

What Constituency Party Associations Do between Elections

When asked what activities they carried out at least once a year, local associations readily provided a diverse list. Table 3.17 summarizes these activities and indicates what proportion of each party's associations reported that they engaged in the particular, identified task or activity at least annually. These various activities fall into four principal groups, each with a somewhat different orientation. First are the primary tasks of organizational maintenance that include fund-raising, membership renewal campaigns and the social events that foster group life. These are the sorts of tasks any voluntary organization must be concerned with if it is to sustain itself. The second kind of activity, policy study and development, is more explicitly political and is central to one of the basic purposes of democratic parties. The third group of activities is concerned with communication, which is the essence of much of modern politics. How does the local association seek to communicate with its members (through newsletters), with the public (through meetings and modern technologies such as cable TV) and listen to its local constituency (through polling)? The last group includes activities with a more explicitly electoral focus: campaign planning or support work for an incumbent MP or an association's nominee. It is of course true that at election time the distinction between these activities blurs considerably. But for the years between, when associations are more quiescent, considering association activity in terms of these four groups reveals much about associations' central preoccupations and the differences between the parties.

As the evidence makes abundantly clear, what we have referred to as organizational maintenance tasks are the most universal. In the three major national parties, far more local associations reported annual fund-raising, social events and membership campaigns than they did other activities. And within that set of activities fund-raising was the single most common local activity. Of all the parties, only Reform associations reported membership campaigns more frequently than fund-raising ones, evidence of the critical importance Reform activists give to expanding their numbers. As we have seen (figure 3.2), the result has been the party's explosive growth in the past four years. On the other hand, NDP associations were least likely to report engaging in these three important organizational tasks. This is an unexpected finding given the NDP's traditions as a mass party relying on strong grassroots organization, especially since it is its Prairie province associations that least frequently report conducting an annual membership drive.

Two-thirds of all the constituency associations reported that, over a year, they worked at policy study and development. Given that

Table 3.17
Constituency association interelection activities
(percentage yes)

Activity	All parties	Progressive Conservative	Liberal	NDP	Reform	Christian Heritage	Incumbent
Organizational maintenance							
Fund-raising	86	89	85	84	86	88	91
Social events	76	83	76	68	84	69	83
Membership campaign	75	76	76	65	96	81	76
Policy study and development	65	67	58	60	94	58	68
Communications							
Public meetings	52	50	34	47	92	75	55
Newsletter	46	38	31	46	74	81	34
Local/cable TV	14	12	10	12	41	10	18
Local polling	9	7	8	7	27	6	7
Electoral							
Campaign planning	45	40	42	46	74	38	50
MP/candidate support	38	59	39	26	29	6	86
Other	7	6	2	13	6	8	5

observers, starting with Siegfried (1906) at the opening of the century, have often characterized Canadian parties as élitist and leader-dominated, with local activists largely interested in patronage, this seems a strikingly high proportion. It challenges the national parties to find a meaningful way to incorporate the output of this activity into their political agendas and campaigns. When they fail to do so they risk eroding the morale of their most active supporters (Clarkson 1979, 159). The data also indicate that, despite their party's image of being more policy-oriented than its opponents, NDP associations are not disproportionately concerned with policy work. It was the local activists of the right-wing parties who most frequently reported policy-related activity: 94 percent of Reform and 67 percent of Conservative associations, compared to 60 percent of those in the NDP.

Of the communications activities, the two traditional methods – arranging public meetings and publishing newsletters – were far more frequently used by local associations than were the newer technologies of local or cable television and opinion polling. Of course cost may be an important consideration for small associations: the newer technologies are also the most expensive and require the greatest expertise. However it may also be that local associations are inherently conservative and slow to adopt new ways of doing things. Some hint that this might be the case can be seen in the distinctive pattern of the Reform Party. They were not only more active communicators, but four times as many of their riding parties regularly used television and conducted local polling as did those of the older parties. Starting from scratch, the associations of the newest party may have simply thought it natural to adopt the most modern communications technologies available. The CHP also stood out as being particularly focused on communication activities, which probably reflects its concern to defend a set of policies that it sees as being quickly abandoned by the wider society. Finally, associations with incumbent MPs were less likely to publish newsletters than were other associations. This is noteworthy because this is the only activity where incumbents' associations were markedly less active than others. Though we have no direct evidence why this was so, one might hypothesize that those associations felt that their MPs' mailings, including constituency householders, made it unnecessary for them to produce local newsletters themselves.

The last category of activities includes those with an explicitly electoral focus: campaign planning and support activities for MPs or, in their absence, nominated candidates. Neither of these was a regular part of the interelection life of most constituency associations, though more Reformers reported planning for the next election than did others. That is perhaps to have been expected given that many of those Reform associations were still facing their first general election. Incumbents' local associations stand out for their support work, which in itself is not too surprising, but it is notable that this was the second most frequently reported activity of MP's associations. The very existence of a MP obviously gives a local association a clear and distinct focus of activity that sets it apart from others in the riding.

Among the five parties, the constituency associations of the Reform Party stand out for the high proportions that reported being involved in various activities. It remains to be seen whether this merely represents an extraordinary burst of energy necessary to build a new party as rapidly as Reformers have, or whether it represents a new pattern of party activity that can be sustained. Given that the NDP, a mass party once noted for the level of participation that characterized its members, is now essentially indistinguishable from the Conservatives or Liberals, the former seems most likely. If that is so, it suggests that once Reform's party-building phase is complete, and its membership stabilizes, the activity patterns of its constituency associations will look much more like those in the three established parties.

The relative frequency with which these different activities were reported varied somewhat across the parties, but the pattern seems remarkably consistent. Fund-raising is almost universal, polling is relatively rare and the other activities are spread out in much the same order within each of the parties. That in itself argues for a distinctive Canadian constituency-party political life.

Although there is a common set of constituency association tasks, not all may regard them in the same light, so the respondents were asked "which of [these activities] would you rank as the most important?" This revealed something of the different priorities of the older parties as compared to the new ones. Fund-raising was the activity deemed most important by the largest number of Liberal, Conservative and New Democratic associations, but membership campaigns were thought to be more important by the largest number of Reform and CHP local parties. However, within the older parties the presence of an incumbent made a difference. In those associations support work for the MP was more often identified as the most important local activity.

There seems also to be a modest regional difference in local associations' perceptions of the relative importance of their activities. In the five eastern provinces fund-raising was identified as the first-ranked activity, but, in Ontario and the West, associations were more likely to rank their membership campaigns as most important. Whether this reflects differences in the country's regional political cultures or the harder economic realities in the East is impossible to say with our data. It does indicate that similar party activity takes on different importance to associations in different parts of the country.

To this point the analysis has been concerned with identifying the range of tasks performed by local associations, measuring how widespread they are and assessing their relative importance. None of that, however, speaks to how many activities any individual constituency association carries out. That can be simply calculated by counting the number of different activities that an association reported engaging in during a typical interelection year. This ranged from a low of 0 to a high of 11, and, while a small percentage of the associations were to be found at both ends of the range, the mean was 4.9, and three-quarters of them carried out between 3 and 7 different activities (figure 3.4). This record of a variety of different activities was closely tied to the associations' own subjective characterizations of their general activity level: those that rated themselves very active averaged 6.9 different activities, those self-described as inactive only 1.6. Table 3.18 reports the average number of different activities taken on by associations in different parties and different regions.

Reform Party associations typically engaged in the widest variety of distinct local activities (their mean was 6.9), New Democratic associations the fewest (averaging just 4.4 each). Though the magnitude

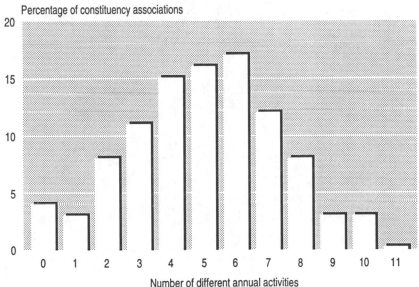

Figure 3.4
Constituency association interelection activities

Percentage of constituency associations

Number of different annual activities

Table 3.18
Numbers of different kinds of activities carried out annually by constituency associations
(mean)

All parties	4.9
Progressive Conservative	5.2
Liberal	4.5
NDP	4.4
Reform	6.9
Christian Heritage	5.2
Incumbent	5.6
No incumbent	4.7
Region	
Atlantic	4.0
Quebec	3.5
Ontario	5.2
Prairies	5.2
British Columbia	6.1

Figure 3.5
NDP interelection activity levels

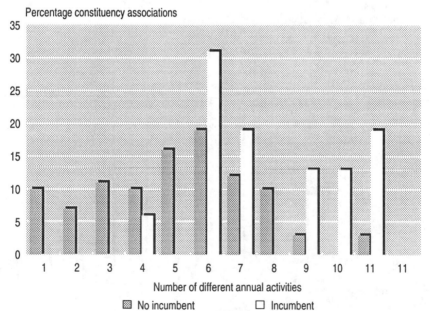

Percentage constituency associations

Number of different annual activities

☒ No incumbent   ☐ Incumbent

of this difference appears small, when we remember that two or three of the distinct activities identified constitute the minimum for organizational maintenance, one has the impression that many NDP associations must be barely surviving, while most Reform ones are unusually lively for Canadian constituency parties. There was a modest difference between associations with and without incumbents, with the former doing more different things during an average interelection year. As we have seen, much of that extra activity seemed to involve work for the MP him- or herself.

This small general increase in the range of constituency association activities fostered by an MP's presence held true for both the Liberal and Progressive Conservative parties. But, as figure 3.5 indicates, the story was radically different in the NDP. Local NDP associations headed by an MP performed a significantly greater number of different tasks (6.9) than did those without one (4.0). We have already seen that those incumbent-led NDP associations had a much larger membership, and membership fee income, than did any in the other two national parties. This evidence reveals that these large, relatively rich, associations were also active in a greater variety of ways in their constituencies. In that they even rivalled Reform Party riding associations. On the other hand, NDP associations without an incumbent MP at their head did fewer things than any other group of riding associations. To a greater extent than in any other party, there appears to be a comparatively large gap between NDP associations that are large, rich and active and those that are small, poor and quiescent.

As table 3.18 also reveals, there were some sharp regional differences in the activity patterns of constituency associations. Those in eastern Canada typically engaged in fewer different activities during the course of a normal interelection year than did those in the five western provinces. This reflects the more robust traditions of grassroots protest-party politics that has characterized much of the western provinces' political experience ever since the First World War. The strength of this tradition and pattern is obviously one of the reasons that the Reform Party associations take the activist shape they do, for they have grown out of this area of the country. These data suggest that the Reform Party may find it needs to modify some of its style and practice of constituency organization if it is to resonate with political activists in Atlantic Canada.

Association Members in the Wider Party
For the largest number of regular party members, involvement in their local constituency association marks the bounds of their participation. For others, however, meetings and conventions held at regional,

provincial or national levels provide an opportunity to represent the association in the wider affairs of the party. The most exciting and potentially significant of these are national leadership conventions (which we consider in detail in chapter 5), but the regular party conventions are also important instruments of internal party democracy. However, as table 3.19 reveals, these conventions provoke limited competition within riding parties: less than a third reported that there was competition for the delegate positions, and close to one in five local parties admitted that recently it had been "a chore to find delegates." This was much less true of the new Reform Party, while finding delegates to participate in party conventions was most difficult in NDP associations. The latter may reflect the distinct structure of NDP conventions, for that party (unlike the Liberals or Conservatives), ties the number of delegate positions to the local membership. Large associations get more delegates and so may be able to provide sufficient opportunity for all those interested in going to conventions. In the significant numbers of very small NDP associations in eastern Canada it is probably harder to fill the delegate slate, hence the larger number of associations in that party reporting difficulty finding delegates.

These differences do not appear to reflect the economic costs of going to conventions, which might bear harder on individual New Democrats, for the competitiveness of the selection of local delegates to regular national party conventions is not related to the ability or willingness of the local association to subsidize them. As table 3.20 indicates, there are some unmistakable differences among the parties in this regard.

The Progressive Conservative associations stand out as being more willing to help their members absorb the costs of participating in party meetings outside the riding. In every instance a greater proportion of them indicated that they subsidized their delegates than did associations in any other party. This is more striking when we remember that Conservative associations typically charge their members significantly

Table 3.19
Competition in constituency associations for party convention delegates
(percentages)

	All parties	Progressive Conservative	Liberal	NDP	Reform	Christian Heritage
Competition	29	33	28	17	72	4
No competition	52	47	51	59	23	78
Chore to find delegates	19	20	21	24	4	18

Table 3.20
Constituency association subsidization of local delegates to external party meetings
(percentage yes)

	All parties	Progressive Conservative	Liberal	NDP	Reform	Christian Heritage
Party meeting outside riding	30	51	28	18	11	19
Provincial level convention	28	48	27	20	6	6
National level convention	52	81	40	44	26	43
National leadership convention	40	58	43	35	6	19
None of the above	41	15	48	52	70	47

lower membership fees. New Democratic associations, for all the party's sense of itself as more internally democratic than the other parties, do not do very well on this score: over half reported giving delegates no financial help to attend any of these meetings. Even fewer Reform Party constituency associations subsidized delegates to external meetings, which is at odds with our portrait of them as being far more active and participatory. Though we have no data on why this apparent anomaly exists, it may well be that Reform members, at this stage of the party's development, are so keen to participate that they do not seek any such help.

Associations' Efforts to Increase Participation

As we discovered in the analysis of constituency association structure, many local parties have specialized branches designed to facilitate the membership of identifiable groups in the electorate. To explore the extent to which local associations were actively seeking to broaden the base of participation in political parties we asked them if they had made "a *special effort* to involve any of [a list of identifiable groups] in an attempt to increase their participation in the central affairs of the local party." Table 3.21 provides a measure of the pervasiveness of such efforts across the five parties.

Three-quarters of the associations reported making some effort to target increased participation, though this sort of mobilization effort was less common in the two new parties. A considerable number of associations reported attempts to attract individuals who were members of visible minority or Aboriginal peoples' communities. The efforts

Table 3.21
"Special efforts" by constituency associations to increase participation
(percentage yes)

Group	All parties	Progressive Conservative	Liberal	NDP	Reform	Christian Heritage
Youth	63	74	58	62	50	58
Women	54	54	49	73	44	24
Visible minorities	32	37	30	38	22	13
Aboriginal peoples	22	14	24	34	24	9
Others	5	2	1	15	4	4
No special efforts	27	21	33	19	41	40

to do so may be greater than the figures in table 3.21 imply, for many constituencies have only small numbers of these groups. Thus, for example, half the associations in ridings where visible minorities "exist in significant numbers" claimed to have made special efforts to involve individuals from those communities in their local association. In contrast, fewer Christian Heritage party associations made extra efforts to recruit these groups, but that is not surprising given that party's appeal to traditional Christian family values. But it is clear that youth and women remain the two groups that most local associations target for special attention. This, of course, may be seen as a version of business as usual, for these are the groups for whom parties have traditionally created special branches and auxiliaries.

Liberal and Conservative associations most frequently reported special efforts to attract youth, while more NDP local parties claimed that they had made such efforts to recruit women. These differences reflect both varying perceptions of the obstacles faced by women in becoming politically involved, and local associations' reception of quite different signals from their national parties. Thus, across all the parties, 29 percent of the constituency associations say that it is harder for women and that "special provisions must be adopted by the parties to ensure fair and equal opportunity." But there is a chasm between New Democratic associations and others: while 73 percent of NDP riding associations agree with this assertion, the figures for the Liberals and Progressive Conservatives are just 20 and 12 percent respectively. There is a similar difference in the associations' reports of how much pressure they feel from their national parties to increase the participation of women. When asked to characterize the situation in their party as either just "talk[ing] a lot" or as "real pressure on our constituency association," the majority of Liberal and Conservative associations claimed it was mostly talk, but 90 percent of the NDP associations said they felt under pressure to do something. In neither instance was there much evidence of a concern for this issue in either the Reform or CHP associations.

The various efforts to increase the participation of women in the local party organizations have not, as yet, borne much fruit. Neither the existence of special local efforts, nor the impact of national party pressure, has significantly altered the percentage of women reported to be association members, or the choice of a woman as the local riding-party president. As we shall see in a later chapter, pressure to involve women does seem to be positively related to the choice of a woman as the local candidate. But of course most candidates lose and so these choices have, for many local parties, a somewhat symbolic character. And without denying the importance of candidates, it must be recognized that change has been slower in local organizational hierarchies.

LOCAL ASSOCIATIONS AND THE STATE

In other chapters of this study we consider the response of associations to various specific proposals for reform, many involving governmental action or regulation. But do local associations, which to this point have had no ties whatsoever to the state, think there is a general case for changing that? Do they think that, as organizations, they need some basic support? The survey allows us to make a very tentative response to those questions. Tentative both because we have only very simple data, but also because there is no consensus among Canadian party associations on these questions.

The respondents were asked to choose which of the following two propositions best represented their opinion: (a) "Political parties should be free to regulate their internal affairs by their own rules, as they think best," OR (b) "Political parties have important public responsibilities and their internal affairs should be subject to at least partial regulation by public law." This question was posed in the context of others about the tie between constituency associations and the state, and sought to ascertain whether local party associations thought some state regulation of their affairs would be legitimate. Just over half did: 56 percent of them agreed with proposition (b). There were some party differences that reflected traditional left–right attitudes to state regulation: 77 percent of the NDP associations were prepared to countenance some regulation, but only 42 percent of the Conservative and Reform associations were. As we shall see in later chapters, the willingness of associations to support particular reforms depends very much upon the policy area involved.

Another question sought to discover if local associations thought they needed basic organizational help to sustain their day-to-day activities. They were asked if they agreed with a proposal to provide local party associations "with office space and furnishings in government buildings." Only one-quarter did. Obviously the vast majority thought they could, or should, do without this sort of patronage. This was a feeling shared across all parties, though as many as 40 percent of the NDP associations were prepared to support the idea, compared to only 20 percent of the Conservatives and 2 percent of Reformers. It was the least active associations that were most predisposed to that sort of government help – which may reflect the difficulties those associations have in simply maintaining a visible presence in their area. An office in a local government building would, after all, provide them with a position and status they are currently not able to achieve on their own. One other difference on this question is worth noting. Over half the local party associations east of the Ottawa River thought this would be a good idea, a far higher proportion than in any other region. This reflects differences in the regional cultures with regard to the provision of government services. It also testifies to a traditional perception of political parties as institutions of the governing élite in eastern Canada, as opposed to the more populist traditions of political organization in the western half of the country.

CANADIAN CONSTITUENCY ASSOCIATIONS

Progressive Conservative and Liberal constituency party associations look much alike: they have rather classic cadre-style membership patterns that reflect electoral cycles, but their activity levels suggest that they have adopted some of the aspects of a mass party. They do not hibernate between elections, and though it is true that much of their activity has an organizational maintenance cast to it, many engage in a wide variety of other political tasks as well. The New Democrats, on the other hand, have associations whose membership profiles look more like those of a mass party, though few have really mass memberships. Their activity patterns do not differ much from their traditional opponents: if anything, they are actually less active than a typical Liberal or Conservative riding party.

Generally speaking the presence of an incumbent makes rather less of a difference to the local party association than might have been expected in a system focused on leadership and driven by the rhythms of the electoral cycle. Ironically, this is more true of the cadre parties than the mass-style NDP. New Democratic MPs head local parties that stand out above virtually all others in the country for their size and activity levels. Whether this is due to the capacity of genuine mass organizations to elect an MP, or whether NDP MPs work harder at building and sustaining these organizations, is impossible to say from the data. What is true of all local parties is that the presence of an MP provides much more of a focus for their activity, and virtually all of them report that support work for the MP becomes a constant task. But, with these provisos, it must be said that while incumbents have larger organizations, and a constituency office provided by Parliament, their local associations do not appear so different from riding parties without an incumbent. We shall see, in later chapters, if this is also true financially or in terms of their electoral capacities.

Our portrait of the Reform Party is a fascinating one, for it captures the party at a moment of organizational take-off: its typical association's membership was large and growing rapidly, and its associations are doing more different things than those in the established parties. There must be some limit to those developments, though our evidence can not tell us what they are. The Christian Heritage party, on the other hand, is a different kind of protest organization. Its membership looks much flatter and more stable. In neither case do these new parties appear to be making an effort to respond to calls for providing new opportunities for women in Canadian political life.

As is true of so much of Canadian politics, there are regional differences in the character of constituency party life. In general these seem to follow a rough east–west gradient. The further west one goes, the larger and more active the associations tend to be. This reflects the traditions of grassroots protest that have often been manifest in western Canada, and currently underlie much Reform Party organization. These appear to be enduring differences for, six decades after the founding of the CCF, many of the same differences continue to characterize variations within the NDP.

But for all these differences, there is a basic similarity to constituency party life in Canada. And while one might wonder why the parties cannot attract more members and stimulate their local associations to become more active, it is also possible to ask why many of these constituency parties continue to exist at all. The answer to this latter question is that the electoral system, and our contemporary assumptions about what makes a national party, require each party to maintain a local association in each riding. This is true whether there is much interest in the party in the district or not. It is rather like a fast-food organization or gasoline company deciding it needs to have a franchise in every community irrespective of the demand for the product. But, unlike the food outlets or gas stations, these partisan franchises must be maintained and run by volunteers prepared to give only intermittent attention to the business of the local franchise.

If we think of parties in this way, as networks of local franchises for electoral competition, peopled by volunteers, the patterns of uneven, unstable membership and variable activity that we have charted in this chapter are not so surprising. After specifying some common organizational framework and rules, there is not a great deal the national office can do to its riding activists beyond encouragement and suasion. Unhappy party members always have the option of "exit," which many clearly choose over "voice or loyalty" (Hirschman 1970). A national party does not have that option, although in extreme cases it can step in to "reorganize" a riding party in organizational turmoil (*Globe and Mail*, 1993). To be credible as a potential government, to obtain a full share of broadcast time, to claim its maximum election-expense reimbursement from the state, it must maintain some local presence, however nominal, in every riding. Ultimately it must be prepared to put itself in the hands of whatever volunteers it can attract and hold.

But, to risk stretching the metaphor, these electoral franchises are not simply in the business of federal politics. Two-thirds of the constituency parties share membership with provincial-level party units, direct some of their energy or activity toward provincial politics or do both. They do so sometimes in compliance with, other times in defiance of, formal party structures. They do so because it suits their local political and organizational needs and allows them to maximize their resources. While we have seen something of the resources available to constituency party associations, the question of their finances – what some have called a black hole in our understanding of Canadian party finance – remains to be explored. This is the subject of the next chapter.

4

FINANCING CONSTITUENCY PARTY LIFE

For over a century the law has required candidates for Parliament to report their election expenses. Since the passing of the *Election Expenses Act* in 1974 the national political parties have had to provide annual returns disclosing their expenditures and income as well as reporting their election expenses. But there is still no provision for recognizing constituency party associations as part of the electoral process, or any requirement that they account for their finances. As a result, beyond some rather idiosyncratic accounts of the affairs of particular associations, virtually nothing is known about the financing of local party activity.

This has been a difficult area of Canadian party life to study. Financial matters have long been considered part of the dark side of political life and kept confidential. The origins of this attitude no doubt lie in the informal, personal-patronage politics of the 19th century. The series of political scandals that marked the history of both federal and provincial party politics (Simpson 1988) likely reinforced this predisposition among party activists. The result was that only those who needed to know for fund-raising or spending purposes were involved in party finance. In a single constituency this generally meant only one or two key people whose instinct was, and often still is, to be secretive. In some cases these individuals would be attached to a local MP rather than the riding party organization itself. As well, many constituency associations have sought to husband local resources and so have been anxious to obscure, even from their own provincial or national parties, their true financial position.

In an age of democratic party organization, this tradition runs counter to the openness and accountability required for the degree of popular control increasingly being demanded by party members. Without a more open, accountable process, party activists cannot hope to hold party leaders responsible for their stewardship, or to establish a meaningful role for themselves in their party's life. In an age in which much of a party's income comes directly or indirectly (via the tax credit system) from the public purse, this tradition of secretive party finance is unacceptable to the taxpayers. Open government requires that there be some scrutiny of the management of public resources, and democratic parties cannot expect, or even long desire, to be free of such scrutiny.

As yet, no official or public records of the sort that provide the rich evidential base for Stanbury's (1991) study of national party finances are available for the local constituency level. Therefore, this analysis of constituency party finance depends upon voluntary self-reporting. We do not have balance sheets, or statements of income and expenditure, and in a number of instances data were reported in terms of categories rather than specific amounts. Nevertheless, the survey responses provide an important first sketch of the constituency associations' inter-election financial affairs. The question of election income and expenditure is taken up separately in chapter 8.

THE FINANCIAL HEALTH OF RIDING PARTIES

Judging the financial health of a constituency association is difficult, and rather arbitrary. There is no absolute standard of need because individual riding parties have quite differing levels of activity and focus. Indeed one of their principal activities is fund-raising (table 3.17), and the country's parties have quite different rules and practices governing revenue and expense sharing across local, provincial and national party bodies. Stanbury (1991) has provided the best analysis to date of the complex world of intraparty finance. Here we simply try to describe the constituency associations themselves as they exist in each party. To obtain a general measure of the nature of local constituency associations' financial positions in the spring of 1991, halfway between general elections, we asked them, "What is the value of the funds your association currently has available to it?" Table 4.1 summarizes their responses by party, incumbency and region, and reveals some sharp differences.

The general picture the data provide is of associations with limited resources. Over half (57 percent) reported that they had $5 000 or less on hand, and almost 30 percent said that they had less than $1 000. At the other end of the spectrum, about one in four claimed to have $10 000 or more available, and 9 percent reported having more than $25 000. Overall, these are not vast sums considering the expenses of sustaining even the small memberships many of them have. Given that these associations knew that they would have to fight an election within

Table 4.1
Funds currently available to constituency associations, 1991
(percentages)

	< $1 000	$1 000–4 999	$5 000–10 000	> $10 000
All parties	29	28	19	24
Progressive Conservative	8	19	18	55
Liberal	29	29	25	17
NDP	53	32	11	4
Reform	9	29	36	27
Christian Heritage	48	39	11	2
Incumbent	8	21	19	53
No Incumbent	36	30	19	15
Region				
Atlantic	43	25	15	17
Quebec	51	17	10	22
Ontario	23	32	16	28
Prairies	23	26	26	25
British Columbia	16	31	31	21

two and a half years, there is little evidence here that many associations build up huge electoral war chests between elections. Nor do these accounts provide much evidence of the large sums Stanbury (1991, chap. 12) reports were paid as expense reimbursements in 1988 and are often assumed to be lodged in constituency accounts (Laschinger and Stevens 1992, 146–47). That is an issue to which we return in chapter 8.

Riding associations with incumbent MPs are something of an exception: over half (53 percent) of them reported having more than $10 000 available, and they constituted almost 60 percent of the ridings that had accumulated these larger financial nest eggs. This pattern of incumbents' associations being comparatively well off is true of all three national parties. It means that incumbents are likely to enter electoral contests with better-financed local associations than are their opponents. But even in these cases, the individual amounts involved seem rather modest, well below what a constituency organization needs to fight a vigorous election campaign. Associations obviously need to depend upon funds they and their candidates can raise at the time of the election, or on outside help from either other elements of their party or the state, through the election expense reimbursement system provided for under the *Canada Elections Act*.

The presence of an incumbent MP obviously helps a local association's financial position, but there are also some clear differences among the parties. The Progressive Conservative associations stand out as being well off. Only 8 percent of them had less than $1 000 on hand, while over half had more than $10 000 available. By contrast NDP constituency associations look quite poor. Over half (53 percent) reported that they had less than $1 000 currently available, though it is also true that virtually all of them were cases where there was no incumbent MP sitting for the riding association. (In over 40 percent of the NDP associations where there was a sitting MP, the local party reported having over $5 000 available to it.) The Christian Heritage party, the other party dependent upon a small stable membership, also reported a high proportion of relatively poor local associations.

Affluent Conservative associations and poor New Democratic ones may coincide with popular images of those parties, but they do not correspond to the resources that membership fees appear to provide. As we saw in chapter 3 (table 3.6), the typical Conservative riding association had a 1990 membership-fee income of just $1 250, well below the balance it had available early in 1991. Meanwhile its opposite number in the NDP collected $3 200 in membership fees, but claimed to have considerably less at its disposal. This confirms our argument that the membership fees paid by Conservatives are not a particularly important part of their constituency associations' finances: they have a more symbolic, bonding value to the party and its members. It also indicates that NDP associations must turn over to (or perhaps never receive from) their provincial offices a large portion of the membership fees of their members.

These differences imply that the extent of constituency associations' financial autonomy varies by party. There appears to be more autonomy in the Conservative party, less in the NDP, which is consistent with Dyck's (1991) models of confederal and integrated party structures. Table 4.2, which records the proportion of associations that reported being regularly engaged in intraparty financial transfers (between elections), provides one measure of the extent of financial integration across the parties. It confirms Dyck's analysis, but also demonstrates that no party conforms to a purely confederal or integrated model. The Conservatives, followed by the Reform Party, have the most financially autonomous local associations, the Christian Heritage party the least. But a third of the Conservative riding parties reported funds flowing to or from higher levels of the party, while 44 percent of the NDP associations claimed to be financially independent in normal interelection years. As expected, the Liberals fall into a position midway between the Conservatives and the New Democrats.

The other aspect of the internal party financial relationship that jumps out from the picture provided by table 4.2 is the relationship

Table 4.2
Constituency association interelection year financial transfers
(percentages)

Flow of funds	Progressive Conservative	Liberal	NDP	Reform	Christian Heritage
To higher levels	32	44	48	30	46
From higher levels	4	5	7	11	33
No significant flows	64	51	44	59	21

between individual local associations and higher party organs that the direction of money flows reveals. In all of the parties, but especially the three large national ones, associations are far more likely to be sending money out than to be receiving it. While this indicates that the parties are still doing a large amount of grassroots fund-raising, it also implies that the national party organizations see the local associations largely in fund-raising terms between elections. There is little evidence here that national (or provincial) party officials put money into the riding parties for local organizational or policy activities.

The only marked regional variation in this pattern of internal party transfers occurs in Atlantic Canada. More associations in that region can be classified as autonomous, but that is simply because they are poorer and hence have less to send to higher party offices. (As we shall see later, the reverse is true during election periods, when the Atlantic region has a far lower proportion of financially autonomous associations – see table 8.9.) The regional differences in local resources can be seen in table 4.1. Put baldly, constituency associations east of the Ottawa River are poorer than those in the other five provinces. This helps explain why associations in the eastern half of the country are less active, more focused on fund-raising and more willing to accept government help for their interelection organizations than are those in the rest of the country.

All but a handful of Conservative, Reform and Christian Heritage constituency associations reported that they held their funds in locally controlled accounts. As befits more integrated parties, a substantial number of Liberal (29 percent) and New Democratic (25 percent) riding parties reported that their local funds were held or controlled jointly with other party offices. This does not necessarily mean that those local associations have less control over how their funds will be used, though that seems a likely consequence. Unfortunately, the survey data are silent on that question.

The Bottom Line

The amount of money a local association has available is only one, indirect measure of its financial health. It may mirror the current balance but it can also represent some long-accumulated funds, perhaps left over from election expense reimbursements to the local candidate after the 1988 election. A more direct indicator of an association's current affairs is whether its annual operating budget showed a surplus or deficit, and what the size of either was. Table 4.3 indicates that, in 1990, 84 percent of all constituency associations operated with a surplus, and 16 percent had a deficit. The number with a deficit was down slightly from postelection 1989 (not reported in the table), and the number running a deficit two years in a row (1989 and 1990) was just 12 percent. Among the parties, the Reform and Christian Heritage associations were most often in surplus. In the three big parties, a larger number of Liberal associations had a surplus than was true of the Conservatives or the New Democrats, which is something of a reversal of the national parties' situation in recent years. Within the parties, the presence of an MP did not alter the likelihood of having a surplus or a deficit.

Constituency associations are not large-scale operations and the size of the typical surplus or deficit reflects this (table 4.4). The size (unlike the presence) of a surplus or deficit is affected by the presence of an incumbent: in both cases it is typically twice as large where there is a MP. Among the three major parties the Conservatives had both the largest surpluses and deficits, perhaps because they had the lowest membership incomes to cushion fluctuations in other income. Individual Reform Party associations appeared to be in the best financial situation in 1990: they typically had a $4 000 surplus. The number of local party members does not appear to make a significant difference: associations with a surplus are, typically, the same size as those with a deficit.

These accounts indicate that constituency associations are generally prudentially run between elections and that they do not pile up financial obligations that they later pay for out of their election appeal. We can assess the extent and nature of their financial activity by looking at patterns of income and expenditure.

LOCAL PARTY INCOME

Annual reports of financial activity for 1990 reveal that there is a considerable range in local riding parties' incomes (table 4.5). Seventy percent of all of them had small incomes – $5 000 or less – but almost one in five took in more than $10 000 during the year. Incumbents' local associations were twice as likely to be in this latter, higher-income

Table 4.3
Constituency association current account balances, 1990
(percentages)

	All parties	Progressive Conservative	Liberal	NDP	Reform	Christian Heritage
Surplus	84	78	86	79	98	97
Deficit	16	22	14	21	2	3

Table 4.4
Constituency association surpluses or deficits, 1990
(dollars, median association)

	Surplus		Deficit	
	Incumbent	No incumbent	Incumbent	No incumbent
All parties	3 000	1 500	2 000	1 000
Progressive Conservative	4 000	3 000	2 500	1 000
Liberal	2 000	1 175	2 000	1 000
NDP	2 250	500	1 100	1 000
Reform	—	4 000	—	—
Christian Heritage	—	900	—	—

Table 4.5
Constituency association income, 1990
(percentages)

	< $1 000	$1 000–4 999	$5 000—10 000	> $10 000
All parties	29	40	12	19
Progressive Conservative	21	40	13	27
Liberal	23	43	14	20
NDP	51	36	6	8
Reform	2	35	26	37
Christian Heritage	40	47	9	5
Incumbent	12	32	14	42
No incumbent	35	43	11	10
Region				
Atlantic	48	43	5	5
Quebec	54	21	6	19
Ontario	21	44	11	24
Prairies	20	44	19	17
British Columbia	21	39	14	25

group. This is in large part because there is a strong association between the activity levels of a riding party and its annual income, and incumbents generally have more active local associations.

Party differences in the activity and overall financial well-being of constituency associations also show up in terms of local income patterns. Of the three major national parties the Conservatives have the largest number of high-income associations, the New Democrats the fewest. Indeed over half the NDP riding parties reported that their annual income was under $1 000, which is probably less than is needed to engage effectively in the most minimal political activities. The two new parties covered by the data are quite different: the growing and busy Reform associations are at the affluent end of the spectrum, those of the CHP seem, like those of the NDP, relatively impoverished. This latter finding deserves attention, for CHP associations are, unlike New Democratic ones, quite active. High activity levels for the CHP do not translate into higher incomes. That pattern reflects the party's relatively narrow appeal and its correspondingly small association memberships.

These party differences are mitigated, within each of the three national parties, by the presence of an incumbent. Figures 4.1 through 4.3 show these income differences. In each of the parties more than three-quarters of the associations without an MP had annual incomes of $5 000 or less. On the other hand, incumbent-led associations (with which these nonincumbent associations must compete) have markedly higher incomes: between a third and a half in each party report an income of $10 000 or more. The patterns vary by party, but the Liberal MPs stand out as having the largest proportion of high (but not highest) income associations. Why that should be so is not clear: their associations are not particularly more active than others. It may well be that Liberal MPs, knowing the weakened state of their national party's finances, have decided to avoid similar problems in their own ridings and work hard at building strong local revenues.

The regional variations are just what one would expect. As table 4.5 reveals, in the five provinces east of the Ottawa River half the associations are in the lowest income group, while Ontario and British Columbia have disproportionately large numbers of the high-income associations. The pattern in Quebec is interesting, for although it is the region with the largest number of low-income associations it also has a surprisingly large number with high incomes compared to the Atlantic provinces. Those differences indicate the current state of the federal parties in Quebec: all but one of the associations with an income of more than $10 000 are Conservative, 58 percent of the low-income riding parties are in the NDP. The very large numbers of constituency

Figure 4.1
Progressive Conservative constituency associations' income, 1990

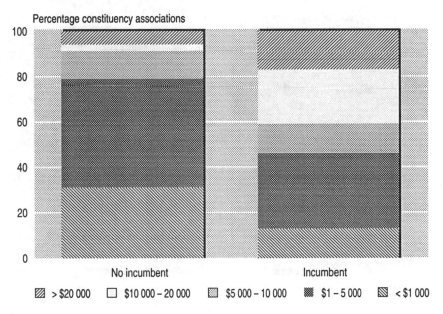

Figure 4.2
Liberal constituency associations' income, 1990

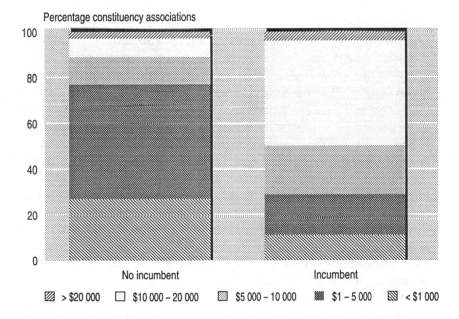

Figure 4.3
NDP constituency associations' income, 1990

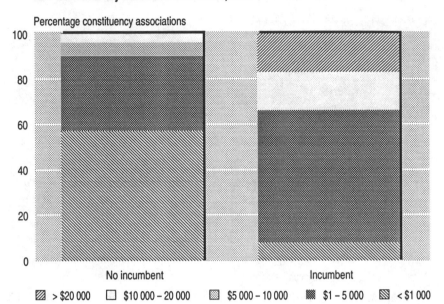

Percentage constituency associations

Legend: ▨ > $20 000   ☐ $10 000 – 20 000   ▨ $5 000 – 10 000   ▨ $1 – 5 000   ▨ < $1 000

associations with limited incomes in the five eastern provinces raise questions as to whether they can play an equal part in the affairs of their party's national organs.

Financial Contributors

Membership fees constitute one important source of local income though, as we have already noted, their size and distribution across party levels varies considerably. A second potential source of income is contributions from individuals. The national political parties, using the appeal of the tax credit and the technology of direct mail, have been quite successful at this (Stanbury 1991). In doing so they have established new attitudes and political giving practices among large numbers of Canadians. Table 4.6 reports the numbers of individuals contributing to constituency associations expressed as a proportion of local party membership size. This measure provides a control for differences in the size of the local association as well as indicating whether the association appears to be significantly changing the level of financial participation in riding party politics. These figures suggest that local associations do not seem to have been generally very adept at expanding the numbers of local givers.

In 1990, constituency parties reported that the number of individuals contributing financially to their association was typically equivalent to 20 percent of their local membership. Among the three big parties it was just 15 percent, just half what it had been in 1988, an election year. While it is almost inevitable that the numbers giving will be highest in election years, it is also true that in the two cadre parties membership numbers fall sharply in the postelection period. A good, institutionalized donation program ought to stabilize the number giving, so that the giver-to-member ratios (in table 4.6) might actually have been expected to rise in 1989 and 1990 if the local associations had had well-developed groups of committed contributors. Obviously that did not happen, though there are some marked differences between the three large parties that are very revealing. They challenge a simple categorization of the Conservatives as a cadre party, the NDP as a mass party.

Conservative associations appear to have the most regular contributors. Their contributor-to-member ratio is most stable and falls only slightly after the 1988 election (from 0.33 to 0.25) and then holds constant from 1989 to 1990. In fact this masks a sharp decline in the actual number of contributors to the typical Conservative constituency association, because the number of members was itself declining (see table 3.5) over this period. Still, this pattern mirrors the institutional discipline and regular attention to maintaining a contributor base that has characterized the Conservative party at the national level in recent years. It is what one might expect of a mass party with a commitment to a regular ongoing organizational life between elections, rather than an electorally focused cadre party like the Tories.

On the other hand, ironically, New Democratic constituency associations' contributor-to-member ratios do look like those of a classic cadre party. Its score of 0.44 during the 1988 election year is the highest reported in the survey, but the sharp fall (to 0.17) the following year hints at a profoundly election-cycle orientation for at least the financial side of its organization. Given that the party's associations have

Table 4.6
Constituency associations' financial contributor:member ratios
(median association)

	1988	1989	1990
All parties	.35	.19	.20
Progressive Conservative	.33	.25	.25
Liberal	.14	.08	.06
NDP	.44	.17	.25
Incumbent	.31	.23	.26
No incumbent	.37	.17	.17

comparatively stable memberships, much of this variation must be in the numbers of local contributors. However, with so much else that characterizes NDP local associations, the data in table 4.6 obscure enormous differences between their incumbent and nonincumbent constituencies. During 1988, incumbent NDP associations had a contributor-to-member ratio that was twice that of nonincumbent associations (1.0 vs. 0.43), while it was four times greater in the two subsequent postelection years. This reinforces the perception we developed in chapter 3 that, in the NDP, the presence of an incumbent transforms the very nature of the local association.

Compared to the Conservatives or the New Democrats, the Liberal riding parties have been far less successful at developing a committed contributor base. Their local ratios are typically far lower, even in an election year. This pattern indicates that the financial difficulties that plague the national party are not being compensated for locally. Liberal incumbents do make some difference, but even there their associations' ratios are typically only a fifth of those of their NDP colleagues.

In both the NDP and the Liberal party, irrespective of the presence or not of an MP, the contributor-to-member ratios were at their lowest in the year the parties had a national leadership campaign and convention: 1989 for the NDP, 1990 for the Liberals. This suggests that many regular partisan supporters, who normally can be counted on to contribute to their local constituency party, may have diverted their annual political contributions to one of the candidates. One of the immediate consequences is that a majority of the riding associations in each party are not able to help subsidize their local delegates' leadership convention expenses (table 3.20). Some, at least in the Liberal party, then turn to the leadership candidates' campaign teams for such help (Wearing 1988, 77). From the perspective of building a strong and responsible party organization this is probably undesirable. It pushes contributors outside the normal association structures, reinforces the importance of personal factional organizations within the parties and keeps the constituency associations from being fully integrated into the parties' leadership politics.

Table 4.6 also demonstrates the general propensity of incumbent-led riding parties to have stronger contributor bases than others. As we have seen this is particularly so in the NDP, but it is characteristic of all three big parties. Even in the absence of incumbents, Reform and CHP associations have relatively high contributor-to-member ratios. That is to be expected given their newness and the fact that, at the time of the survey, they were operating primarily in areas of strength. Whether they will be able to maintain that pattern after nationalizing their activity remains to be seen.

Fund-raising

The analysis of constituency associations in chapter 3 revealed that fund-raising was the most universal interelection activity and the one most frequently ranked as "most important." The two other activities identified by the vast majority of associations as part of their normal interelection year activities were membership campaigns and social events.

The constant imperative of fund-raising means that constituency associations must employ a range of different techniques if they wish to be successful. Table 4.7 indicates the frequency with which various fund-raising methods are regularly used by riding parties. It reveals that social events and the annual membership campaign have, for a large majority of associations, important fund-raising dimensions beyond their manifest purposes. For both Liberal and Tory associations social events are the most common fund-raising devices, for the other three parties the membership campaign claims pride of place. Only two other methods – personal canvassing and direct mail – are used by over half the local associations. Among the traditional parties the Conservative associations seem keener on the new technology of direct mail (remember they are far more likely to own a computer – table 3.8), the New Democrats on the traditional practice of a personal canvass. Reform Party associations more frequently reported using all these methods. Seminars or other policy-related events are not a common fund-raising tool of the old parties (and they were reported less frequently by NDP than by PC associations), although almost half the Reformers use them.

Constituency associations commonly have youth or women's branches attached to them, but the data suggest that their activities are not seen as an important part of the associations' fund-raising activities. But if they do not serve financial ends, this strengthens the argument sometimes heard that these units exist not only to mobilize those groups in the electorate but also to keep them segregated from the main business of the constituency association.

One fund-raising method that did not show up very commonly among constituency associations in the three large parties is the rather old-fashioned device of a public meeting with a featured speaker. Yet 14 percent of the Reform Party local associations spontaneously reported using such meetings to raise money. In large part that indicates the tremendous appeal and effort of the party's leader, Preston Manning, in the establishing and building of the party. The last Canadian party leader to have done anything like this was Réal Caouette, who built the Ralliement des Créditistes in a similar fashion in the early 1960s.

Though the Liberals and Conservatives have programs of leader dinners (Stanbury 1991, chap. 10), they are used to fill the national coffers rather than to help individual constituencies. Indeed the pressure put on activists in the metropolitan areas to sell and buy tickets to those dinners may very well deprive constituency associations of fund-raising energies and potential income.

Table 4.7
Regular constituency association interelection year fund-raising activities
(percentage yes)

Activity	All parties	Progressive Conservative	Liberal	NDP	Reform	Christian Heritage	Incumbent
Membership drive	76	74	74	69	96	89	72
Social events	75	76	78	68	80	69	84
Personal canvassing	56	48	57	61	69	53	44
Direct mail	56	62	47	42	78	79	60
Policy-focused events	19	17	10	15	49	24	13
Women's group events	5	5	6	7	—	2	4
Youth group activities	7	11	6	5	—	7	9
Other	8	6	3	12	18	11	2

Table 4.8
Most important constituency association fund-raising activities
(percentage associations ranking activity first)

Activity	Progressive Conservative	Liberal	NDP	Reform	Christian Heritage	Incumbent	No Incumbent
Social events	38	38	10	9	14	48	19
Membership drive	22	30	46	49	51	21	40
Personal canvassing	16	22	27	16	21	14	23
Direct mail	22	8	10	18	7	17	12

When asked which fund-raising method was the most important for their association, riding presidents most often chose social events or their annual membership drive (table 4.8). Conservatives and Liberals favoured the former, NDP, Reform and CHP associations the latter. There is a marked distinction between incumbent and nonincumbent associations, with the former preferring social events. That difference, however, is largely an artefact of the party differences. MPs do seem to make successful fund-raisers: NDP associations with MPs were six times as likely to identify social events as their most important method as were nonincumbent NDP associations.

Of the four most common constituency association fund-raising methods, direct mail was the one least likely to be identified as the most important. That is partially because it is a new method that requires some technological investment, but also because the economies of scale involved do not always allow it to be efficiently used in constituency-sized populations. At that level mailings can go to identified supporters, but building and renewing lists of donors through prospecting may not be particularly cost-effective. Among the three national parties the Conservative associations seem to have gone the furthest in attempting to use direct mail. More of them report using it, and more call it their most important tool. In this the local associations again mirror national party activity, for the Tories have been more successful than the New Democrats and the Liberals in sustaining a direct-mail program.

Associations do not rely on a single fund-raising style or event: the secret to raising money is to ask often and to ask in as many ways as practicable (Sabato 1981; Warwick 1990). Almost inevitably, then, income levels will be related to the number of methods employed: thus constituency associations with an income of $1 000 or less in 1990 reported using an average of 2.4 different methods, those with an income of $1 000 to $5 000 claimed to use 3.1 methods, and those whose income ranged between $5 000 and $10 000 used 3.5 different methods. In table 4.9 we have a summary of the numbers of different kinds of fund-raising methods the typical constituency association regularly uses in nonelection years.

These patterns reflect the general differences in activity levels of constituency associations by party and region (compare to table 3.18), because so many local party activities have a fund-raising dimension. Reform and CHP associations use the most diversified fund-raising strategies, New Democratic Party associations the fewest. Regionally, the by-now familiar east–west gradient appears. East of the Ottawa

Table 4.9
**Numbers of different fund-raising activities
carried out annually by constituency associations**
(mean)

All parties	2.9
Progressive Conservative	2.9
Liberal	2.8
NDP	2.6
Reform	3.8
Christian Heritage	3.1
Incumbent	2.8
No incumbent	2.9
Region	
Atlantic	2.6
Quebec	2.4
Ontario	3.0
Prairies	3.0
British Columbia	3.2

River, associations use below-average numbers of fund-raising methods, west of it they use more, with British Columbians employing the most of all.

Direct Mail and Constituency Finance

The use of national direct mail has been the most important single instrument in the transformation of Canadian party finances over the past decade. It has allowed the party's national offices to bypass constituency associations and reach members and supporters directly. It has provided a vehicle by which the parties, with the aid of the tax credit, are able to collect large numbers of relatively small amounts from individual donors. Both aspects of the national programs threaten the constituency associations: the first by making them superfluous to a mass financial participation scheme, the second by threatening their natural base. Highly professional national campaigns are arranged with little attention to the schedule or structure of local events and so may usurp comparatively amateurish local efforts. And, when direct mail is used at the national level, there is little impulse to share income with local associations, whereas when the initial collection is local some will almost inevitably stay in the constituency.

When asked, "Do local party members complain about the number of appeals for party funds they now get?" 52 percent of the riding party presidents say yes. That is most true of the Liberals (62 percent), which is ironic given that they have had the least success using direct mail. Perhaps Liberals are simply getting sick of appeals to retire the party's debt that have persisted since 1984. Christian Heritage (7 percent) and Reform (43 percent) association presidents are the least likely to report membership complaints about financial appeals. That may reflect something of the ethos of protest-party supporters who are, almost by definition, at the core of the direct mailers' universe.

For constituency associations the question is what has been the impact of the growing use of direct-mail campaigns upon their ability to raise money. Has the potential threat identified above materialized? Or has direct mail, by stimulating awareness and interest in the party, helped local fund-raising? Of course a third possibility is that it has had no impact. Table 4.10 summarizes the constituency association presidents' experience. About half in all the parties indicated that it had no impact on local fund-raising. But among the half that thought it had made a difference to them locally there were sharp party differences on the nature of that impact.

In those cases where the national party direct-mail program was perceived to make a difference to local fund-raising, Conservative and Liberal associations overwhelmingly (by ratios of approximately 6:1 and 9:1 respectively) reported its impact to be negative. The New Democrats were also negative, but far less so (approximately 2:1). The Reform and CHP respondents, on the other hand, were more likely to see the national direct-mail campaign as having a positive local impact. That makes sense. As new parties trying to establish themselves, their local associations know that direct mail is another tool to spread their message and so it ultimately helps them at the local level. As we have already noted (table 4.7), local CHP and Reform associations more often use direct mail themselves.

Local direct mail fund-raising programs are spreading: 56 percent of all constituency associations now report using them, though that is

Table 4.10
Impact of national direct-mail campaigns on local fund-raising
(percentages)

Impact	All parties	Progressive Conservative	Liberal	NDP	Reform	Christian Heritage
Hinders	38	44	44	37	29	13
Helps	14	7	5	17	31	37
No impact	48	50	50	46	40	50

true of only about a third of the associations in the five eastern provinces. Given that one of the purposes of direct mail, besides collecting money, is to expand the base of association contributors, the data on the number of association contributors can be taken as one measure of these programs' impact. Figure 4.4 reports the contributor-to-member ratios for 1988 through 1990, distinguishing between those constituency associations that used direct mail, and those that did not, as a regular part of their local fund-raising activities. In each year the direct-mail associations had a higher ratio, evidence of a broader base of contributors. The difference was largest in 1988, suggesting that local direct mail may be specially effective at stimulating campaign giving, but it clearly has a positive impact on local giving generally.

Local direct-mail programs not only increase the proportion of members contributing regularly, they also mobilize interest and contribute to increasing a constituency association's absolute membership. In this way they have a double effect, so that the sheer numbers of individuals contributing to riding parties that run direct-mail programs is typically two to three times larger than in those that do not. This being so we can expect more constituency associations to adopt them in the future.

Figure 4.4
Local direct-mail use and contributor:member ratios

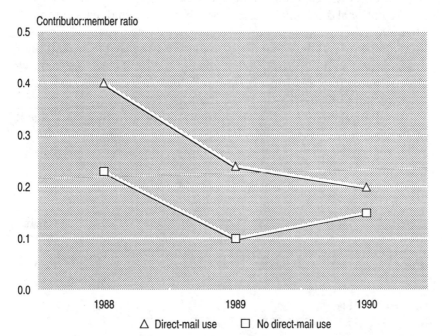

Contributor:member ratio

△ Direct-mail use   □ No direct-mail use

Table 4.11
Constituency association willingness to share mailing list
(percentages)

	Progressive Conservative	Liberal	NDP	Reform	Christian Heritage
Share list with central office	62	81	88	98	98
Hold list for local use	38	19	12	2	2

The most valuable resource available to the direct mailer is a list of proven donors or known sympathizers. Therefore, constituency associations are under considerable pressure to share their mailing lists with provincial- or national-level party offices. In the Liberal party access to membership mailing lists has been such an ongoing problem that it became one of the central issues at the party's constitutional reform convention in February of 1992. Unable to agree on a national membership list, the reform convention delegates finally supported a system that would give the national party access to provincial-level lists. Given the stakes involved, this is a problem that confronts all the parties.

To ascertain how this issue is now affecting constituency party behaviour, associations were asked whether they "Freely share [their] mailing lists with central party offices," or whether they "Guard [their] own lists to protect [their] local fundraising ability." Table 4.11 indicates that a large majority claim to share their local mailing lists, though that practice is most common in the new parties, and least common among Conservative associations. In the latter case, over a third of the party's riding parties claim not to be sharing their lists. This propensity for maintaining exclusive mailing lists, rather than sharing them, is twice as common among Tory riding associations that use direct mail as among those that do not, suggesting that more than a uniquely Conservative party dynamic is at work here. From this perspective, the growth of local direct mail financial activity may be one of the parochial forces at work slowing the development of a fully integrated national party membership.

LOCAL PARTY EXPENDITURES

Given that a large majority of constituency associations have a surplus on their annual financial accounts there are no big surprises in the expenditure patterns (table 4.12). Over three-quarters of the riding parties typically spend less than $5 000 a year between elections, just 11 percent

Table 4.12
Constituency association expenses, 1990
(percentages)

	< $1 000	$1 000–4 999	$5 000—10 000	> $10 000
All parties	39	38	12	11
Progressive Conservative	23	43	16	18
Liberal	33	39	18	10
NDP	66	24	6	4
Reform	19	51	14	16
Christian Heritage	56	39	2	2
Incumbent	12	36	28	25
No incumbent	49	39	7	6
Region				
Atlantic	61	27	9	2
Quebec	53	23	10	14
Ontario	30	44	12	13
Prairies	33	44	16	7
British Columbia	40	33	11	26

more than $10 000. More Conservative (18 percent) and Reform (16 percent) associations are big spenders, while large proportions of New Democrat (66 percent) and Christian Heritage (56 percent) associations manage to spend less than $1 000 a year. And, mirroring regional differences in income patterns, over half the constituency parties in Atlantic Canada and Quebec have annual expenses of less than $1 000. The data also reveal that incumbents, despite having offices in the constituency provided at public expense, are more likely to have big-spending constituency associations. Over half report annual expenditures of more than $5 000, while just 13 percent of those with no MP spend that much.

What do constituency party associations spend money on between elections? Table 4.13 summarizes those things identified as "important costs." Clearly they are principally concerned with servicing their local members (membership events/printing and postage) and doing local publicity work (PR/printing and postage). Only a quarter mentioned spending anything on "policy work" and significantly it was associations in the new protest party (Reform) that most frequently reported this as an important cost. This is consistent with our portrait of very active and growing constituency associations in the Reform Party, but it also confirms that much of their activity has a policy dimension. They are, to use a colloquialism, putting their money where their mouth is. By contrast, the NDP, which has long prided itself on being the party most interested in and serious about policy development, had the fewest

Table 4.13
Important interelection year constituency association expenses
(percentage yes)

Activity	All parties	Progressive Conservative	Liberal	NDP	Reform	Christian Heritage	Incumbent
Printing and postage	87	87	86	80	100	96	89
Membership events	67	64	68	67	65	72	69
Local PR	39	47	32	26	51	59	51
Policy work	23	26	18	17	35	24	29
Office rental	7	12	9	5	16	2	9
Paid staff	3	3	2	3	2	2	3
Other	20	18	17	31	18	6	23

Table 4.14
Expenditure ranked most important by constituency associations
(percentage ranking item first)

Activity	Progressive Conservative	Liberal	NDP	Reform	Christian Heritage	Incumbent	No Incumbent
Printing and postage	45	45	40	68	62	37	53
Membership events	13	23	22	18	21	20	19
Local PR	19	6	6	5	13	19	7

associations reporting that policy work was an important area of local expenditure.

A number of constituency associations apparently count their participation in wider party bodies as a major local expense. In each of the three national parties about 7 percent of the associations listed sending delegates to other party gatherings as an important cost. Twelve percent of New Democratic associations reported that financial obligations to higher levels of the party (described as dues and/or debts) resulted in one of their major annual expenditures. To put this in perspective we should recall that rather fewer (just 7 percent) of local NDP associations claimed to receive interelection financial help from other levels of the party (table 4.2).

Finally, table 4.14 reports the associations' assessment of the expense that was most important for them. In every case it was printing and postage. While the incessant upward drift in Canadian postal rates is the bane of many voluntary organizations, this also reflects the rather limited scale and scope of most local political activity. These are the expenses of organizational maintenance, and perhaps some traditional approaches to proselytizing. There is nothing in this assessment of local expenditures to suggest that individual constituency parties play a significant, active part in the political life of the nation – or of their members – between elections.

THE RICH AND THE POOR

Constituency associations are rather like citizens when it comes to money. Though they vary a good deal, there are fairly predictable differences in their behaviour and condition. One of the most enduring is that some riding parties are rich and some are poor. Undoubtedly the condition of individual associations changes over time. Thus many Quebec Conservative riding associations must have gone from a state of relative penury to one of comparative ease after the 1984 electoral landslide changed the political complexion of that province. But, whatever the changed circumstance of a particular association, differences between those with no financial problems and those with no financial prospects persist.

Identifying the rich and the poor is somewhat arbitrary, though the data on income (table 4.5) and funds on hand (table 4.1) provide two criteria for an operational definition. *Rich* constituency associations can be identified as those with a (1990) income of $10 000 and having at least $10 000 available to them; *poor* associations those whose income was under $1 000 and which had less than $1 000 available. Together they make up almost one in three of all associations, with the poor ones (18 percent) outnumbering the rich ones (11 percent) by nearly two to one. As one would expect, poor associations are most common in the most economically disadvantaged parts of the country (the provinces east of the Ottawa River). The survey failed to turn up a single rich riding party in all of Atlantic Canada, while 43 percent of those in Quebec fell into the poor category. At the same time, Quebec stands out as having the most economically polarized local parties – 54 percent were either rich or poor, almost twice the proportion of any other region. That seems to reflect the feast-or-famine pattern that has characterized parties' electoral success in the province since 1917.

The parties vary in the proportion of their constituency associations that are either rich or poor (table 4.15). The Conservatives have

Table 4.15
Rich and poor constituency associations, by party, 1990
(percentages)

	Progressive Conservative	Liberal	NDP	Reform	Christian Heritage
Rich	20	7	3	21	—
Poor	6	14	39	2	31

three times as many rich as poor riding associations, but the situation is reversed among both the Liberal and NDP constituency parties. The Liberals have twice as many poor as rich associations, the New Democrats thirteen times as many. This high ratio in the NDP reflects the fact that fully 39 percent of its associations are poor. That is a huge number and clearly indicates that the party's local presence is hardly more than a nominal one in many parts of the country. It is hardly surprising then that 42 percent of the NDP candidates failed to reach the 15 percent electoral quota necessary for election expense reimbursement in the 1988 general election.

The balance of rich and poor constituency associations in any area is important to note because rich and poor ridings differ. As the summary below reveals, in 1991 two-thirds of the rich associations had incumbents and half described themselves as very active, while only a handful of poor associations had an MP and almost none were very active. Rich associations reported (on average) almost five times as many members, and a contributor-to-member ratio that was two and a half times as large, as that of the typical poor association. Over half the country's rich constituency associations were Conservative (another 20 percent were Reform) but half the poor ones were in the NDP. This partisan cast to rich and poor makes a difference for, as we shall see, an association's financial position colours its perceptions of the need for reform.

Who Are the Rich and the Poor?

	Rich	Poor
Incumbent	69.6%	7.5%
Very Active	50.0%	2.5%
Conservative	56.5%	10.0%
New Democrat	6.5%	52.5%
1990 membership	515	110
Contributor/Member	0.71	0.28

PROPOSALS FOR REFORM

We began this chapter by observing that Canadians have made the financial affairs of candidates for Parliament and of the national parties matters for public concern. For almost two decades now the Canadian state has been deeply involved in the financial affairs of both. It provides large income subsidies through election expense reimbursements and tax expenditures (via the income tax credit) that support the parties in interelection years as well as for election campaigns. The state now regulates expenditures, at least during the election period, through a system of candidate and party election-expense spending limits. With all this has come a system of registration and both annual and election-period reporting, to provide for a measure of public accountability.

However, the system deals only with candidates and registered national parties. It misses, or ignores, the local constituency associations of the parties which are the key organizational link between the two. In Canadian parties it is the constituency association that nominates the candidate, that organizes and staffs the local election campaign, that sustains party activists between elections and that sends the majority of the delegates to party policy and leadership-selection conventions. Thus it is not surprising that there have been calls to extend the regulatory framework governing political money to include riding party associations. These have been justified both on the grounds of providing for a comprehensive, integrated system by incorporating now-neglected parts, and by a more pragmatic argument that there are specific problems with the financing of nomination and leadership campaigns that need to be addressed in the same way election expenses have.

The interparty consensus that exists over the current national regime governing party finances does not appear to include extending the system to the constituency associations – at least, not among the local association presidents who would be those most affected by such a change. Though there are particulars on which local presidents agree (generally to maintain the status quo), some aspects of each area of proposed reform provoke differing responses. To a large extent variations among association presidents are predictable, reflecting ideological and economic differences. Right-wing party associations are less supportive of extending government regulation or public spending; the same is true of rich riding parties (table 4.16).

One approach to supporting lively and participatory constituency-level politics is to ensure that local associations have sufficient income to maintain a minimal presence and activity level in the riding.

However, there is no agreement on how that might be achieved, for the association presidents differed over a series of suggested reforms. Over half the New Democrats supported the proposition that "The government should provide matching funds up to some amount (for example, $5 000) raised locally," but only a quarter of the Tories agreed with that idea. Even the poorest associations do not appear to be particularly enthusiastic about that plan: presumably if you do not have much now, matching it would not give you a lot more. An alternative to providing some basic support for all associations would be to limit the incomes of some. Practically, this might be tried (as it has been in the province of Quebec) by limiting "the amount an individual could give to a constituency association in a given year." Though New Democrats were again prepared to support this possible reform, it engendered the least interparty agreement of all.

A third suggestion for regulating constituency association income proposed restricting the right to donate to a local constituency association to resident electors. That would exclude individuals who do not live in the riding, on the grounds that riding associations ought to be left securely in the hands of local constituents. It would exclude nonvoters, such as businesses, trade unions or interest groups, on the grounds that local parties should be responsive to voters, not interests.

Table 4.16
Proposals for reforming constituency association financing regime
(percentage agreeing)

	Progressive Conservative	Liberal	NDP	Rich	Poor
Income issues					
Government match funds between elections	26	40	53	7	49
Limits on individual's annual donation	26	41	71	37	69
Only resident voters allowed to give	11	17	19	15	27
Spending					
Regulation of interelection spending	16	40	58	13	51
Tax credit issues					
Constituency associations to issue tax receipts	17	25	44	33	36
No forced remittance of locally raised funds	38	47	36	31	54
Accountability					
Register and submit annual financial report	24	41	57	39	41

It would, of course, also exclude non-Canadians and those below the voting age, even if they were regular party members. In any event, this was one of the few questions on which association presidents were pretty much agreed: they opposed any such restriction on their fund-raising.

The spending side of the financial equation also saw marked inter-party differences. Asked whether party spending should be regulated between elections as well as during the campaign only 16 percent of the Conservative riding presidents said yes as compared to 58 percent of the New Democrats. The gap between the rich and poor ridings was about the same.

One of the most potent devices employed in soliciting donations from individuals has been the federal income tax credit. Making it more accessible to individual constituency associations might well help them stimulate local giving. But when asked whether they should have the right to issue tax receipts or whether that authority should remain with the national party (to prevent abuses), the majority in all parties opted to deny themselves. They supported leaving this authority with party headquarters. In much the same way, most local presidents admitted the right of the national parties to use their control of the receipt books to extract a share of locally raised funds from riding parties. The poorest associations were the only ones in which a majority seemed to resent that practice by their party.

Finally, any major changes to the system that involve regulating the nomination or leadership process, or the finances of constituency parties, are bound to raise questions of transparency and accountability. The Canadian solution to those problems at the national level has been registration and annual reporting. But when asked if constituency associations should be obliged to register and report on their finances annually, only a quarter of the Tory, and 41 percent of the Liberal, local presidents said yes. Fifty-seven percent of the New Democrats said yes. On this question there was no difference between the rich and poor.

The differences revealed in table 4.16 indicate that there is no clear local-level consensus on how much state regulation of constituency party affairs is appropriate. On the other hand, nothing in the data indicates widespread demand for change. Except for some enthusiasm (limited to NDP and poor associations) for limiting individuals' annual donations, the general impression is that the majority would prefer to leave the system, that is, their association's place in it, pretty much as is.

CONSTITUENCY ASSOCIATIONS AND NATIONAL PARTIES

At the end of the previous chapter I suggested that constituency associations were rather like local franchise organizations. They differ from commercial ones in that they are staffed by volunteers, and appear to be closed a good deal of the time. A small group of committed activists keeps them in place between elections, but the national parties do not do much for them. If anything, the fairly unidirectional flow of funds (upwards) suggests that head office sees them largely as another source of income for the national party organization. Certainly most associations do not have sufficient financial resources to make much of a local impact between elections.

From another perspective, however, the national extraparliamentary party is the sum of its constituency associations, and it is often very difficult for a democratic political party to be more than the sum of its parts. This leads us to consider what the profiles of these constituency associations, as developed in these last two chapters, tell us about the parties. In this discussion we are primarily concerned with the three big parties in Parliament for only they, to this point, have contested elections with the declared aim of forming a government.

The single-member constituency electoral system, and contemporary assumptions about the nature of national elections, require serious parties to have constituency associations and candidates in every electoral district in the country. Some proportion of these represent token efforts, as the record of lost electoral deposits (all parties lose some in every normal election) would imply. The questions are, then, can we identify these purely nominal constituency organizations, and what does the pattern of them tell us about the nation's parties and its political competition?

Party activists have a name for these token or nominal local organizations that is taken from the lexicon of European mass parties. They call them *paper branches*. This is because they exist on paper, on the mailing lists of politicians or party headquarters, but one would be hardpressed to find much evidence of them on the ground. The Canadian equivalent of those paper branches are constituency associations that do nothing and have no money. With our constituency data we can now measure the prevalence and distribution of such local parties. To be considered a paper, as opposed to real, constituency association, a local party must be both poor (defined above as having neither income nor money) and self-confessed (see chapter 3) as inactive. The data in table 4.17 provide an estimate of the proportions of Canadian constituency associations whose existence is probably more nominal than real.

Within the five parties, about one association in five appears to be a paper branch. The Reform Party has none, the Tories very few (5 percent). At the other extreme, however, over half (55 percent) of the NDP constituency parties fall into this category. Indeed the data provide something of a puzzle. The Conservative and Reform parties are traditionally thought of as cadre parties, the NDP and CHP as mass parties, yet the former pair has the most real constituency associations, the latter pair the fewest. Some of this can be explained by the importance of incumbents, most of whom have real local parties in their constituencies, while a good deal of the rest is rooted in the regional vagaries of Canadian politics.

Comparatively few constituency associations in western Canada are paper organizations. This is a region with a long tradition of grassroots political activity and it obviously persists in the contemporary parties. In Quebec, on the other hand, an extremely high proportion (52 percent) of its constituency associations fall into the category defined as largely token political organizations. That might be because Québécois are not very interested in national politics, but it might also be a reflection of the one-party cast to federal electoral outcomes in that province. The two explanations are not necessarily mutually exclusive but it is possible to choose between them. If the reason for the large number of paper branches in Quebec has to do with a lack of interest in federal politics, then the proportions of nominal riding parties ought not to vary too much by party. If, however, the explanation has to do with the province's penchant for returning large numbers from one party at any given time, then there will likely be big differences between the proportions of paper branches in each party in Quebec.

Table 4.17
"Paper branches": poor and inactive constituency
associations, 1990
(percentages)

All parties	22
Progressive Conservative	5
Liberal	16
NDP	55
Reform	—
Christian Heritage	21
Incumbent	6
No incumbent	29
Region	
Atlantic	32
Quebec	52
Ontario	15
Prairies	12
British Columbia	13

It turns out that the one-party dominance explanation is correct. Almost none (the survey found one) of the Conservatives' Quebec constituency associations met the paper-branch criteria. But 50 percent and 94 percent of the Liberal and NDP associations respectively did. It does not stretch the imagination very far to think that 10 years ago, when Mr. Trudeau dominated federal politics in Quebec, the Liberal and Tory figures would have been reversed – indeed the Conservatives might have looked even weaker than the Liberals do now.

On this same logic one might expect the Liberal party to have a fairly large number of purely nominal constituency associations on the Prairies, where they have suffered an electoral drought since the Diefenbaker realignment a generation ago. But no such pattern exists. Indeed the survey revealed that none of the Liberal constituency associations in the three Prairie provinces fell into this category. This testifies to the enduring national vocation of the Liberal party.

The balance between real and paper constituency associations in each of the three national political parties tells us much about them individually and hence about the character of Canadian party competition. Figure 4.5 charts the real-versus-paper association regional profiles of the parties. Except for the weakness already discussed of the Liberals in Quebec, both the two historic parties are genuinely national political organizations. The large majority of their constituency associations in every region are real and thus constitute the core of potentially effective and meaningful political vehicles in national politics. The same is not true of the NDP. For all intents and purposes the party can hardly be said to exist east of the Ottawa River. In 95 percent of the ridings of Quebec and the four Atlantic provinces, the local NDP riding parties are, by their own admission, paper branches. This is particularly striking for Quebec, where the national party made major organizational commitments, and spent large sums of money, during the years immediately preceding the 1988 general election.

This analysis of Canadian political parties from the perspective of the constituency associations forces us to conclude that the NDP is not a genuinely national party, or at least not one in the organizational sense that the Liberals and the Progressive Conservatives are. If that is the case, and if constituency associations are critical elements in the democratic process of competitive elections, then the NDP cannot be considered a full player in the electoral process in half of the country. This is but a confirmation that the party systems of the two halves of the country are structured quite differently, and that it is the Quebec–Ontario border that marks this fundamental division in Canadian party life.

Figure 4.5
Party regional profiles, 1990

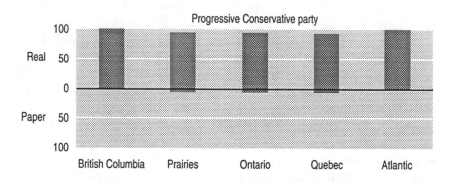

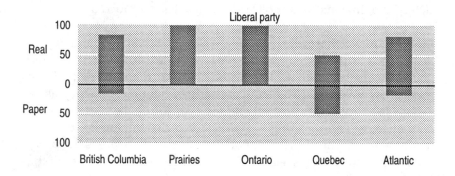

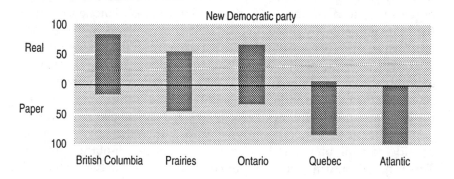

5

CANDIDATES, DELEGATES AND INTERNAL PARTY DEMOCRACY

THERE ARE THREE moments when Canadian political parties' constituency associations spring to life and when their activity can change the political landscape. The first is at election time, when associations compete with others for the support of the wider electorate. That is a public process, much of which is now regulated by statute. The other two instances are moments of internal party democracy, when party members gather to nominate their candidate for Parliament or to elect delegates to a party leadership convention. On the most momentous of these latter occasions, such as the Liberal leadership convention of 1984, those delegates then go on to choose a new prime minister for the country. But whether it is to select a candidate or convention delegates, these activities are treated as the private business of the parties' constituency associations and left unregulated by the state. In theory, the exercise of constituency association democracy is governed by each party's constitution. In practice, there is a long and valued tradition of local autonomy, a good deal of variation from riding to riding, and limited amounts of democracy if we equate democracy with an open, electoral competition for position. This chapter explores candidate nomination and delegate selection in the constituencies.

In choosing candidates and selecting delegates, individual local party members have the greatest opportunity to make a personal impact on the system. Despite the formal role of the party's membership in policy making, the exigencies of parliamentary politics and the rhythms of electoral competition mean that that activity is largely the domain of the professional politicians. But local activists control access to the political class through their dominance of the nomination process, and they have a powerful capacity to shape their party's leadership through their predominance in the selection of leadership convention delegates (for a dramatic example, see Blake, Carty and Erickson 1988). In both instances, long-established norms dictate a participatory democracy with local party members having a vote in a general meeting of the constituency association membership. Nominating candidates is a regular activity driven by the electoral cycle; selecting delegates to a leadership convention is invariably more episodic, dependent as it is on the vagaries of party leaders' careers.

Widely shared assumptions about representation underlying the country's single-member constituency politics (Courtney 1978) assure that the parties' basic approach to nominating candidates is quite similar. However, differences in conceptions of internal party democracy, and in the corresponding rules and structures, mean that delegate selection has a different character in cadre-style parties like the Conservatives or Liberals than it does in a mass party like the NDP. In the analysis that follows, the focus is largely on the three major national parties. Many of the Reform Party's constituency associations will really only be getting their first taste of a full electoral cycle during the next election.

The localism that has long been at the heart of much Canadian political organization has meant that the parties' constituency associations have traditionally been relatively free to order their own affairs as they saw fit. An almost inevitable concomitant has been the limited capacity of the national party organizations to play a significant role in important activities such as choosing candidates. Though the national parties have tried to set standard rules and delineate common processes, they have had only a limited ability to defend or enforce them. It is in just this situation that the parties are coming under increasing pressure to alter the practices of constituency politics. Among the most insistent of these demands has been the call for the parties to nominate more women candidates. But if constituency associations do not voluntarily change their behaviour, that will require a significant change in the relationship between riding and national party organizations.

Two dimensions of contemporary constituency-level party democracy have attracted a good deal of comment, both inside and outside the parties themselves, and demand attention. The first is the phenomenon of "instant" party members. This refers to the practice of aspiring candidates, for either a local nomination or the party leadership, signing up large numbers of individuals as party members just before a local nomination or delegate-selection meeting in an attempt to swamp the vote on their behalf. It is often alleged that such new members have little knowledge of or interest in the party per se, do not become involved beyond the single meeting for which they are recruited and often displace the real long-serving partisans who are the mainstay of a local constituency party. To the extent this is so, it might be argued that parties are correspondingly impoverished as viable instruments of democratic participation in a parliamentary system. On the other hand, given the conception of membership in the cadre-style Conservative and Liberal parties, the (re)mobilization of partisans is naturally tied to occasions of electoral competition and choice (see figure 3.1). After all, instant members are not necessarily instant supporters or instant partisans. Of course some may be, but it is still an open question how constituency associations interpret this practice. Many riding parties may therefore see the cycles of membership renewal as having a positive, invigorating impact, bringing individuals into the fold just when the association needs them for electoral work.

The second issue is the financing of constituency association contests. Internal party elections, like all others, cost money. During the 1980s the press was full of reports of the increasing costs of such contests, be it thousands for a local nomination or millions for a party leadership. The parties have a legitimate concern about the extent to which money is now a determinant in their internal affairs, but there are also important public-policy questions. After all, in areas of one-party dominance the nomination contest may be harder fought than the general election itself, and in leadership contests the prime ministership may be at stake. The control of election spending is now seen as a legitimate part of ensuring fair democratic competition. The question now is, does the election expense regime need to be extended to control internal party elections as well? That would be a change in our conception of parties, moving in the direction of viewing them as a kind of democratic public utility (Epstein 1986) rather than as an instrument of a group of interested citizens mobilized to control the state. Evidence from the constituency survey allows us to put the problem of money in internal party elections into perspective and explore the extent to which it really has become a serious problem.

The analysis proceeds by examining the two faces of internal party democracy in the constituencies – nominations and delegate selection - in turn. That provides the basis for a consideration of local party activists' views on whether the system is working satisfactorily and what, if any, aspects of it need reform or regulation.

NOMINATING CANDIDATES

The right to determine who will be their candidate for Parliament is a traditional prerogative jealously guarded by local party activists. Though sitting MPs are generally renominated with comparatively little difficulty, they have always been expected to submit themselves to the will of the local association before every election. Nomination challenges

are not commonplace, they can be messy, but they have long been part
of constituency politics in Canadian parties. Accounts of local party
activists denying James Beaty a renomination in 1887 (*Globe* 1887, 5), or
W.F. Maclean, the "Dean of Parliament," one in 1926 (*Globe* 1926, 1) make
for familiar reading today. Though the practice by national campaign
leaders of reserving seats for star candidates is not unknown in any of
the parties, resistance to it from Liberal activists during the 1988 general
election (Fraser 1989, 164–65) indicates that it is often seen and resented
as an illegitimate intrusion into the business of the riding party.

The rules of the game were changed in 1970 when the *Canada
Elections Act* was amended to provide for the use of party labels on the
ballot. The mechanism adopted required that the local nominee be cer-
tified by the party leader (or his or her representative) as an endorsed
candidate. In effect this gave the party leader a new, enforceable veto
over a riding association's nomination. Leaders have used this power
sparingly, however, because large numbers of local activists continue
to believe that the party leader should always have to accept the candidates nominated by constituency associations (Carty and Erickson
1991, table 3.1). Inevitably then, its use – or demands for its use – has
the potential to engender considerable internal party conflict. But constituency association presidents understand that the vagaries of the
nomination process may require it. As we shall see below, a majority
of them now support the veto. The notion that the wider party has an
interest in who the local nominee is, and how she or he is chosen, is
clearly taking root among those most responsible for the management
of the constituency parties.

For all that local nominations are one of the few moments when
constituency associations can make their mark, there is little evidence
that most organize in a fashion that might allow them actively to do
so. Their role, more often than not, is essentially a passive one: the processes of internal party democracy are more often those of quiet accountability than of active participatory decision making. In a comprehensive
study of the nomination processes used by constituency associations in
the three major political parties for the 1988 general election, Carty and
Erickson (1991) reveal that a majority of local nomination meetings are
uncontested. That study describes the typical nomination process as
open, relatively unstructured, easily permeable and generally inex-
pensive. Of course not all contests are typical, and some involve high
levels of conflict and expensive campaigns, but they do appear to be the
exception.

Responses to a series of questions in the constituency association
survey about their local nomination experience confirm the basic

portrait provided by the Carty and Erickson study, and its details do not need to be redrawn here. In that study the authors were primarily concerned with the dynamics of the nomination process itself. Here we shift the focus to consider what nomination activity reveals about the parties' constituency associations and their operations. The basic parameters of constituency nominations are determined by the fundamental reality that the majority are not openly contested, including over 40 percent of those that have no incumbent but are considered a safe seat by the local association (Carty and Erickson 1991, table 3.18). This can be seen in table 5.1, which summarizes constituency association reports of recent nomination experience as well as the numbers of nominees acclaimed in 1988.

Association presidents were asked to characterize the nomination experience of their local constituency party as either a "source of local conflict," "competitive," "no competition" or "a chore to find a candidate." This was done to assess the character of the formal competition, as described by the number of candidates, as well as to detect any underlying competition that did not surface in the form of a contested nomination meeting. The latter is always difficult to quantify but it clearly exists. One-quarter of the associations that had just one candidate contest their nomination in 1988 (i.e., an acclamation) rated their recent experience as either conflictual or competitive, suggesting some behind-the-scenes competition that was resolved without a formal decision of the membership at a nomination meeting. And in all the different constituency association groupings reported in table 5.1, the proportion with acclamations was always higher than the proportion reporting that they had no competition for the nomination.

Table 5.1
Finding candidates: nomination politics in the constituencies
(percentages)

	Conflict	Competition	No competition	Chore to find candidate	1988 acclamations
Progressive Conservative	11	40	38	12	64
Liberal	23	35	32	11	50
NDP	7	40	35	18	57
Paper branches	12	16	39	33	73
Candidate's finish, 1988					
First	12	46	41	1	59
Second	16	37	30	17	55
Third	11	34	34	21	60

These data demonstrate some modest but quite understandable differences in the extent of competition over the local nomination among the parties. It is highest in the Liberals, lowest in the NDP. No doubt the higher levels of competition in the Liberal party reflect the large number of normally good Liberal seats without an incumbent in 1988 as a result of the Conservative landslide of 1984. In many of those same seats the presence of an incumbent would have inhibited nomination competition in the Conservative associations. The NDP pattern is superficially puzzling, for the party prides itself on its internal democracy, and one might have hypothesized that that would be reflected in more frequent local contests. In fact, as we saw in chapter 4, the NDP has far more paper associations than the other two major parties (table 4.17), and those are the types of associations most likely to have non-competitive nominations. Thus, the NDP had acclaimed nominations in 71 percent of their paper branches but in only 43 percent of their other associations: 39 percent of all the party's nominations were acclamations held in paper branches.

Few riding parties that ultimately won their local constituency election in 1988 reported that it was a chore for them to find a local candidate, but one in five of those which finished third did. Given Canada's multiparty system, and the fact that candidates are expected to be connected to the riding and not simply paying their dues before moving on to safer seats (as in the United Kingdom), there are inevitably considerable numbers of nominations that are relatively undesirable. These the parties have to work to fill. As one might expect these patterns match those of constituency association activity: a majority of the ridings that described themselves as active had a competitive local nomination politics, while 41 percent of those that admitted they were inactive reported that it was generally a chore for them to find a local candidate.

There are no sharp regional differences in the competitiveness of nominations, though the lower levels of constituency association activity in the provinces east of the Ottawa River (see chapter 3) result in somewhat less competitive nominations there. Interestingly, it was on the two peripheries, Atlantic Canada and British Columbia, that constituency associations most frequently admitted that it was a chore to find a local candidate. In part that reflects the real (1991) weakness of one of the federal parties in each region, the New Democrats in the east, the Liberals on the west coast.

Despite the fact that nominating candidates is one of the local associations' most important tasks, and the one in which individual party members can make a significant difference, the majority of local associations continue to seek and to choose their candidate in a relatively informal fashion. As table 5.2 indicates, most reported not having a regular candidate search committee. More New Democratic associations claimed to have one (44 percent), but, as we have already noted, that does not translate into more competitive nominations for the party as a whole. Within each of the parties, acclamations are less likely when there is a constituency search committee in place, which suggests that a more structured process can alter the character of local nomination contests.

Even fewer associations have "formal rules governing spending on nomination campaigns" in place, though again these are more common in NDP associations than in either of the two other parties. This lack of nomination-spending rules, despite stories about excesses that regularly appear in the press, appears to reflect a NIMBY (not in my back yard) view of the issue. Only 3 percent of all constituency party presidents thought that excessive nomination spending had been a problem in *their* riding association, and 89 percent said it simply was not an issue. For them there seems little incentive or reason to put sets of local guidelines in place.

Though the nomination process is organized in a rather casual fashion in the constituency associations of all three parties, the same can not be said for local attempts to increase the number of women candidates. In response to the question whether "any special efforts [have] been made to recruit women candidates by your association" only a third of the Conservative and Liberal associations said yes, while 80 percent of the NDP associations answered in the affirmative. This is striking evidence that the NDP's local riding associations have begun to take this issue seriously and put policies and structures in place to deal

Table 5.2
Local nomination process characteristics
(percentage yes)

	Progressive Conservative	Liberal	NDP
Regular search committee	17	25	44
Spending rules	12	13	24
Efforts to recruit women candidates	34	32	80
Membership time requirement			
One week or less	23	14	10
One month or more	23	47	67
Core group pretty well decides	42	49	36

with it. The problem with this, as far as increasing the number of women parliamentarians is concerned, is that the NDP has very few winnable seats to offer the women candidates it recruits.

Here the operative word is "recruits." Constituency associations in all three parties that reported making a special effort to recruit women candidates were more than twice as likely to have had a woman candidate in 1988 as those who said they made no such effort (27 percent as opposed to 11 percent). And these special efforts to recruit women candidates in 1988 were not random affairs. Local associations that reported feeling "real pressure" from their national party to increase the participation of women in party affairs were twice as likely to have made such efforts as riding parties that thought the national parties were engaged in more talk than action (62 percent to 31 percent). As we noted in chapter 3, NDP associations feel that kind of pressure from their national party far more frequently than do their Liberal or Conservative counterparts. This suggests that riding associations are open to moral suasion from their national parties on locally sensitive questions such as their nomination strategy, but also that they will respond only when they are convinced the party is serious.

The parties obviously differ on the degree of commitment they expect of their supporters in terms of how long individuals have to be members before they are entitled to vote at a nomination meeting. This period is popularly referred to as the "membership cut-off." It provides one indication of how open the nomination process is to newly recruited supporters, and thus how permeable a constituency association is to outside political forces. Two-thirds of the New Democrats require individuals to have been party members for at least one month; less than a quarter of the Conservative riding parties make that demand. But these are essentially differences of degree: membership cut-off variations of this magnitude did not affect the competitiveness of local nominations in 1988. As we shall see below, in practice these variations make little difference to the mobilization of instant members. Rather, the cut-off rule differences between the New Democrats and its two cadre-style opponents signal different attitudes toward membership and the openness of the party organizations to unrestrained internal competition.

Finally, one might infer from the large number of uncontested nomination meetings that, in many local associations, the nomination process is managed behind the scenes. Forty percent of the constituency association presidents confirmed that in their riding a "core group of the association pretty well decide among themselves on who the candidate ought to be, then work to get that individual nominated." When some set of key players in the local party is managing the process, contested nomination meetings are less common: 61 percent of those cases ended up with an acclamation in 1988 as compared to just 44 percent where no such élite manipulation was practiced. As the data in table 5.2 indicate, the interparty differences on this are not particularly large. Élite dominance is more frequent in the Liberal party, less so in NDP associations, but the differences do not support sharply contrasting models of the parties characterizing the Liberals and Tories as élitist and the New Democrats as democratic in their internal electoral choices.

Mobilizing Members and Nominating Candidates

One of the realities of the nomination process that Carty and Erickson's study demonstrated (1991, table 3.10) was that would-be nominees routinely recruit supporters to join the party and come to the nomination meeting. This is commonplace in contested nominations, but also seems to happen in almost half of all uncontested nominations. That this practice is widely accepted as part of the normal politics of party nomination can be seen from the fact that the large majority of these recruitment campaigns do not cause a local controversy. Yet that same study reported (ibid., table 3.13) that the press gave disproportionate attention to the limited number of conflicts that arose over local membership recruitment campaigns, emphasizing the negative impact such conflicts could have on local party organizations.

In 1988, constituency parties with competitive nominations were typically bigger and more active associations (see figure 5.1). This was true in all three parties, though the size differential appears to have been smaller in the NDP than in either of its two bigger rivals. That is partially accounted for by the general size differences between NDP local parties and those in the Conservative or Liberal parties during an election year. In all three parties, the associations that reported it was a chore to find a candidate had a comparatively small local membership.

There is, however, something of a chicken-and-egg character to this relationship between constituency association size and the competitiveness of its local nomination, for it is often the presence of a nomination contest itself that leads to membership growth. While most local association memberships typically grow during election years in cadre-style parties such as the Conservatives and Liberals, aggressive recruitment campaigns should still generate more election-year membership growth in ridings with competitive nominations than in others. The patterns in figure 5.2 demonstrate that this was the case in 1988, but also reveal some considerable interparty differences. Perhaps most striking is the relatively small difference in the growth of the typical

Figure 5.1
Constituency association size and nomination competitiveness, 1988

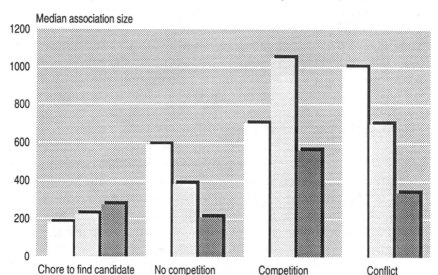

Median association size

Chore to find candidate   No competition   Competition   Conflict

☐ Progressive Conservative   ☐ Liberal   ▨ NDP

(median) NDP local association made by a local nomination contest. This is consistent with the mass-style membership of the party's constituency associations (analysed in chapter 3), but it does suggest that NDP associations are little affected by nomination contests. For NDP associations, nomination contests are the private internal affairs of a well-established membership. Certainly they do not appear to use the opportunity, and incentives, provided by a contest to recruit and involve new members and in so doing broaden their base in the constituency. It is quite the contrary in the cadre parties.

In the governing Conservative party's constituency associations, membership growth was largest in situations where the nomination was contested. In particular, where the riding president described the association's nominations as a source of local conflict, the median 1987–88 growth rate (at 145 percent) was two-and-a-half times that of competitive riding parties (58 percent), and five times that of those reporting it a chore to find a candidate (29 percent). This pattern might be thought of as a classic cadre-party experience. The Liberals, by comparison, provide a much more dramatic example of what nomination mobilizations can do to local membership numbers. Its typical (median) competitive nominations produced membership increases (150 percent) in the order of five times those of its associations with noncompetitive nominations (31 percent), but still only half that of

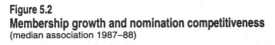

Figure 5.2
Membership growth and nomination competitiveness
(median association 1987–88)

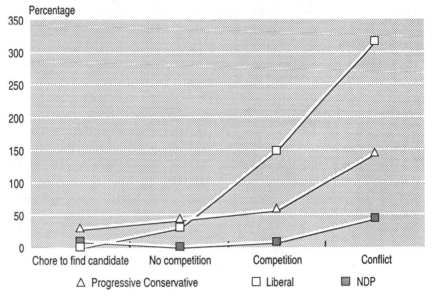

the instances where the nomination stimulated a local conflict (317 percent). These extraordinarily large Liberal recruitment drives reflected some very hard-fought nomination battles in ridings opened up by the defeat of 1984 but which the party expected to win back in 1988. It is just these sort of cases that attract media attention but also colour party activists' attitudes about the merits of recruitment drives. That being so, we might expect these party differences to be reflected in the perceptions of local parties about the consequences of the instant-member phenomenon for their local association.

One of the principal arguments for requiring party supporters to have held their membership for some nontrivial fixed period before being eligible to participate in constituency association elections is to prevent instant members flooding into an association only days, or even hours, before a nomination meeting. Few Canadian constituency associations have requirements (such as six months or a year) that might hinder and discourage outsiders from a last-minute campaign to take over the riding association meeting, though some try to frustrate them by having a membership cut-off period that is longer than the required notice of meeting. It may be that attention to the issue of membership requirements has been exaggerated, for the constituency membership data indicate that, at least in 1988, growth rates were not associated with nomination meeting participation rules (table 5.3). Short time requirements do not produce larger waves of instant members. Thus, for example, the typical Liberal association requiring individuals to be a member for one week or less saw its size grow at about the same rate as those that required members to have been in good standing for at least one month. In the Conservative and NDP cases, it was the local associations with more, rather than less, stringent requirements that generally experienced the largest growth rates. This being the case, the cut-off period is not as important for its impact on the numbers of instant members in local parties as for what it signals about both the parties' openness to new members and their determination to maintain the integrity of their internal democratic processes.

The recruitment of a significant number of new members and their infusion into the constituency association in the context of a nomination contest can often have consequences long after that contest, and even the subsequent election, are over. The very process can result in new people, interests and ways of conducting local politics being imposed on a constituency association so that old members are displaced and their experience lost. Sometimes new members stay involved and help sustain new levels of party activity. However, given that they entered party life largely to help a particular individual win a specific contest, their level of interest may prove to be ephemeral and their participation fleeting. When that occurs the constituency association is left weakened and worse off than it was before the invasion of instant members.

Bell and Bolan (1991) provide examples of how two such excessive nomination contests rebounded against the local party, in their study of constituency campaigning in Ontario during the 1988 federal election. In Markham, the Liberal association was swamped by over 2 000 new members recruited to support the candidate favoured by one ethnic group. The process was so disruptive that the local party executive resigned, leaving the new candidate to fight (and lose) with-

Table 5.3
Constituency association growth by nomination meeting cut-off periods
(median association 1987–88 growth in percentages)

Membership requirement	Progressive Conservative	Liberal	NDP
One week or less	83	40	3
One–two weeks	20	37	7
Two weeks–one month	27	83	4
One month or more	83	44	10

out much help from the established party organization. In Perth–Wellington–Waterloo a Liberal nomination fought over abortion divided a swollen riding association, and, when the candidate tried to downplay the position that had won him the nomination, supporters apparently defected and the party lost the constituency battle in the general election.

These examples suggest that electoral-period mobilization can pose significant problems for cadre parties. Thus, it is necessary to ask about the incidence of local mobilization campaigns during the nomination process, and the consequences for local constituency associations. Just under half (48 percent) of the constituency party presidents in the three major parties reported that their local association had had some experience with the recruitment of instant members in local nomination battles. That sort of activity in association nomination contests is common all across the country, though it appears to be less prevalent (33 percent) in the Atlantic provinces than in other regions. However there are marked differences among the parties in the proportion of their associations that have had nominations marked by the recruitment of instant members into their local party. Only 25 percent of the NDP, compared to 50 percent of the Conservative and 70 percent of the Liberal constituency parties, reported having had to deal with the phenomenon. It is also evident that there are party differences in terms of the impact of these instant members on the respective constituency associations (see figure 5.3).

Among both the Conservatives and New Democrats, riding parties were twice as likely to interpret their experience of instant members recruited in nomination contests as positive rather than negative. On the other hand, Liberal constituency associations were one-and-a-half

Figure 5.3
Experience of instant membership in nomination contests

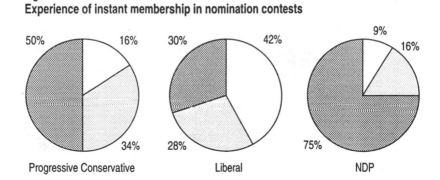

Progressive Conservative	Liberal	NDP

□ Positive   □ Negative   ▨ Not happened

times more likely to rate their experience negatively than positively. It might be assumed that this difference is rooted in some highly publicized battles over Liberal nominations in Metro Toronto in 1988. However, such a geographical account is inadequate. Though over half of the Liberal riding associations with a negative view of instant membership were in Ontario, only a handful were in the Toronto area, and almost as many Toronto associations claimed instant membership was positive as negative. A clue to a fuller explanation of the interparty difference is to be found in the scale, rather than the location, of instant-member mobilization campaigns in the Liberal party: they were both more frequent and larger in its riding associations than in those of the other two parties.

In both the Conservative and New Democratic parties, local associations that thought instant members had a positive impact had grown more (over 1987–88) than those that saw the process in negative terms (table 5.4). They had obviously interpreted the influx of significant numbers of new members as a boost to the local association. The reverse was true in the Liberal party. Its associations with negative views of instant members had grown 50 percent more than those that saw nomination-driven membership mobilizations in a positive light. As we noted above (figure 5.2), the very large Liberal membership growths were associated with the most conflictual nominations. The comparison between Liberal and Conservative local parties, both of which expect election-year membership growth as a matter of course (figure 3.1), suggests that there may be a threshold beyond which a cadre party association cannot cope. In 1988 some Liberal associations may simply have grown too much, and too aggressively, so that the process shifted from being normal and functional to being pathological and dysfunctional for the regular ongoing party membership. That seems to have been the problem faced by both the Markham and Perth–Wellington–Waterloo Liberal constituency associations (Bell and Bolan 1991) during that election.

Table 5.4
Constituency association growth by perceptions of "instant" members
(median association 1987–88 growth in percentages)

Perception of "instant members"	Progressive Conservative	Liberal	NDP
Positive	100	100	180
Negative	45	150	25
Not happened	14	14	0

Money and Nominations

Election expenses are now regulated, nomination expenses are not. This raises two problems: one for the parties, the other for the public. The first is that large sums of money may help determine just who is able to run for office as a party candidate. Given the relatively informal and open character of most association nomination procedures, this can deprive the local party organization of control over the choice of its nominee. The second problem is that in many ridings a party nomination may be tantamount to election itself. Certainly that was the case over the 1970s and 1980s for Conservatives in Alberta. But unlimited and unmonitored nomination expenditures can make a mockery of the election expense regime. Popular accounts (Lee 1989, 120–21), and those arguing for increasing the participation of women and minorities (Brodie 1991), suggest that nomination spending is now a problem; constituency party presidents do not agree.

Only 2 percent of local riding respondents agreed that excessive nomination spending was a major problem. Eighty-nine percent said it was not an issue, while the rest indicated that it was something that needed to be watched. This general lack of concern flows from the reality that in the majority of cases only modest sums are being spent on nomination contests. The winner of a nomination in 1988 typically spent just $200, though this low number includes all the uncontested cases as well. Not surprisingly, there were some marked party differences in 1988 – the typical Liberal winner spent three to five times more than his or her Conservative or New Democratic counterpart – in part because more Liberal nominations were contested in 1988. As table 5.5 makes clear, more money is spent on contested nominations. Contested Conservative winners spent more for their nomination than did Liberals, but Liberal runners-up outspent Conservatives in the same situation. The two cadre parties stand in sharp contrast to the NDP. With winners having spent only $300, money is clearly not a significant factor in the typical NDP nomination contest.

Nominations are not being bought by individuals with more money than others. In all three parties, fewer than half the nominees outspent their opponents. About a fifth of the contested nominations were won by an individual who spent less than his or her rival, while in the remaining cases (from one-fifth of the Liberals to three-fifths of the New Democrats) the winner and runner-up spent the same amount (table 5.6). And in the cases where the winners were able to outspend the runners-up, the differences were typically not large: from just $200 in the NDP to $800 in Conservative associations.

Though the largest proportion of nomination contests involve only a few hundred dollars, there are some where substantial sums are

Table 5.5
Nomination contest spending, 1988 general election
(dollars, median amount spent)

	All winners	Contested	
		Winners	Runners-up
Progressive Conservative	300	1 500	800
Liberal	1 000	1 000	900
NDP	200	300	200
Nomination contests in riding			
Source of local conflict	1 000	2 750	1 000
Competition	500	850	500
No competition	0	200	0
A chore to find a candidate	50	500	50

Table 5.6
Winners vs. runners-up: who spends most in nomination contests?
(percentages)

	Winners	Runners-up	Both equal
Progressive Conservative	47	19	34
Liberal	49	19	18
NDP	25	18	57

expended. The most expensive nomination battles in 1988 saw winner and runner-up each spend $5 000 or more. Eight percent of the local associations had such a contest. The majority of these contests (58 percent) occurred in the Liberal party, and they constituted some 14 percent of the Liberal nominations in 1988. It is very likely that the location and frequency of such contests are election-specific, reflecting institutional factors as well as the political context. Thus, in 1988, while there were obviously more Liberal seats to be won back, it is also noteworthy that a disproportionate number of these nomination contests took place in ridings marked by large boundary changes. In 1984 there were probably more of them in Conservative associations.

Expensive nomination contests sensitize local party officials to the problems created by excessive spending. Though only 9 percent of all local presidents thought nomination spending was an issue to be watched, 42 percent of those in whose association there had been one of these extravagant contests indicated they thought it was a potential problem. However, local associations do not appear to be effective in controlling nomination spending. Those associations with their own formal nomination-spending guidelines (admittedly a weak arrangement given the lack of any legal sanction) were just as likely to have had such a free-spending contest as those without them. But of course some may not really want to limit expenditures. Unlike they do for elections, local associations do not feel obliged to raise the funds needed to cover the costs of a nomination contest: candidates do. From the riding party's perspective a vigorous nomination contest may be a good way to enrich its coffers at a critical time.

Contested nominations, especially in the two cadre parties, go hand in hand with mobilization campaigns to bring in new members, increasing the size of the local association. For a constituency association new members mean, among other things, a higher membership-fee income. The implications of this are different for each of the three major parties. The Conservatives have significant nomination-year membership growth but low fees, the New Democrats have high fees but relatively little growth. Neither will therefore have as large income increases from nomination contests as the Liberal riding parties, which typically have both high growth and moderately high fee levels. Table 5.7 indicates what the impact of this pattern was during 1988 in each of the parties. New members' fees added $175 to the income of the typical NDP association with an uncontested nomination, $500 to the Conservative and $600 to the Liberal one. The significant financial impact comes with contested nominations: for the median Liberal local association they added $2 500 to its income. However, this undoubtedly underestimates the impact of a vigorous nomination contest. In Liberal associations the *mean* fee-income increase was considerably more – $5 900 – and in a few instances this amount ran well into five figures.

The membership fees of many of the individuals recruited into the party for a nomination fight often end up being a charge upon the would-be nominee's campaign. This is because instant members can be induced to come to a nomination meeting but they will often not pay to do so, leaving the candidate little choice but to pay for them. Thus these membership fees, which effectively constitute little more than the charge for attending a nomination meeting, represent a kind of poll tax: but one that, levied by the local association, falls on the candidate rather than the voter. This means that local associations, especially in the Liberal party, have it in their power to lower at least one of the financial barriers to nomination. They need simply reduce their membership fee. However, that would reduce local party income in election years, just when they need it most, and open them even

Table 5.7
Income from new memberships for 1988 nomination meetings
(dollars, median association)

	Acclamations	Contests
Three major parties	500	1 750
Progressive Conservative	500	500
Liberal	600	2 500
NDP	175	900

Note: Income was calculated as constituency association's 1987–88 growth times its membership fee.

more to penetration and the capture of their nomination by outsiders. Constituency associations have little incentive to do either.

CHOOSING DELEGATES TO LEADERSHIP CONVENTIONS

The second set of party decisions that allow local activists to contribute to the shape and direction of the party is the choice of their delegates to party conventions. Constituency association representatives constitute the majority of those voting at party conventions, so the selection of these delegates is important. Several individuals are normally chosen from each riding association (the numbers vary by party), and the time and financial obligations of delegates are clearly defined and limited. This means that, unlike they do in a nomination, many ordinary party members do not need to confine their participation to voting at the selection meeting but can hope to be elected themselves. As we noted in chapter 3 (table 3.19), in most cases there is rather little competition for delegate positions to the parties' regular biennial policy conventions. It is a different story when the party leadership is at stake.

At the beginning of this century André Siegfried (1906, 118–19, 136) commented on the importance of leaders to Canadian parties, and their pre-eminence has not waned over time. Indeed the invention of extraparliamentary leadership conventions and leadership reviews has probably only reinforced the leadership focus of Canadian parties (Perlin 1988; Carty, Erickson and Blake 1992). In recent years, leadership conventions have spilled down into the local constituencies, involving far more activists in increasingly lengthy preconvention leadership campaigns (Carty 1988a). Leadership candidates have a strong incentive to penetrate local associations in an attempt to mobilize and capture support at the delegate selection phase of the process. That inevitably increases the extent and amount of competition within the constituency associations. In the most recent NDP (1989) and Liberal

(1990) leadership contests, the number of contested delegate selection meetings in local associations was about three times larger than it was for those held for their other regular national party conventions.

Leadership contests are more sporadic events than are constituency nominations, which routinely come with every general election. Untied to a common electoral process, they also vary much more by party than do nomination contests. The cadre parties structure participation to ensure equal representation from every constituency association irrespective of its size or level of activity. In recent years both the Conservatives and Liberals have also required that the associations' delegations meet particular age and gender requirements. In that way the Liberals were able to ensure that half of the constituency delegates to their 1990 leadership convention were women. By contrast, the NDP's mass-party concern for member democracy has led it to structure its constituency representation differently. Their local associations' delegations are tied directly to membership size: big associations have more delegates than small ones. Thus, in 1989 there were nearly two-and-a-half times as many constituency delegates from the 14 ridings in Saskatchewan as from the 107 in the five provinces east of the Ottawa River (Archer 1991, table 1.2).

As both the Liberals and New Democrats held leadership conventions during the period that our constituency association survey covered, it is possible to explore the impact of those contests on those two parties' riding organizations. While the Progressive Conservative party's structure differs in some important ways from the Liberals', previous research on the 1983 Mulroney and 1984 Turner leadership conventions has demonstrated that the delegate selection process was remarkably similar in both parties (Carty 1988a). Thus the Liberal experience can be taken as representative of the Conservatives', and the Liberal–NDP comparison can tell us something about the differences between the contemporary constituency-level leadership politics of cadre- and mass-style party organizations in Canada. In both cases, the NDP in 1989 and the Liberals in 1990, the parties were in opposition, so that the contests were not exaggerated by the prime ministership being at stake.

In a leadership contest every delegate's vote is important, as it can contribute to a candidate's final total. This means that winning delegate selection contests is as important in weak as in strong riding associations. Indeed, other things being equal, candidates' campaign teams have had a greater incentive to move into weak local associations, where delegates might be won at lower cost (in energy and goodwill) than in well-organized, strong riding parties. That is why, in the 1983 and

1984 Conservative and Liberal contests, candidates more often organized delegate slates in areas where the party had traditionally had limited support (Carty 1988a, 91–92). This pattern is quite different from that of the nomination contests, for those are precisely the areas where the seat cannot be won and so there is little incentive to contest a nomination (Carty and Erickson 1991, Part 3). This logic leads to the proposition that, over all, leadership delegate selection contests will be more competitive than nominations. As such competition increasingly involves mobilizing new members, that would help explain the very high 1990 Liberal association memberships reported in table 3.5.

The evidence suggests that this strategic model holds with respect to Liberal constituency associations, but not for those in the New Democratic Party (figure 5.4). Among Liberal riding parties, more of the delegate selection than nomination meetings were contested, and a higher proportion of them were characterized as a source of local conflict as opposed to being simply competitive. Whereas over half of all Liberal leadership delegate selection meetings generated conflict, only 1 percent of the New Democrats' did. Despite the relative paucity of ridings that offered a good prospect of election, NDP nominations were more vigorously contested than the leadership delegate selection meetings held the following year.

Figure 5.4
Liberal and NDP nomination and delegate selection meeting competitiveness

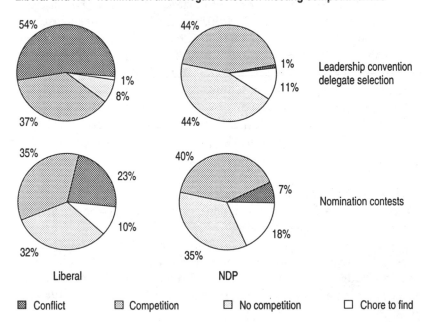

| Conflict | Competition | No competition | Chore to find |

These sharp differences in the constituency-level processes of the Liberal and New Democratic associations do not simply reflect the contests that were going on in the two parties. The Liberal leadership was always a one-person race: Jean Chrétien was widely seen to be the front runner, and he subsequently won rather easily on the first ballot. On the other hand, the NDP contest was an unpredictable affair from the start, and Audrey McLaughlin took four ballots to win it. The explanation for the differences in constituency-level competitiveness lies in the nature and structure of the parties.

As a party whose organization is defined by electoral imperatives, the Liberals believe in mobilizing individuals for electoral competition, even within the party. Liberal candidates were encouraged to develop a strategy to contest the smallest riding associations, for all their associations have the same number of delegates as the biggest and strongest local parties. On the other hand, the New Democrats see leadership contests as the business of their established activists, and do not welcome members who join for the occasion (Morley 1992). The party's many small local associations do not have enough delegates to make it worthwhile trying to capture them. Its large associations, with their correspondingly large convention delegations, would be very difficult for a candidate to penetrate and monopolize. With these differences go very different attitudes to leadership campaign spending (the Liberals fixed a candidate limit of $2 million in 1990, the New Democrats $150 000 in 1989), so that NDP candidates could not hope to mount an intense pre–delegate selection campaign in most constituency associations in the way Liberals might.

Constituency associations' leadership delegation selection processes are not dissimilar from those for the nomination: members are mobilized to come to meetings to vote, in this case for supporters of particular leadership candidates. As figure 3.2 indicates, the impact of this on Liberal association memberships in 1990 was dramatic. More than half of them reported that their local membership was greater in 1990 than at any time over the 1987–1990 period, including the election year of 1988 (when 80 percent of the Tory associations hit their peak). No such new-member mobilization wave disturbed NDP associations: only 3 percent of them said that 1989 (their leadership convention year) marked their largest membership over the four-year period, and their typical constituency membership actually dipped that year (table 3.5). NDP leadership campaigns are obviously not vehicles by which either candidates or the party seek to mobilize support or recruit new members. Only 6 percent of the local associations reported such activity, down from 25 percent in the nomination contests of the year before.

In cadre parties like the Liberals, leadership campaign–driven membership mobilizations differ from those in nomination contests in one important regard. Whereas nominations revolve around the ambitions and capacity of local candidates, delegate selection contests are driven by external forces and decision makers. Leadership candidates and their campaign teams target particular local associations in terms of their wider national strategies and resources, and move into a riding in an attempt to capture its delegates. This means that the recruitment of instant members is more widespread, producing the pattern of association growth described above. Thus only 19 percent of Liberal associations said they had no experience of instant members being recruited for convention delegate meetings, compared to 30 percent that had not had to deal with them in their nomination process. Sometimes these external pressures increase local competition; in other instances an effective campaign by one candidate will scare off competitors or force coalescent strategies among opponents in a riding. The net result is that the growth and eventual size of a constituency association are not as strong indicators of the degree of local competition within a riding party in a leadership year as they are in an election year (figure 5.5).

Externally motivated mobilizations of instant members were not welcomed in the majority of local Liberal associations in 1990, which described them as negative and a very disruptive force. Twenty-five

Figure 5.5
Liberal and NDP constituency association size for nomination and delegate selection meetings

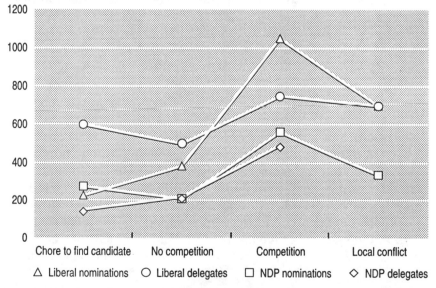

percent more associations saw instant memberships this way than they had during the 1988 general election. This attitude toward efforts to swamp delegate selection meetings was particularly prevalent among constituency parties that had not experienced instant-member campaigns during their nomination process. No doubt this generally negative perception reflects the impersonal, machine-like way in which national leadership campaigns now move in and out of local ridings, with their limited concern for the consequences of disrupting local memberships or the impact of pushing local élites and long-serving activists aside.

If constituency delegate selection was once a rather informal, semi-automatic business, with local officers and notables being chosen (Power 1966, 372), it is no longer so. A study of the 1983 Conservative and 1984 Liberal experience revealed considerable variation among local associations. It also identified a range of practice which suggested a hierarchy of organizational intensity in local selection processes (Carty 1988a). Five stages characterize the process in the constituency parties: (1) delegate positions are contested; (2) would-be delegates identify themselves with a particular leadership candidate to indicate their position and attract support; (3) slates of prospective delegates are put together to maximize the impact of organizational effort; (4) slates are identified with candidates; and (5) identified slates find themselves contesting other identified slates in what has been called trench warfare. This is, strictly speaking, not a rigid hierarchy, for delegates on slates (stage 3) need not themselves be identified with a candidate (stage 2), or even find themselves contested (stage 1) at the selection meeting. Indeed the very existence of an organized slate may well discourage a contest. But as one moves from stage to stage greater organizational resources are required, and the selection process does become more intense. However, this transformation of the delegate selection process is an ongoing one, still largely confined to the two old cadre parties. This can be seen in the differences between the New Democratic and Liberal parties during their recent leadership contests, and in changes in the Liberal party between 1984 and 1990.

Archer's (1991) study of the NDP's 1989 leadership convention indicates that delegate selection in its constituency associations was highly individualistic and not strongly tied to the declared candidates' campaign organizations. Just 51 percent of the delegates reported having to contest their position while, at the other end of the spectrum, only a tiny 2 percent reported that they had been engaged in a trench warfare situation. As figure 5.6 dramatically illustrates, the contrast with the highly organized Liberals could hardly be more revealing. In an analysis of Perlin's (1991a) survey of the 1990 Liberal delegates,

Figure 5.6
Delegate selection contests, NDP, 1989, and Liberal party, 1990

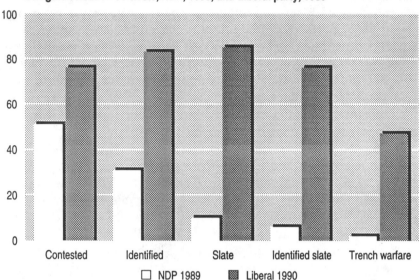

Sources: Data from Archer (1991) and Perlin (1991).

Hanson (1992) discovered that over three-quarters of them had found it necessary to fight for their place at the convention and that almost half (47 percent) had been in trench warfare battles.

These differences speak to the quite distinct orientations to internal party democracy held by mass- and cadre-style parties such as the NDP and the Liberals. However, it is also true that Liberal party practice has been evolving so that the differences between the parties have increased over the last decade. Figure 5.7 compares the Liberals' constituency association delegate selection in 1990 with that for 1984, the party's previous leadership convention. Though the numbers of constituency delegates who were contested hardly changed, there was a significant increase in all the other categories. The proportion of previously identified delegates grew by 102 percent, the numbers on identified slates by 216 percent and the cases of trench warfare by 292 percent (Hanson 1992). The Liberals' 1990 leadership candidates simply picked up on the experience of 1984 and expanded the scope and intensity of their organizational efforts.

The 1984–1990 Liberal comparison is particularly telling because the stakes were considerably higher in 1984 than in 1990. In the former contest the winner automatically acceded to the prime ministership,

Figure 5.7
Liberal delegate selection battles, 1984 and 1990

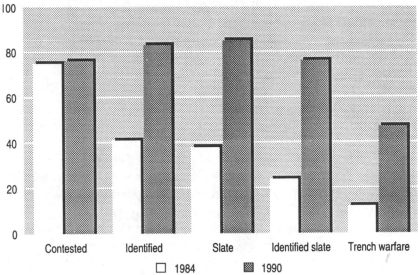

Sources: Data from Carty (1988a) and Perlin (1991).

in the latter the prize was only the right to lead the Opposition. Given this, there is no reason to think that the pressure to build comprehensive personal organizations capable of penetrating constituency associations would be any less in future leadership contests operating under the same rules. That seems as true for the Conservatives as the Liberals.

The highly structured selection process that now takes place in the cadre parties fundamentally changes the position of the local delegate and by extension the place of the constituency association in the extra-parliamentary party. Internal party democracy loses its immediacy and intimate grounding in the constituencies. Delegates, when elected with the support of a leadership campaign team, become agents of that campaign. By attaching themselves to a national campaign they sever the claims of the local association and inhibit their capacity to represent local party members in anything but a mechanical fashion. Inevitably, this must make constituency associations merely stages on which the same personal contest is fought out time and time again. By treating all associations equally as they do, the Liberals and Conservatives ensure that this process will go on unimpeded. Indeed, by giving weak riding associations as many delegates as strong, active ones, the parties may accelerate this process, for it is just those weak associations that are most vulnerable to outside manipulation. The New Democrats' resistance to treating associations, rather than members, equally may be one of the explanations for their ability to escape the worse excesses of these developments in Canadian leadership politics.

Constituency associations in cadre parties expect to have membership influxes around election contests, including leadership races that are, strictly speaking, internal to the party. That these should be closely managed by national campaign teams may be hard on particular activists or local organizations, but they are not inherently destructive of the fabric of the party itself. What does make the process problematic, however, is the very openness and minimum of structure and regulation that facilitates the participation of almost anyone who chooses to do so. Individuals representing narrow interests, as well as those seeking to rebuild the Liberals' or Conservatives' broad coalitions, may mobilize interest-group supporters to take over parts of a party. The Liberal campaign of 1990 was subject to just such an effort.

Tom Wappel's leadership candidacy was generally interpreted as a part of a wider public campaign by the pro-life movement to generate attention and support from and in the Liberal party. In 1988, its supporters had helped him get elected to Parliament; in 1990 groups such as Liberals for Life and the Saskatchewan Pro-Life Association worked to recruit individuals to come to delegate selection meetings and support delegates committed to Wappel. The impact of their efforts can be seen in figure 5.8, which compares the experience of Wappel delegates with that of those supporting other candidates, in terms of the proportions that had interest-group help in getting elected. As the figure makes clear, group support was four times as common for Wappel delegates, irrespective of competitive strategy employed, as it was for the other constituency association delegates. There is no doubt that this was the pro-life movement in action, for 93 percent of Wappel delegates with interest-group help indicated that it was the pro-life movement that supported them (Hanson 1992). While Wappel finally received less than 6 percent of all the votes cast at the convention, almost three-quarters of his supporters reported that their election had been helped by a pro-life group.

Wappel's interest-based campaign ultimately had little impact on the outcome of the leadership contest in 1990, but it might have been different had the contest been closer and the convention taken more than one ballot to choose a winner. There have, after all, been several close leadership conventions in which the outcome has depended on a few votes cast at a critical juncture. In that event, a block of disciplined delegates, devoted to a cause rather than attracted to a

Figure 5.8
Interest-group basis of Tom Wappel's leadership campaign

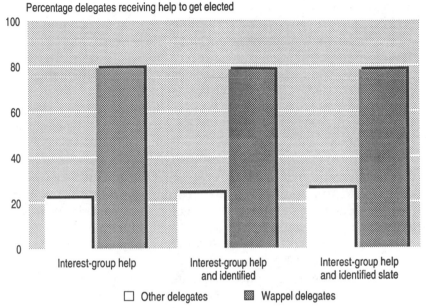

Percentage delegates receiving help to get elected

Sources: Data from Hanson (1992) and Perlin (1991).

personality, might well play a critical role in determining the final outcome. And while both the Liberals and Conservatives seek to embrace
a wide range of interests, it would hardly be desirable for them to have
their leadership seen to have been decided by some particular organized interest group.

From the perspective of the individual constituency associations,
this sort of interest-group invasion also entails some distinctive costs.
When a regular leadership candidate's campaign penetrates a local
association, even to the extent of swamping it with instant party members, it prefers to have them support known local party activists as the
association's convention representatives. The campaign's principal concern is whether the potential delegates will commit themselves to support the candidate at the convention throughout the balloting. The
capture of a constituency will leave local political fences to be mended,
but a contest won by known partisans can usually be grudgingly
accepted as a legitimate aspect of internal party democracy. In contrast,
when an interest group takes over a local association, it seeks to have
proven interest-group loyalists selected as delegates. The result is that
those associations end up not only with instant members voting at the

selection meeting, but also with instant members as their delegates. As often as not these individuals have but limited interest in the party and a marginal attachment to it. Regular party members particularly resent this kind of take-over. They know that those individuals' commitment to a single cause will almost certainly lead them away from party activity, with its messy compromises and concern for issues across the entire public agenda. And when individuals who have represented the constituency's members at a leadership convention leave, the local association loses an important connection to the wider party. It can no longer count on a cadre of local members who have had the experience of participating in one of the party's most important national events.

Evidence of this phenomenon can also be seen in the 1990 Wappel leadership campaign. Figure 5.9 reveals that the instant party members recruited by the pro-life groups supporting Wappel tended to select instant members as delegates. Thus over half of the delegates supporting Wappel at the convention had only joined the party during the course of the campaign, while just 13 percent of them had been Liberals for at least five years. This pattern stands as a mirror image of the delegates supporting all the other candidates. Despite the fact that the majority of them had been chosen in local races managed by external organizations, more than two-thirds of them had been Liberal party members for over five years, and just 15 percent had joined during the leadership race (Hanson 1992). Though the Perlin (1991a) survey from which these data are drawn cannot tell us how long the associations that supported Wappel held their delegates as members, a process that produces instant Liberals as delegates is just as likely to produce instant ex-Liberals.

This portrait of the leadership process, and the comparisons we have been able to draw between the Liberal and New Democratic parties, indicate that there is a considerable difference between the cadre parties, with their constituency-structured processes, and the New Democrats with their classic mass-membership orientation toward internal party organization and democracy. The nomination processes of the parties, tied as they are to the electoral imperatives of the single-member plurality electoral system, do not vary in the same fundamental way. One might expect that this distinction between the two principal exercises of internal party democracy would have sharp implications for the design of a regulatory framework. The parties ought to find it easier to agree on a common framework for the nomination process than for leadership selection. The evidence suggests that this is not the case. Local activists, across the three national parties, are prepared to support an agenda of only limited change.

Figure 5.9
Tom Wappel's instant Liberals

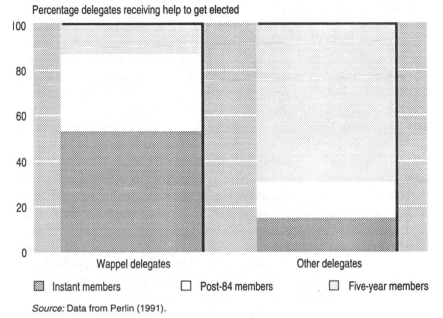

Percentage delegates receiving help to get elected

Instant members   Post-84 members   Five-year members

Source: Data from Perlin (1991).

STATE REGULATION AND PARTY DEMOCRACY

Much of the discussion about reforming the mechanisms of internal party democracy centres on issues of money. That is to be expected. Many individuals and groups believe it now constitutes a formidable barrier to entry and participation by regular party members. This perception was given a powerful boost when Lloyd Axworthy, a prominent and highly regarded MP, was forced to drop out of the 1990 Liberal leadership race because he did not have the financial resources to compete effectively with Jean Chrétien or Paul Martin. A second reason for this focus is that the financing of general election campaigns by both parties and candidates is regulated, and it would appear natural to extend the principles that govern that regulatory regime into the party processes for electing candidates and leaders.

The Canadian election expense rules are designed to try and level the financial playing-field on which political opponents operate. They do this from both ends of the money cycle. At the income end, the system provides candidates who demonstrate (albeit after the fact) that they are serious competitors with a reimbursement of a proportion of their election expenses. This allows them the financial security to wage at least a minimum campaign. At the same time there is a system of tax credits to induce private individuals to support the candidates/parties of their choice. As Stanbury demonstrates in his magisterial study *Money in Politics* (1991), the result of this combination has been to give the (three big) parties and their candidates large amounts of both public and private money to compete with one another. At the expenditure end of the money cycle, the system sets spending limits for election expenses so no party can spend so much as to smother its opponents. It is this two-pronged approach, regulating both income and expenditure, that levels the field at both ends.

Constituency association presidents were asked whether they were in favour of extending this framework to the nomination and leadership processes in their parties. To do so would imply accepting a measure of state regulation of internal party affairs. Given that parties have been seen as the instruments by which citizens control the state, such regulation has traditionally been resisted in Canada. Some principled opposition to state regulation persists. Forty-four percent of the associations thought "political parties should be free to regulate their internal affairs by their own rules, as they think best," while the other 56 percent accepted the general notion that "their internal affairs should be subject to at least partial regulation by public law." The parties differed on this: a majority of the Conservative and Reform associations opted for the self-regulation position, while a majority of the Liberal and NDP local parties accepted that there was a case for some outside regulation.

General predilection for, or opposition to, regulation disguises the fact that, even within the parties, there is a considerable issue-specific variation in the extent of support for specific changes. Tables 5.8 and 5.9 report the proportions of local associations that endorsed a set of five changes that would bring the nomination and leadership processes into line with the electoral process. The tables are organized with changes that commanded the greatest support at the top of the list, those with the least at the bottom. Two things strike one about these tables immediately. First, the rank order of the items is remarkably similar, and second, there is relatively little difference between them. As one might expect, there is somewhat less grassroots support for regulating the nomination process, for that is the activity that touches a local riding party's ongoing life most directly.

On all but one issue there is a general left–right continuum that defines support for change. The Conservative (and Reform and CHP for that matter) associations tend to be toward the status-quo end, the New Democrats toward the reform end, though none of the parties were overwhelmingly in one camp or the other on even a single issue.

Table 5.8
Support for proposed reforms to nomination process
(percentage associations in favour)

	All three parties	Progressive Conservative	Liberal	NDP
Limit spending	69	59	69	81
Use tax credits	52	48	57	52
Allow voters only	47	58	53	28
Government to reimburse expenses	35	26	35	46
Election law to govern process	33	22	35	44
Abolish leader's veto	34	30	39	34

Table 5.9
Support for proposed reforms to leadership selection process
(percentage associations in favour)

	All three parties	Progressive Conservative	Liberal	NDP
Limit spending	76	66	78	86
Use tax credits	65	53	76	66
Allow voters only	49	62	53	30
Government to reimburse expenses	40	29	40	54
Election law to govern process	31	20	32	43
Elect by direct all-member vote	59	52	68	57

The parties reverse ends on the question of who ought to be allowed to vote in the parties' nomination and leadership selection proceedings. A majority of the cadre-party associations favour limiting the right to those eligible to vote in an election. A large proportion (70 percent) of NDP associations reject that position and advocate participation by all party members, even if they are under the voting age or otherwise (e.g., non-Canadian) ineligible to vote. That difference is rather ironic, for the NDP has far fewer ineligible (under-age) voters participating in its leadership conventions than do the Liberals or Conservatives (see the Archer 1991 and Perlin 1991a surveys).

The changes that attract the support of a majority of local parties are those that will bring something of the level financial playing-field to internal party contests. The general system of election spending limits is now widely seen as satisfactory (by 79 percent of local associations), and riding parties are prepared to extend it, and the use of tax credits for fund-raising, to the internal party processes of nomination and leadership selection. The majority, however, oppose public reimbursement of candidates' expenditures. Local party officials may think that by openly taking public funds (as opposed to the indirect tax credit) they would not be able to resist demands for closer regulation of their activities.

This is a salient point, because local parties are opposed to state regulation of their internal electoral processes. When asked whether the law should set standards and principles governing candidate nomination and leadership selection, or whether the parties should be left entirely on their own to decide those principles and standards, about two-thirds of the local party associations argue for leaving these matters to the parties themselves. They do not want the business of the local associations to become part of a legal system that would standardize and nationalize their organization and practice. In this the associations reaffirm their opposition to having to register and provide annual financial reports (table 4.16).

As key players in local party politics, many constituency association presidents have naturally come to believe that the system they manage works well. Other activists may not have as conservative an orientation. Evidence that this is so can be seen in figure 5.10. It compares the responses of 1990 Liberal leadership convention delegates (Perlin 1991a) to those of their constituency association presidents on our five basic reform proposals. It indicates that, on every one of the five issues, constituency activists were more supportive of increased regulation than the local party officials. But still the basic pattern of enthusiasm for spending limits and tax credits, coupled with opposition to reimbursements and common legal rules, held. The one issue on which delegates differed the most from association presidents was the participation of non-voters in nomination and leadership elections. On this, Liberal activists were simply less ambivalent than constituency officers: 87 percent of them reported that they would forbid it.

The data on reform proposals also report local association reaction to specific suggestions for changes to both the nomination and leadership selection processes. One important change to the existing nomination process would be the abolition of the legal veto on party candidates that now rests with the party leader. It exists because in the absence of any formal recognition of constituency associations, some party-endorsement mechanism is required to put party labels on the ballot. A change to the status of local associations that saw them become reg-

Figure 5.10
Leadership selection reform proposals: support from Liberal delegates and association presidents

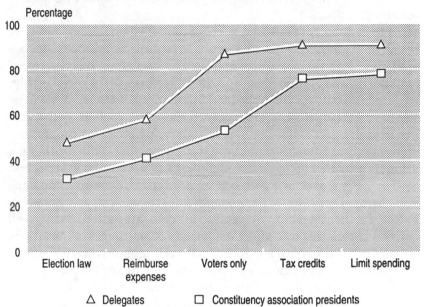

Source: Data on delegates from Perlin (1991).

istered entities would make this superfluous, and free local associations to reassert their traditional autonomy in this matter. Despite the rhetoric of local sovereignty, two-thirds of the constituency association presidents rejected the prospect (table 5.8). Perhaps they saw it as a check on the very openness and permeability of their association membership.

The process by which parties choose their leaders has come under much scrutiny in recent years (Perlin 1991b; Carty, Erickson and Blake 1992). Several provincial parties, including the Parti québécois, the Ontario, Prince Edward Island and Alberta Conservatives, and the Ontario and Nova Scotia Liberals (see Latouche 1992 and Woolstencroft 1992 for accounts of the first two) have opted to choose recent leaders by some variant of an every-member vote. Perlin (1991a) and Archer (1991) report that a majority of delegates at the last Liberal and New Democratic Party leadership conventions favoured moving to a direct-vote system. It is no surprise, then, to see that a majority of constituency association presidents also favour it (table 5.9). Liberals reported the greatest enthusiasm for such a system, and their party adopted one in early 1992. In this the Liberal party may be replaying the events of the early second party system (Carty 1992). It was then the first national party to move from caucus to conventions to choose its leader, and, if the process is seen to be successful when the Liberals come to replace Jean Chrétien, the party may again pioneer a major shift in Canada's leadership politics.

The national Liberals' new process, modelled on the experience of the Ontario Liberal Party, will continue to be centred on a delegate convention. Constituency association delegations will have their first (convention) ballot vote tied directly to the preferences of the membership, as determined by a vote in the local association, but delegates will be free to vote their personal preferences on subsequent ballots. With membership in each constituency's delegation being allocated proportionately among candidates, mobilizing instant members will not offer the same exaggerated winner-take-all pay-offs as the current system, and so the strategy and tactics of local association leadership campaigns will change. Direct appeals from candidates to regular party members before the membership vote, and to all delegates after it, may well increase. How this will affect the party's constituency associations remains to be seen. What is clear is that the riding association is destined to continue as the principal organizational focus of most partisans' participation in the democratic life of their party.

PARTY DEMOCRACY IN THE RIDINGS

It is no simple matter to come to some general conclusions about local organizational democracy in Canada's national political parties. For one thing, they continue to differ in their approach to internal organization and their willingness to experiment with new structures and processes. The Liberals have plunged into a whole new approach to leadership selection, which entails giving every member a direct vote, with only a limited view of how it will work nationally. This was hardly forced upon them. Perlin (1991a) argues that an important force leading to this change was Liberal activists' views of what was appropriate given changing Canadian conceptions of democracy. New Democrats, by contrast, appear much more cautious about experimenting with their leadership processes. They have only agreed to study the idea of an every-member vote, despite the fact that it has quickly been adopted by several other parties across the provincial party systems as well as by the federal Liberals. They are also reluctant to alter the organizational basis for leadership choice in the party. Archer's (1991) survey of the 1989 NDP leadership convention delegates found that 87 percent of them thought that their party should not move to a system of allowing all constituency associations equal representation but should stick to its practice of tying delegation size to local memberships.

The parties also vary in the extent to which they are prepared to change long-standing relationships between national-level organizations and the constituency associations. The New Democrats, for instance, have moved furthest toward imposing a gender-balanced candidate selection process which of necessity will reduce constituency association autonomy and the ability of local activists to choose their own candidate. Of course the NDP's ability to do so reflects the large number of ridings without an NDP incumbent as well as the party's genuine concern about the issue.

However, this chapter has also demonstrated how much variation there is across the riding associations within individual parties. This is quite consistent with the accounts of local organization, activity and finance in chapters 3 and 4, but it also testifies to the power and impact of local conditions on practice. Though both nominations and delegate selection take place within a fairly clearly defined set of common norms and rules, party activists make constituency association democracy work in ways that suit them, as best they can. Given that these are entirely voluntary bodies that bring people into political life intermittently, and for a variety of motives, it may well be that this very opportunity for a constituency association to shape and infuse its own democracy is one of the continuing strengths of Canadian local party organization.

6

CONSTITUENCY ASSOCIATIONS AND ENUMERATION

IN HIS LAST REPORT to Parliament Jean-Marc Hamel, the former chief electoral officer of Canada, argued persuasively that Canada was suffering from a "crisis in electoral administration" (Canada, Elections Canada 1989). This crisis is, in large part, a result of the collision between the *Canada Elections Act* and the *Charter of Rights and Freedoms*, but it also flows from the inability of the system to cope with the patterns of rapid socio-economic and demographic change that are transforming the country and the electorate. Not the least important part of this system is the process, institutionalized by the 1938 *Dominion Elections Act*, by which a voters list is prepared.

Canada is unique among Western liberal democracies in that it has no permanent voters list or system of personal electoral registration. Instead it carries out a universal door-to-door enumeration in the days immediately after an election has been called, to establish a list of eligible electors. The process inevitably extends the period between the call and conduct of an election beyond that in other similar parliamentary systems. This mechanism of election-specific enumerations has generally been defended on the grounds of ensuring a current, complete and cost-effective voters list. However it is now increasingly clear that the failings of the enumeration process form part of the ongoing crisis in electoral administration that the chief electoral officer described. In his account of the 1988 general election he reported that he had been forced to invoke special powers overriding provisions of the *Canada Elections Act* to deal with 17 distinct problems. Five of them (involving up to 76 electoral districts) were related to difficulties in finding enough enumerators and then ensuring that they had enough time to do their work.

This problem concerns parties because they have an immediate interest in the voters list. It involves the constituency associations because they have an immediate role to play in the enumeration process.

The *Canada Elections Act* makes the candidates and their local parties important actors in the administration of the system.

When an election is called, the returning officers in each electoral district must appoint and train large numbers of enumerators promptly. For example, in 1988 this required finding and putting some 90 000 people to work within a week. It is at that point that the parties' constituency associations become involved, for the Act requires that the returning officers await the nomination of enumerators by the candidates (and in practice their local parties) who finished in first or second place in the riding during the previous election. In urban polling divisions these enumerators work in pairs and thus, in theory, serve as a partisan check on one another. In the rural polling divisions enumerators are allowed to work alone. This difference reflects both the realities of finding sufficient personnel to cover the ground and the provisions for election-day voter registration at rural polls.

Such a system traditionally served the interests of both state and party. The state was provided, at short notice, with a list of available workers who had an interest and concern that the job be done quickly and well. The local party, on the other hand, benefited in several ways. First, it received a source of small-scale patronage with which it could reward its loyal activists at a time when it was going to be calling on them for volunteer help. Second, many of these enumerators would move directly from enumeration to party work, and the information and knowledge that they had gained in the door-to-door canvass was often valuable to local campaign managers. Finally, at least in some areas, there was a tradition that enumerators contributed some of their earnings to the campaign chest of the local association that appointed them.

Canada's demography and political culture have changed in the half-century since this system was established, and some would argue that many local constituency associations no longer derive much benefit from it. The income to be earned is not such that many active partisans now view an appointment as an enumerator as a plum. As often as not, a well-organized local campaign team can make better use of volunteers during this period on strictly partisan activities. And now that parties and candidates are able to raise substantial funds in many other ways (Stanbury 1991), any contribution from enumeration income to a local campaign is likely to be relatively minor.

Beyond the loss of positive benefits, many constituency associations may simply be unable to find sufficient enumerators. Changes to the labour force, the modest remuneration provided and the reluctance of many people to go knocking on every door in unfamiliar neighbourhoods in the evenings have reduced the pool of potential enumerators. This is what ultimately shows up in the chief electoral officer's report of enumeration failures. In any given constituency such an outcome represents the failure of the local party associations, and the two strongest of them at that, to fulfil one of the basic functions the state asks of them. This brief chapter looks at the workings of this enumeration process from the perspective of contemporary constituency parties.

Finding Enumerators

As we have already noted, the law assigns the privilege, or task (depending upon one's point of view), of naming enumerators to the parties that finished first or second during the previous election in the constituency in question. That effectively decentralizes the responsibility so that it varies by party over time in the same riding, and from riding to riding in the same election. In practice, a majority of Conservative and Liberal associations regularly have to find enumerators while only a minority in the other parties do. Among the respondents to the constituency association survey, 84 percent of the Conservative associations reported finding enumerators in 1988, compared to 61 percent of the Liberal ones and just 35 percent of the New Democrats'. These differences need to be kept in mind in the discussion that follows, for it focuses primarily on the experiences of those associations that were responsible for providing lists of enumerators for the 1988 general election.

Just half (49 percent) of all the associations involved in naming enumerators in 1988 reported that they were able to "provide enough names easily," while 18 percent reported the opposite experience, indicating that they were "not able to find enough." The rest claimed that they "barely managed to name required number." Table 6.1 reveals that the success with which constituency associations were able to find enumerators varied both by party and by region. Fifty-seven percent of Liberal associations reported easily finding enough enumerators, compared to 49 percent of the Conservatives but just 38 percent of the NDP. The latter figure is striking for, unlike those of the two large parties, as many NDP associations admitted not being able to find enough enumerators. One might have expected that a mass party like the NDP with its more stable membership would be better able to find needed individuals. Part of the explanation for this rests with the smaller size of the typical NDP constituency association (see chapter 3). Large associations are able to find enough enumerators more readily than small ones. The typical (1988) membership size of all associations easily finding their allotment was 955; that of those not able to do so was just 550.

Table 6.1
Ability of constituency associations to find enumerators
(percentages)

	Found easily	Unable to find
Progressive Conservative	49	12
Liberal	57	17
NDP	38	38
Region		
Atlantic	65	0
Quebec	79	2
Ontario	36	25
Prairies	49	22
British Columbia	28	32

A local party's ability to find enumerators also depends on the region of the country it inhabits. As table 6.1 makes abundantly clear, the Ottawa River again stands out as a significant boundary in Canadian political life. In the five provinces east of the river, whose economies are weaker and whose politics are dominated by traditional Liberal–Conservative competition, local party organizations apparently have little difficulty finding enumerators. The survey did not turn up a single riding party in the Atlantic provinces that said it could not find enough enumerators. By contrast, in Ontario and the four western provinces, constituency associations had much more trouble finding enumerators, and in British Columbia more actually reported they could not find enough than said they did so easily. Here, of course, is another dimension underlying the party differences noted above, for the NDP is generally a nonplayer in the eastern end of the country (see figure 4.5), where enumerators are plentiful.

The system makes different demands on rural and urban party organizations – though many constituencies have a mix of both rural and urban polls – for urban polls require twice as many enumerators. It is also in the metropolitan areas where the challenges of finding suitable and willing enumerators are often greatest. Thus it is not surprising to discover that associations reporting they found enough enumerators had, on average, just 61 percent of their polls classified as urban, while those claiming not to have been able to find enough had, on average, ridings in which 83 percent of the polling divisions were urban ones.

The ease with which a constituency association is able to find enumerators has a dramatic impact on its general evaluation of the system. Those associations that easily found enough people viewed the right to name enumerators as "an advantage for their campaigns" rather than a disadvantage ("ties up people who would otherwise work in the campaign") by a ratio of six to one. On the other hand, associations that could not find enough enumerators were split evenly in their estimation of the value of the prerogative. As many (30 percent) saw it as a disadvantage as an advantage. It is also true, however, that the advantages that accrue to a constituency association from its right to nominate enumerators may be more apparent than real, and more valued in their absence than their exercise. At least that is what one might infer from a comparison of the views of all the local parties in the survey. Seventy-one percent of the associations that had not named enumerators in 1988 reckoned it was an advantage to a riding party's campaign, but only 55 percent of those who had actually been through the exercise shared that judgement. Nearly twice as many of those that had been responsible for naming enumerators as those that had not (18 percent as compared to 10 percent) considered that it was, on balance, a disadvantage.

Given this *mélange* of experience and attitudes it is not surprising that most associations are not committed to the existing system. Two-thirds of them, including a majority in all parties, favour extending the right to name enumerators to all parties. This reform is supported in all regions, and most enthusiastically among those who did not have the opportunity in 1988. The only substantial group of local associations that oppose a change to their pre-eminence in this matter are Quebec riding parties now naming enumerators. As we have noted, Quebec associations find it easy to recruit enumerators. It remains to examine the extent to which those individuals are subsequently put to work in the local associations' campaigns.

From Impartial Enumerators to Partisan Campaigners

Once the enumeration is completed, and the election campaign begins in earnest, local associations seek to mobilize as much volunteer help as possible. Naturally enough, many local associations that have been in the position of being able to name enumerators will turn to them for campaign help. Certainly that sort of patronage exchange was for many years the essence of much traditional local Canadian party organization. The questions to be asked now are: Does this enumeration system still feed the constituency associations' and candidates' campaign resources? And, if so, how important is it to the local parties?

There are two aspects from which we can assess the impact of enumerators' contribution to campaign work. The first is that of the enumerators themselves, and what proportion of them go on to work for the party. The greater the patronage component of the relationship, and of local party organization, the higher this ought to be. The second is that of the local party campaign. The party's need for volunteers depends on the kind of campaign it chooses to run. The impact and contribution that any or all of the enumerators make will consequently depend on the size and character of the local campaign. Table 6.2 provides estimates of the contribution enumerators made to 1988 constituency campaign staffing from both these perspectives.

Constituency associations that named enumerators in 1988 were asked whether "most," "some," "a few" or "none" of them later worked in the local party campaign. The left-hand columns of table 6.2 report the proportions of associations, in each of the three major parties and across the country's five regions, that responded with either "most" or "a few"/"none". The first point to note is that in none of the parties, and only in Quebec among the regions, did a majority of the associations report that most of the enumerators they had named subsequently became partisan campaigners. The second is that only east of the Ottawa River, and in the Liberal party, did more associations respond with most rather than a few or none. This confirms the perception, developed in the discussion on finding enumerators, that more traditional patterns govern enumerator–association relationships in the eastern half of the country. But with 35 percent of all the associations reporting few or no enumerators working for them, as opposed to 29 percent reporting most did, it would appear that enumerators can no longer be counted on by the campaign organization in the postenumeration period.

Table 6.2
Participation in local campaigns by enumerators

	Most[a]	Few/none[a]	% of volunteers[b]
All parties	29	35	10
Progressive Conservative	28	42	10
Liberal	32	30	13
NDP	26	28	10
Region			
Atlantic	33	25	10
Quebec	52	19	30
Ontario	19	44	10
Prairies	25	33	10
British Columbia	25	42	5

[a]Percentage of constituency associations reporting this response.
[b]Enumerators as percentage of volunteers in median constituency association.

Campaigns run by associations strong enough to be in the position of naming enumerators are, almost by definition, normally going to be better staffed than those organized by others. In 1988, 45 percent of the riding parties naming enumerators claimed to have as many volunteers as they needed, compared to only 22 percent of those who had not had to name them. Some of this difference may have been the result of having some enumerators volunteer, but table 6.2 indicates that enumerators' contributions were limited. In the typical association 10 percent of the volunteers had been enumerators, though that figure was considerably higher in Quebec and rather smaller in British Columbia.

When the constituency associations were asked what proportion of the enumerators they had recommended "contributed some of their enumeration income to the local campaign" two-thirds replied none: we found only two associations that reported most had. Given the rather overwhelmingly one-sided response to the question, there was little regional variation to be seen, though Quebec associations more often reported that some of their enumerators had made a financial contribution than did those in other regions.

The Importance of Enumerators to Constituency Association Campaigns

These measures of the contribution made by enumerators to local associations' electoral campaigns suggest that it is rather modest. What this quantitative information cannot reveal is the qualitative impact those individuals make on the campaign and thus how important they are to it. When asked about individual enumerators who eventually worked in the campaign, over half (57 percent) of all the associations rated them as either "very important" or "somewhat important." Not surprisingly, those that did so were twice as likely, compared to those who rated them "unimportant" to the campaign, to believe that the right to name enumerators was a distinct advantage to a local party. Interparty variation on the importance of these individuals to the local campaign is trivial: it ranges from a high of 59 percent in the NDP, through 58 percent of the Liberals, to 53 percent of the Conservatives.

As figure 6.1 demonstrates, there is a distinct regional pattern, by this point familiar, to the importance accorded party-named enumerators in local campaigns. It is higher in the eastern end of the country, low in the West. Over 70 percent of Quebec's constituency associations, but under 40 percent of British Columbia's, rated their enumerators-turned-campaigners as important to their local campaign effort. The organizational impact of the enumeration system has turned out to be primarily a regional one.

Figure 6.1
Enumerators "important to local campaign"

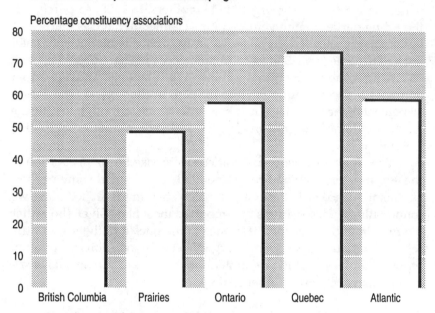

Percentage constituency associations

Enumerators, Riding Parties and Regional Political Style

Whatever differences exist between the cadre-style organization of the Conservatives and Liberals, and the mass-organization character of the NDP, they do not show up in the respective constituency associations' capacity to find enumerators for the state and then convert them into local campaign resources. Thus, a departure from the current system of preparing voters lists would not appear to have differential partisan consequences. The impact would play itself out in the constituency associations east of the Ottawa River.

The major differences we have identified are regional, and the pattern is a consistent and cumulative one. As the summary opposite indicates, on five traits that characterize the traditional patronage model of the relationship between a constituency association and the state's enumerators, Quebec and Atlantic-region associations rate comparatively highly: the relationship then gets progressively weaker as one moves west. In effect, the assumptions about the benefits that flowed to constituency associations, and therefore their incentives to accept these state responsibilities, are now probably valid only in the five eastern provinces. West of the Ottawa River constituency associations are not tied to the enumeration system and draw little from it.

	B.C.	Prairies	Ontario	Quebec	Atlantic
Find enumerators easily	L	M	M	H	H
Think prerogative an advantage	M	L	L	H	H
Most enumerators/campaign workers	L	L	L	H	M
Enumerators as percentage of volunteers	L	M	M	H	M
Enumerators important to campaign	L	L	M	H	H

Notes: L=low   M=medium   H=high

This argument suggests that abandoning the current enumeration system will have an observable impact only on the parties' local associations in eastern Canada. As we saw in chapters 3 and 4, many of those associations are financially weak and numerically small. The change would amount to kicking out some of the last, though perhaps marginal, props of their old system of local organization whose roots go back into the 19th century. Riding parties in other regions of the country have demonstrated that constituency associations can thrive without it. At election time most are just anxious to get on with the contest.

7

ELECTORAL ORGANIZATION AND ACTIVITY IN THE CONSTITUENCIES

WHEN AN ELECTION is called the life of Canadian parties' constituency associations is transformed overnight. Organizations that are normally somnolent quickly rouse themselves to work; those that are regularly active mobilize dozens of volunteers within days. It is, as one prominent Progressive Conservative party strategist describes it, like moving from a peacetime state to a wartime condition. Constituency associations strain to accomplish as much as possible within the allotted seven weeks, knowing that they usually will have but one chance every four years. Most local activists can influence the national outcome only through their constituency's individual campaign: success will make all their preparation and effort worthwhile, failure will condemn them to a long wait in the political wilderness.

For all the variety that marks the 295 constituencies across the country, there is a consistency in the structure and organization of constituency associations' local campaigns. This is, in part, the consequence of the fundamentally similar tasks involved in any constituency campaign: nominate a candidate, define issue positions, identify support, communicate a message and get out the vote. Differences among the parties' local campaign organizations reflect differences in the resources they, and their opponents, have in any particular case to do these jobs. But this consistency in party constituency campaigns flows also from deliberate attempts by the national parties to provide support and help for their local organizations. Publicly this approach is obvious in the standardized advertising logos or common-design lawn signs that spring up during elections. Privately it goes much deeper to include intensive campaign colleges, regional strategy meetings of riding campaign managers and extensive training manuals (in print or on tape) designed to help even the most inexperienced build a classic campaign organization and run a model campaign with whatever resources they have available. As Preyra argues in his study of two Nova Scotia constituency contests in 1988, "one striking result of all this coordination [is] that campaign structures and management processes at the local level, both within parties and between parties, [are] virtually identical" (1991, 147).

However, for all our sense that constituency campaigning has come under homogenizing, nationalizing influences, we know little about the basic parameters that govern this vital local party activity. There is a small literature that describes constituency party electoral organization (e.g., Meisel 1964; Land 1965), but it is almost all based on case studies of individual ridings. The Royal Commission on Electoral Reform and Party Financing's series of paired-comparison studies of the relationship between local campaign activity and the media (Bell and Fletcher 1991) provides a rich lode of material on contemporary (1988) constituency-level party competition, but it does not define or specify the range and bounds of riding party electoral structure and operation. This chapter provides just such a benchmark. Readers should keep in mind that much of the detail in the analysis to follow refers specifically to constituency associations' experiences in the 1988 election.

The analysis of basic constituency party structure and activity in chapter 3 demonstrates that the Liberals and Progressive Conservatives are classic cadre parties whose organizations are driven by the imperatives of the electoral cycle. The NDP, on the other hand, bears the marks of a mass party's organization, though it seems able to mobilize a mass membership in only a limited number of ridings. In many other ways, however, it looks and acts like its larger opponents. In this analysis we shall be concerned to discover which conception – essentially similar or different – best characterizes the parties' electoral organization and activity. As for the Reform and Christian Heritage parties, the 1988 general election was the first one that most of their constituency organizations fought. No doubt they all learned from that experience and may operate differently in subsequent electoral contests. That will certainly be the case for the Reform Party, which promises to have much greater resources its second time out. The analysis of both these new parties must be read in this context, recognizing that the data for both may now be somewhat dated.

It is not possible, in a broad survey of hundreds of constituency associations' campaign organizations, to detail how the idiosyncrasies of individual constituencies or politicians shape a local contest. It is clear that local *issues* can influence individual outcomes (see Bernier's

1991 account of Outremont in 1988), that superb *organization* can help carry a riding (Bell and Bolan 1991, on Markham), and that individual *candidates* can make a difference (Sayers 1991, on Vancouver Centre). But it is also clear that there are some common patterns in the structure and staffing of local campaigns, in the activities of volunteer activists and in the ways in which local parties and candidates attempt to communicate with their electorate.

Local parties must struggle with the reality that election "campaigns revolve around a discussion of national leaders and the national issues" (Preyra 1991, 143), but that the geographic basis for organization and competition means that "the degree of intraparty integration in campaign strategies [is] limited" (Sayers 1991, 43). On election day it is the local organization that must deliver the vote, but for a party campaign increasingly overwhelmed by national media and national appeals that may or may not have much local salience or resonance. As Sayers' account of Kootenay West–Revelstoke suggests, it is as if local organizations are, at once, in both a highly structured national environment and a local vacuum. We have already seen how they find a candidate and meet their obligations to find (i.e., register) the electorate. This brings us to the most important moment in the life of a local Canadian constituency party association, the election itself.

CREATING A CAMPAIGN ORGANIZATION

In practice, most constituency party associations do not wait for an election to be called to begin their campaign work. As we noted in chapter 3 (table 3.17), almost half of them report that election campaign planning is one of their regular, ongoing interelection activities. Two events bring their preliminary planning to a head and signal a new level of activity. One is the nomination of a candidate, the other the establishment of a campaign organization. In Carty and Erickson's detailed analysis of the nomination process they demonstrate that, at least in the three national parties, most nominations are now held over the months immediately before an election is called. Thus, in 1988, about four out of five of their constituency parties had held their nomination in the period between January and the October 1st call, and this proportion was even higher among the governing Progressive Conservative party's associations (Carty and Erickson 1991, 112 and table 3.5).

Obviously there is often good reason to delay putting the campaign organization into place until the candidate is nominated. That ought to make it easier to assemble a group of people capable of working together harmoniously and effectively in the high-pressure atmosphere of an election. Presumably the desire to do just this is one of the forces leading more local associations to hold their nominations before the election is called. But it is not always necessary or desirable to wait until the nomination to set a campaign team in place. Where an incumbent is running the nomination is often only a formality, where the party is weak the identity of the candidate is often only a technicality and where the party has real hope the nomination is often delayed to facilitate attracting a star candidate. In all those cases a local association might well choose to put a campaign organization in place before choosing its nominee. In 1988 about one-third of the constituency associations did so.

Figure 7.1 reveals that there were some differences among the parties in terms of when local associations put their campaign organizations in place. Of the three established parties, NDP associations set their campaign organization up before their candidate was nominated more often than either Conservative or Liberal riding parties (46 percent compared to 37 percent and 28 percent respectively). That fits with the portrait of the NDP as a more bureaucratic, mass party, for one would assume its local constituency executives would be less inclined to wait for, and defer to, a candidate than would those in the cadre-style electorally oriented Progressive Conservative and Liberal parties. The two

Figure 7.1
Timing of local campaign organization establishment

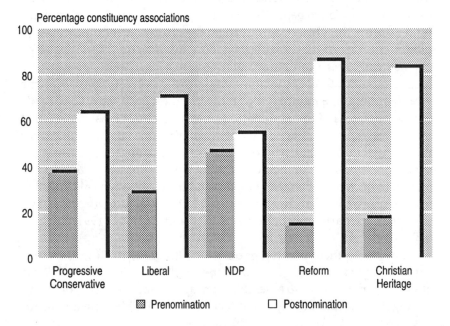

Percentage constituency associations

new smaller parties stand out for having very few campaign teams in place before they nominated a candidate. That is an indication of a lower degree of organizational stability and continuity at the riding level. But it is probably also common to most marginal or new parties: until a local association finds a willing and acceptable candidate, they cannot be sure which ridings they will be contesting.

Until the summer of 1988 it was not clear what constituency boundaries would be in place for the election. For constituency associations with major changes to their local boundaries, such an institutionally induced disruption of their existence might have played havoc with their ability to set up a campaign organization. In fact it does not appear to have done so: there were few differences between riding parties facing large boundary changes and those facing few or none, though those coping with major disruptions were somewhat more likely to nominate first. Whatever else the organizational impact of boundary changes may have been on local party associations, they do not seem to have inhibited associations very much in establishing their campaign structures.

There were, on the other hand, some regional differences in the willingness of riding parties to set up a campaign team in the absence of a nominated candidate. Quebec associations were almost twice as likely as those in British Columbia (46 percent compared to 24 percent) to put their campaign organization in place before nominating. Local parties on the Prairies were more like those in British Columbia, while those in Ontario and the Atlantic provinces fell between the two extremes. Whatever differences we can attribute to the parties themselves, it is apparent that organizational traditions in the regions continue to exercise a distinctive pull on election planning and management at the riding level.

Once the campaign team is established, its task is to design a campaign strategy and implement a tactical plan to meet its objectives. At that point the constituency association, through its executive, may back off and leave the campaign to be run by the campaign's own organization, or it may continue to be intimately involved in electoral decision making. To pursue the metaphor raised in the chapter's opening paragraph, the issue is whether the wartime generals are allowed their head, or whether they are expected to answer to the democratically accountable executive of the riding party. The cadre-party model would presume the former, while a mass party might be expected to be more concerned with organizational accountability. By requiring that an official agent named by the candidate, rather than the local party organization, be accountable for the finances of the campaign, Canadian law appears to assume cadre-style candidate-centred campaign management. That of course is consistent with the approach to electoral politics long practised by the Conservative and Liberal parties that created the Canadian party system.

Riding parties were asked to characterize this relationship between their local association executive and the party's campaign team as one of the following: (1) the association executive maintains control; (2) control is completely delegated to the campaign team; or (3) there is a balance struck between those two positions. It seems likely that the responses reflect intention and local theory as much as practice. In most riding organizations there is inevitably some personnel overlap between executive and campaign team (with the same individuals simply wearing different hats), so that the relationship is apt to be a relatively fluid one, depending on the issues and problems involved. Nevertheless, the data in table 7.1 indicate considerable interparty differences that conform to our perception of the Liberals and Conservatives as being different kinds of parties than the NDP. In both the two old cadre parties only a handful of local associations reported that the executive maintained control of the campaign team, while over half of them said it was delegated entirely to the campaign organization. Just a third reported trying to balance the two approaches. The dominant approach in both those parties is to give their wartime generals (the campaign managers) full responsibility. In this the Liberals and Conservatives clearly reveal their cadre-party organizational style and their compatibility with the assumptions underlying the current reporting provisions of the *Canada Elections Act*.

New Democratic local associations are different. More (but still just 10 percent) try to leave their association executive with responsibility for the campaign, and fewer than half delegate control to the campaign team. The largest group attempts to find a balance between these two positions as they strive for a more collegial style of electoral decision making. This difference appears to reflect a distinctive party organizational culture, and not simply its many fewer incumbents or strong candidates, for NDP riding associations that won their local seat did not differ on this dimension from those that lost. Carty's (1991) study of candidates' official agents noted a similar interparty difference in agents' participation in local campaign planning, which reinforces this portrait of the NDP as having more party-responsive campaign organizations than the candidate-centred machines of the Liberals and Conservatives.

Table 7.1 also indicates that Reform Party associations claim to have the least candidate-focused campaign organizations of all of the five parties surveyed. To a certain degree that finding may reflect the very newness of the party and the extraordinary prominence (even by

Table 7.1
Relationship between constituency executive and campaign team
(percentages)

	Association executive maintains control (1)	Control completely delegated to campaign team (2)	Balance between positions (1) and (2) (3)
All parties	8	52	40
Progressive Conservative	5	62	34
Liberal	6	56	38
NDP	10	44	46
Reform	18	38	45
Christian Heritage	5	44	51
Campaign manager appointed by			
Local executive	14	38	48
Candidate	6	60	34

Canadian standards) of its leader, Preston Manning, who overshadows local candidates. But it is also congruent with the party's populist culture and its members' enthusiasm for grassroots participation. By all accounts the NDP's predecessor, the CCF, had these same organizational characteristics in its early years. It may well be that the NDP pattern provides the best glimpse of the Reform Party's future in this regard.

Quebec stands out from the other regions: twice as many of its constituency associations (as the national average) report that they maintain control of the campaign team. Given that there is no difference across the three major parties in Quebec on this aspect of their electoral organization, despite the current dominance of the Conservatives and the paper-branch character of most of the New Democrats, this difference may be rooted in the province's modern organizational culture, which has reshaped its provincial politics and provides the basis for its unique system of *financement populaire* that influences provincial party organization.

The data in table 7.1 also indicate that when the candidate personally appoints the campaign manager the electoral organization is much more likely to be autonomous than when the local association has a hand in the appointment. That is not surprising, and it indicates that the appointment of the campaign manager is not only a crucial decision but also serves as a powerful signal of the kind and style of campaign team in place in the riding.

Figure 7.2 demonstrates the sharp differences that exist between these cadre and mass parties' electoral organization styles in terms of

Figure 7.2
Constituency campaign appointments

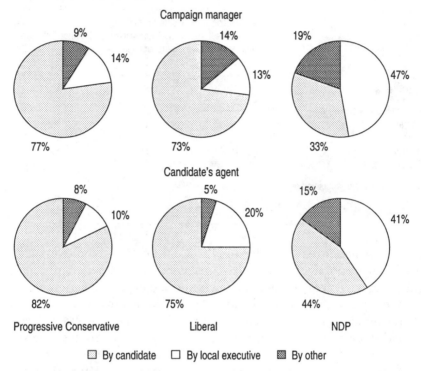

Source: Data on agents from Carty (1991).

the appointment of the two key officials in a contemporary local campaign: the campaign manager and the official agent. In Conservative and Liberal associations these appointments are made, in the vast majority of cases, by the individual candidate. In the NDP the local party executive is far more influential and actually appoints the campaign manager more frequently than do its candidates. That is not true in ridings the NDP won, but even among those associations the candidate named his or her campaign manager only 38 percent of the time.

Campaign Managers

At the centre of every campaign organization stands a campaign manager. The territorial logic of the electoral system, and the geographic cast of representation in Canada, might seem to be most directly served when local individuals manage their riding party's campaign. To the extent that the manager is a local party activist, the campaign is more likely to reflect the impulses of the local association and to resonate with the agenda and the concerns of the constituency and its parochial interests. Table 7.2 indicates that over three-quarters of all constituency campaigns are managed by individuals who are also regular members of the local party association. There is not much party or regional variation in this feature, though it is least common in the NDP and in Ontario. There is something of a reinforcing effect there, for only 61 percent of Ontario's NDP associations reported having a regular local member as their campaign manager.

Constituency associations may resort to using an outsider to manage their campaign for several reasons. In urban areas party activists may not be concerned with local residence, assuming instead that they should find the best individual available in the area. In 1988, for instance, over half the campaign managers in Metro Toronto ridings were not local party members. But finding an outsider to manage a campaign is still not the norm in Canada, and so is likely to take place either where the party thinks an infusion of special talent might pay electoral dividends or where the situation is so desperate that there is no local available to take on the job. Table 7.2 gives evidence of this first scenario: outsiders were markedly more common in situations where the party ran second than where it finished either first or third. It is precisely in second-place constituencies that a party might be tempted to install an outsider in an effort to give those campaigns a special boost.

The NDP has become particularly adept at pursuing this strategy. Not only does it use more outsiders as campaign managers, it also

Table 7.2
Local activists as campaign managers
(percentage regular member of constituency association)

All parties	78
Progressive Conservative	79
Liberal	76
NDP	71
Reform	93
Christian Heritage	88
Region	
Atlantic	82
Quebec	84
Ontario	70
Prairies	82
British Columbia	82
1988 finish	
First	83
Second	69
Third	75

attempts to put them into ridings where it hopes for some electoral advance. Thus in 40 percent of the seats where the party ran second in 1988 it had appointed an outsider. There is, of course, always some risk of alienating local activists if external party officials are too ham-handed in their attempts to insert an outsider into a constituency to run its campaign. Preyra (1991) reports how such an effort engendered hostility among Halifax activists in the 1988 campaign. That disruption may well have been one of the factors that contributed to that riding party's vote-share decline of 13 percentage points.

The second scenario, where a constituency association resorts to using an outside campaign manager for want of an alternative, is not as common but it does happen. Twenty-four percent of the campaign teams in the three major parties' paper branches had such management in 1988. Clearly the party was not sending in its top people in those situations. Sayers' (1991) account of the 1988 Liberal organization in Kootenay West–Revelstoke provides an example of just this sort of case. He reports that the provincial party office in Vancouver recognized "the weakness of the local association" and sent them a young volunteer campaign manager who had energy and enthusiasm, but commanded very limited financial resources (ibid., 37). He was there to run a campaign in a riding where the Liberal candidate was expected to do little more than carry the party banner.

Commitments made by the parties to increase the number of women candidates have been slow to materialize (Erickson 1991). The same is generally true with respect to campaign managers, although more women occupied that position – 28 percent in 1988 – than were candidates. New Democratic Party campaigns were more likely to be managed by women (38 percent) than were those of Liberal (29 percent) or Conservative (20 percent) associations. Women were not left to work in the parties' hopeless seats in 1988: there was as high a proportion of women campaign managers in winning constituency campaigns as in losing ones. Indeed, paper associations had a disproportionately low number of women campaign managers, while the number of women among the paid campaign managers was disproportionately high, an indication that women were not simply being assigned, or confined, to marginal ridings. It is true, however, that women were more likely to recognize the managerial abilities of other women. Among women candidates who appointed their own campaign manager, the proportion of women in the position was markedly higher (40 percent).

Constituency campaign management is increasingly becoming a full-time, specialized job. As a result more campaign managers are now being directly paid (as opposed to awaiting some political pay-off) for their services. Table 7.3 reports the proportions of campaign managers who were paid in 1988, and indicates that there are some sharp differences among the parties in this regard. One in five managers was paid, but this proportion was much lower in the associations of the new parties (4 percent for both Reform and the CHP), and very much higher in the NDP. Forty-three percent of the NDP managers were paid, a proportion almost three times as high as that of the Conservatives.

This big interparty difference in the rate of paid campaign managers is partially an artefact of the election expense regime. As Stanbury (1991, chap. 12) reports in his analysis of candidate expenditures, the salaries of party and trade union officials who work in the campaigns must be reported as expenses and charged against the legally allowable limit. On the other hand, as Preyra's study of Halifax reports, many Liberal and Conservative campaigns are able to call upon the services of local lawyers who act as unpaid campaign managers with "the expectation that the firm will be appropriately rewarded after the election" (1991, 174). It is notable, but not surprising, that when party officials (other than the local executive) are forced to find a manager, or when an outsider must be drafted, the campaign is much more likely to have

Table 7.3
Paid campaign managers
(percentage of constituency campaigns)

All parties	21
Progressive Conservative	15
Liberal	18
NDP	43
Reform	4
Christian Heritage	4
Region	
Atlantic	16
Quebec	19
Ontario	25
Prairies	18
British Columbia	18
Appointed by	
Candidate	16
Association executive	27
Other*	47
Local member	16
Nonlocal	40

*"Other" (11% of all cases) consists primarily of party officials outside riding.

to pay for the help. As we have already seen, those are also both factors that vary by party. Table 7.3 indicates that there is little regional
variation in the use of paid campaign managers, but that obscures
important differences within the NDP, the party whose local campaigns
most commonly use them.

As figure 7.3 dramatically reveals, there is a significant east–west
gradient in the proportions of paid campaign managers among NDP
associations. Almost three-quarters (73 percent) of the party's campaigns in British Columbia reported using one, while only 7 percent of
those in Atlantic Canada did. As for so many of the other aspects of
the party discussed in earlier chapters, the Ottawa River is the significant dividing line. East of it the party has little prospect of winning
many seats and so is far less likely to employ campaign managers. The
party uses its resources, including professional campaign managers,
to defend existing seats (recall the large local association incomes of
NDP incumbents – table 3.7), or where there is a good prospect of victory. Thus, in 1988, 75 percent of the winning NDP campaigns had paid
campaign managers, compared to 60 percent of those finishing second
and just 33 percent of those placing third.

This account of several key elements in the establishment of a local
campaign organization points to systematic differences between the

Figure 7.3
Paid NDP campaign managers

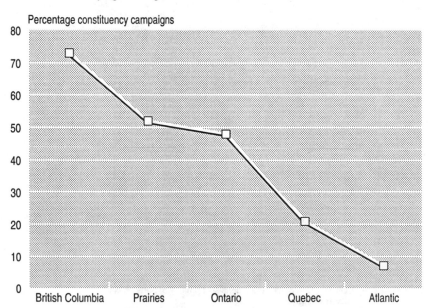

Percentage constituency campaigns

New Democrats and its traditional opponents. These differences reflect the organizational imperatives of a mass party as opposed to the electoral orientations of cadre parties. As such they are quite congruent with the analysis, in earlier chapters, of the interelection organization and activity of these parties' associations. In summary, we might characterize the mass-party style as more bureaucratic, that of the cadre party as more traditional. In terms of the measures used here, the bureaucratic campaign organization would be one in which *party officials* (local or otherwise) appoint a *paid* campaign manager. A traditional campaign would be one in which the *candidate* appoints a *volunteer* campaign manager.

By labelling this distinction as traditional versus bureaucratic, I do not mean to imply that one of these management techniques is more efficient than the other. Rather, the assumption is that each offers distinct advantages to the parties that use them because those techniques are congruent with their organizational instincts and personnel needs. Figure 7.4 reveals just how different the three national parties are in terms of their approach to campaign management. While two-thirds of the Liberal and Conservative cadre-style local associations have what we have defined here as a traditional campaign organization, less than

Figure 7.4
Traditional vs. bureaucratic campaign management

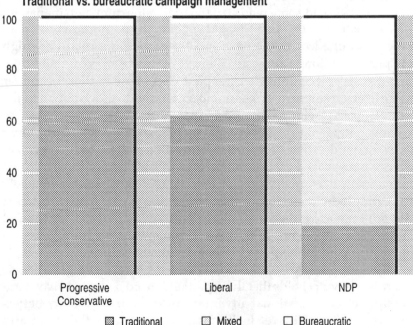

one in five of the NDP campaigns still retains this old Canadian form. Twenty-three percent of the NDP associations now have a more modern bureaucratic style, compared to just 2 and 3 percent of the Liberals and Conservatives respectively. And more NDP associations are in an intermediate, mixed, situation, indicating that they have adopted at least one of the two elements of the bureaucratic model. This sharp difference is particularly pronounced among the most successful NDP associations – those that elected an MP in 1988. Forty-four percent had a bureaucratic type of campaign set-up, while only 6 percent were still using a traditional pattern.

Staffing Constituency Campaign Organizations

The great bulk of the individuals who work in a constituency campaign are local activists who are volunteering their time and effort. This centrally important group will be discussed in a separate section below. Here the focus is on two distinct groups: those who are paid to work for the campaign and those who have come into the riding from outside. Accounts of the earliest Canadian campaigns record that both types of campaign workers have always played some part in Canadian elections. The constituency party survey provides the first systematic estimates of how important they are, and how widespread the practice of using them now is.

As table 7.4 indicates, just under 40 percent of the riding party campaigns in 1988 had some paid staff (including the campaign manager). As the analysis to this point would suggest, the proportion with paid help was quite low in the new, smaller parties, but relatively high (57 percent) among NDP associations. But the data reveal more than that. Of the associations that use paid staff, those in the NDP are far more likely to employ a larger number of individuals. Over half of the NDP campaigns with paid staff had more than two individuals on the payroll, compared to just over a quarter of such campaigns in the other two large parties. (Fraser reports that the NDP's national campaign managers assume that a typical campaign will have two or three salaried individuals: 1989, 169). And NDP associations are also far more likely to employ individuals from outside the riding as paid help (63 percent did so) than are either their Conservative (14 percent) or Liberal (18 percent) opponents. In the case of the new parties, the few associations that paid for help used local individuals exclusively.

There appears to be a theoretical paradox here. Duverger's classic mass-party model holds that those parties depend on their active membership for organizational advantage over the traditionally better-financed cadre parties. Yet, in this case, we find that it is the mass party

Table 7.4
Constituency campaigns' use of paid staff
(percentage of constituency campaigns)

	All parties	Progressive Conservative	Liberal	NDP	Reform	Christian Heritage
Use paid staff	37	33	39	57	9	14
Where paid staff used						
Pay more than 2 individuals	37	26	28	54	25	14
Pay locals	66	86	82	37	100	100
Pay outsiders	8	6	6	13	—	—
Pay locals and outsiders	25	8	12	50	—	—

(the NDP) that is paying for help, a good deal of which is imported. In part this puzzle is phony, and can be explained by the reporting requirements of the election expense law referred to above, which requires the salaries of many of the types of individuals managing NDP campaigns to be claimed as regular election expenses. For the rest, the reality is that mass parties of the left such as the NDP also have a bureaucratic imperative. That imperative prods them to routinize and pay for specialized electoral labour. In a regionalized party system like Canada's, the plurality electoral system forces a third-placed party like the NDP to rationalize its efforts and focus on winnable ridings. The result of that imperative is that many election employees come from outside the riding.

Paying campaign staff is, however, a practice that varies across the country. Overall, constituency associations in the four western provinces are considerably less inclined to do so than are those in the other regions. Fewer than half as many British Columbia associations claim to pay campaign staff (21 percent) as do those in Atlantic Canada (47 percent) or Quebec (45 percent). In this there is an echo of the regional differences observed in the proportions of enumerators engaging in campaign work (see chapter 6). It points to the more populist cast of local political organization and action that is part of western Canada's political tradition and is currently most visible in the Reform Party.

The data in table 7.5 indicate that the campaign manager's job was the one that constituency associations in all three major parties most commonly had to pay someone to perform. However, the data also indicate that the NDP used paid staff more commonly, and in a larger variety of roles, than did its larger opponents. Particularly notable is its use of paid election-day coordinators. That task is critical to an effective get-out-the-vote (GOTV) campaign, and the relative frequency with which the NDP pays individuals to do it is a mark of their campaigns'

Table 7.5
Principal tasks of paid campaign staff
(percentage constituency campaigns)

	All parties	Progressive Conservative	Liberal	NDP
Campaign manager	21	15	18	43
Canvass organizer	6	—	—	24
Office manager	10	7	12	16
Clerical	8	13	9	7
Election-day coordinator	3	—	1	12

bureaucratic professionalism. This is most obvious in ridings the NDP wins: in 1988, 44 percent of them had paid election-day coordinators.

The analyses in chapters 3 and 4 of constituency associations' membership and finances demonstrated that, of the three national parties, it is the NDP that is most marked by severe regional imbalances (see figure 4.5). The analysis here, of the party's use of professional campaign management and staff, reveals that they are not employed to compensate for those weaknesses. To the extent the party is committed to these techniques, it reserves them for areas of existing strength. While this is no doubt a prudent strategy as far as the party and its current MPs are concerned given a winner-take-all electoral system, it is essentially a conservative, defensive one. It leaves the NDP's weaker associations to adopt the traditional campaign styles the party considers second best. Of course it is precisely those associations that occupy the ridings where its opponents are best at playing their preferred, traditional campaign game. This is not a formula designed to improve the NDP's electoral position or change the organizational character of many constituency election contests in eastern Canada.

To the extent that our image of Canadian party organizations as networks of franchise-like organizations populated by volunteers is a valid representation of one aspect of their reality, then the use of paid staff during elections offers an important mechanism by which the central party apparatus might impose some order and discipline on their local franchise's campaign planning and activity. Employees brought in from outside the constituency, especially if the funds to pay them also come from outside, or if their future careers are going to be influenced by the judgements of party officials, are bound to be amenable to following the campaign directives of the central party. As table 7.6 indicates, a substantial proportion of riding parties using outside

Table 7.6
Sources of funds used to pay for non-local campaign employees
(percentage of associations using paid outsiders)

	All parties	Progressive Conservative	Liberal	NDP	Reform	Christian Heritage
National/provincial party organizations	43	27	38	45	100	83
Trade unions	16	—	—	29	—	—
Business	1	—	—	2	—	—
Interest groups	2	4	—	2	—	—
Don't know	13	32	32	2	—	—
Candidate	9	5	25	7	—	—
Constituency association	42	27	13	57	—	50

Note: Percentages do not add to 100 because individual constituency associations could check as many sources as relevant.

employees reported that those individuals were paid from outside the constituency. It is tempting to speculate that this development is diluting the parochial cast of constituency contests that has long been a central feature of Canadian electoral politics, as well as contributing to the nationalizing of electoral campaigns.

Table 7.7 reports the number of constituency associations that had individuals from outside the riding working in their 1988 campaign (irrespective of whether they were paid or not), and table 7.8 summarizes the principal tasks for which they were utilized. The picture is by now relatively familiar, for the NDP stands out as having the largest proportion of ridings with outside helpers (note, however, that this is despite the fact that it has the lowest proportion, of the three main parties, of winnable seats). But both the Liberals and Conservatives also report substantial numbers of ridings with such cross-border help. Party activists choose to work in ridings other than their own for a variety of reasons. In his study of campaigning in British Columbia, Sayers (1991) gives examples of two. In one instance the appeal of a candidate (Svend Robinson) and his advocacy of a particular issue (gay rights) led a number of NDP activists to leave their home riding. The second instance was one in which Liberal party workers left their riding to work for the campaign in an adjacent riding (John Turner's in Vancouver Quadra) that they believed could make more profitable use of their efforts. As it happens it was Vancouver Centre campaigns that were left in both instances, and while the NDP and Liberal campaigns to which those

Table 7.7
Outsiders working in campaigns
(percentage of constituency campaigns)

All parties	44
Progressive Conservative	46
Liberal	41
NDP	58
Reform	21
Christian Heritage	35
Region	
Atlantic	37
Quebec	48
Ontario	51
Prairies	44
British Columbia	31

Table 7.8
Campaign work done by outsiders
(percentage associations using outsiders)

	All	Progressive Conservative	Liberal	NDP	Reform	Christian Heritage
Volunteer workers	68	80	72	52	60	74
Strategists/managers	34	38	39	31	30	13
Paid organizers	26	10	13	56	10	7
Other	8	8	13	1	—	27

activists moved were successful, neither was particularly close. On the other hand the Conservatives ended up just squeaking through in Vancouver Centre in what turned out to be the seventh-closest race in the entire 1988 general election, one decided by 269 votes (Eagles et al. 1991). Though one cannot assume that those deserting workers made the critical difference, there is no doubt that their efforts could have had a much greater impact in their home constituency.

By far the most common role for outsiders in a constituency campaign is general volunteer work (table 7.8). This is particularly true in the old cadre parties and the newer small protest parties. New Democratic associations stand out because more of them report that they have outside help working as paid organizers than as volunteer campaigners. This is the campaign staff–level concomitant of the NDP's generally more bureaucratic approach to local campaign management.

CAMPAIGN VOLUNTEERS

Local campaigns, if they are to be successful, have three critical tasks: they must target their support, communicate their chosen message and mobilize their vote on election day. Even when paid staff are used to lead and coordinate this work, the campaigns depend on small armies of volunteers to operate (Brook 1991, chap. 11). Campaign volunteers are particularly important in Canada because the highly volatile system leaves many seats politically marginal and susceptible to turnover (Blake 1991). The election campaign, especially local canvassing, can make a significant difference: Heintzman estimates "the campaign effect to be, at a minimum, twice that of the incumbency factor" (1991, 143). Bell and Bolan's account (1991) of the 1988 Markham constituency contest illustrates the vital role that volunteers can play in a local campaign. In that case, the Tory campaign assembled more than ten times as many workers as its nearest rival, and that organization played an important part in mobilizing its winning vote. This section looks at these armies to discover how big they are, who joins them and why (associations think) they do so.

Riding parties are not all agreed on how many volunteers are required "to run an effective local campaign in [their] constituency." Ten percent claim that they can manage with 35 but, at the other extreme, 7 percent say that they need at least 500. The typical (median) association reports that it needs 150 volunteers. Of course not all associations have as many as they need. In 1988 only 16 percent said they did, and the median campaign organization reported having just two-thirds of its requirements. Tables 7.9 and 7.10 provide portraits of the volunteer base of riding campaign organizations in the 1988 general election.

There is not a great deal of interparty or regional variation in the typical riding party's contingent of campaign volunteers. Of the three major parties, the Conservatives typically thought they needed more (200) than either the Liberals (150) or the New Democrats (123), and they had more. The median Conservative campaign had just over 90 percent of the volunteers it needed, while the other two parties typically had to make do with something over 60 percent of their needs. We have seen, however, that there are really two worlds of NDP constituency organization – the real associations and the paper ones (see chapter 4). Table 7.9 indicates the dramatic differences in the volunteers available to those two distinctive groups in 1988. The volunteer resources of the campaigns in the real associations looked much more like those in the two larger parties, while the ones in the paper associations were much more modest. Those associations only had about a quarter of the (far fewer) volunteers they thought they needed.

Table 7.9
Campaign volunteers needed and available, by party and region
(median association)

	Volunteers needed	Volunteers in 1988	1988 volunteer availability rate*	1988 volunteers as % 1988 local membership
All parties	150	94	.67	20
Progressive Conservative	200	150	.91	24
Liberal	150	100	.67	15
NDP	123	70	.60	23
Real	200	140	.68	24
Paper	100	21	.27	19
Reform	225	35	.20	25
Christian Heritage	100	30	.60	23
Region				
Atlantic	100	100	.73	20
Quebec	150	81	.67	20
Ontario	200	100	.67	23
Prairies	200	50	.70	14
British Columbia	200	100	.67	25

*Calculated as volunteers available in 1988 divided by volunteers needed.

Table 7.10
Campaign volunteers needed and available, by selected association characteristics
(median association)

	Volunteers needed	Volunteers in 1988	1988 volunteer availability rate*	1988 volunteers as % 1988 local membership
All parties	150	94	0.67	20
Paid campaign manager	200	125	0.80	18
1988 winner	200	200	1.00	23
Rich association	300	250	1.00	30
Poor association	100	40	0.40	20
Paper association	100	30	0.39	20

*Calculated as volunteers available in 1988 divided by volunteers needed.

In the two new parties local campaigns typically reported that they had only small numbers of volunteers working for them. The difference was that Reform associations believed they needed far more (they reported the largest demand for volunteers of any of the five parties) than did those in the CHP. This low volunteer availability rate (i.e., the number needed divided by the number available) in Reform associations is a reflection of their ambition and the commitment to grassroots politics which their very newness thwarted in 1988. It does foretell something of the shape of their campaign strategy for future elections. Reform associations would seem to be planning for campaigns based on the largest possible armies of local volunteers working the ridings.

The final column of table 7.9 is instructive, for it measures the size of the median constituency association's volunteer team in the 1988 campaign as a percentage of the association's membership in that year. The size of a constituency party's core of election volunteers is normally about one-fifth that of its local membership. Put another way, one might argue that a typical local association would have to increase its membership by five for every extra campaign volunteer it wants. But an interparty comparison suggests that this is probably an overestimate, distorted by the Liberal associations, which, as we noted in chapter 3, grew the most (except for Reform) in 1988. As we shall see below, part of this Liberal story is bound up with their experiences of instant nomination memberships.

Regional differences in the volunteer base of campaigns hardly exist, despite the many regional differences we have discovered in other aspects of local constituency organization. More than anything, this is testimony to the ubiquitous nature of the tasks election campaigns require volunteers to perform. The slightly lower numbers of volunteers parties east of the Ottawa River report needing reflect the very high proportion of NDP paper associations in that end of the country; the low volunteer-to-member ratio on the Prairies reflects the very large size of some of that region's NDP associations.

Table 7.10 portrays the volunteer base of five groups of campaigns in 1988. Three, those with paid campaign managers, those that won and those run by rich associations, all had larger-than-average volunteer contingents. Two, the poor and the paper branches (categories, it will be remembered, that overlap – all paper branches are by definition poor, though the reverse is not true), had far more modest-sized groups of volunteers. It is not possible to sort out completely the dynamics that lie behind these linkages (do lots of volunteers produce winners, or do winners attract lots of volunteers?), but the patterns are clear enough. Two elements deserve particular mention. First, the median campaign organizations of both 1988 winners and rich associations claimed they had all the volunteers they needed, but these were the only sets of campaigns that reported doing so. Clearly large numbers of local parties are not engaging all the individuals they could, or even want to, in election activity. Bell and Bolan (1991) report that several candidates they interviewed in their study of two Ontario constituency contests stated that this was a problem for their campaigns. Thus riding parties are suffering a significant electoral participation deficit and the political system pays a price for it: opportunities for citizen involvement are missed, and parties and candidates are not able to present their message to the electorate or to harvest the vote on election day as effectively as they would like.

Second, of the five campaign groups examined in table 7.10, those with paid campaign managers have the lowest ratio of volunteers to local association members. It is not possible to demonstrate any causal effect here, but it does raise the question of whether the use of paid election workers discourages local activists from participating on a volunteer basis. Of course this may be a chicken-and-egg problem. Paid managers may be used to compensate for a volunteer deficit but then their presence, in turn, only increases it. This may be a dilemma that party associations are going to have to confront in the future, forcing them to balance the pressures of organizational expediency with the voluntary character of local activity that has been the essence of much constituency party organization in Canada.

Party membership is not particularly stable in many riding associations, and it generally grows in election years as more individuals turn their attention and efforts to politics. This is particularly true of the Liberal and Conservative cadre parties with their electoral orientations (figure 3.2). It is generally assumed that this membership growth reflects the remobilization of party activists who are returning to work in the campaign. The volunteer and membership data allow us to see if this is really what is going on. Table 7.11 provides a first estimate of the impact of local association election-year membership change on the numbers of volunteers who subsequently work on the campaign. To allow us to focus on cadre-style political organization, it includes data from only Liberal and Conservative party associations. Big membership increases do not seem to lead to larger numbers of volunteers. The most striking feature of the data is the evidence that, as membership growth increases, the ratio of volunteers to members decreases. In other words, as an association gets bigger, it cannot count on a correspondingly bigger coterie of election volunteers. This suggests that much of the election-year party membership surge represents a pretty limited assertion of commitment. It undoubtedly brings in some income, and a reaffirmation of political identification, but perhaps little more in most cases.

Table 7.11
Conservative and Liberal volunteers needed and available, by membership growth
(median association)

	Volunteers needed	Volunteers in 1988	1988 volunteer availability rate*	1988 volunteers as % 1988 local membership
Membership growth, 1987–88				
< 0 %	200	100	0.67	40
0–24 %	150	87	1.00	27
25–50 %	200	95	0.63	22
50–74 %	100	100	0.87	20
75 % +	200	100	0.78	14
Experience of instant members for nominations				
Positive	200	150	0.80	18
Negative	150	76	0.67	14

*Calculated as volunteers available in 1988 divided by volunteers needed.

In many cadre-style party associations, election-year membership growth is tied to nomination contests. As we saw in chapter 5, local parties are quite divided on the value to the association of those sorts of membership campaigns. The bottom portion of table 7.11 tells part of this story. Associations that reported a positive view of nomination-contest membership recruiting apparently had good reason to do so. Compared to those which had a negative response, such associations saw a definite pay-off in terms of producing campaign volunteers in 1988. Not only did they have a smaller volunteer deficit, the numbers of volunteers they had (as a percentage of the local membership) was higher. Indeed, in associations reporting a negative experience, the volunteer-to-member ratio was as low as in any other set of campaigns we have examined (tables 7.9–7.11). No wonder those associations reported a negative experience – they had a good empirical basis for that judgement. They took in large numbers of new members and allowed them to participate in choosing the candidate, but then found few of them working in the subsequent election campaign.

In some instances this dynamic can be turned on its head. Bell and Bolan's (1991) account of the Markham Liberals describes how 2 000 new members were faced with the resignation of the local executive after a disruptive nomination contest. In effect, this was a case in which many new, potential party volunteers were deserted by a local establishment which had been outmanoeuvred in an instant membership battle. And the consequence was that there was not much experienced campaign leadership left to use and direct these volunteers and the riding contest was lost.

However much these data tell us about constituency campaigns' ability to recruit volunteer help, they say little about the individual volunteers themselves. The constituency association survey cannot provide much personal information, but it does reveal something of their continuing involvement in the local association. Associations were asked to estimate the proportions of their 1988 volunteers that were "regular party members," "regular financial contributors to [their] association," and "worked in the 1984 general election." The median responses are summarized in table 7.12. In all parties, and across all regions, the vast majority of the campaign volunteers are drawn from regular local party members. There is little evidence here that election campaigns involve many who are not already committed enough to the political process to have joined one of their local parties.

On the other hand, there are considerable differences among the parties in terms of the proportions of volunteers who are committed enough to be regular financial contributors as well as members. The proportion is highest in the new protest parties, lowest in the old established cadre parties. NDP associations estimated that twice as many of their election volunteers were also regular financial donors as did the Conservative or Liberal riding parties. This is a significant difference and points to a more episodic and intermittent party involvement on the part of active Liberals and Tories, compared to the regular financial obligations assumed by New Democratic activists. Quebec certainly stands out on this variable as a distinctive region, though why this should be so is not readily apparent. There does not seem to be a party effect at work within the province, for this general pattern holds across all three federal parties: the members of the dominant Conservative associations were no more or less likely to be regular contributors than were New Democrats.

Continuity as well as change must be an important dimension of most volunteer campaigns, for the typical association reported that about half of its volunteers also worked in the 1984 general election. Without any comparative data it is difficult to know whether this proportion is particularly high or low. Quebec again appears to stand out, but in this instance the low figure (29 percent) for the proportion of returning volunteers in local campaigns is entirely a function of the NDP. The median riding campaigns in both Liberal and Conservative associations in Quebec reported a 50 percent volunteer return rate,

Table 7.12
Partisan activity characteristics of local campaign volunteers, 1988
(percentages, median constituency association)

	Regular party members	Regular financial contributor	Volunteered in 1984
All parties	90	50	50
Progressive Conservative	80	25	60
Liberal	90	30	50
NDP	85	60	50
Reform	100	75	—
Christian Heritage	100	80	—
Region			
Atlantic	90	50	60
Quebec	90	11	29
Ontario	80	50	50
Prairies	90	50	50
British Columbia	90	50	40

which is not significantly different from those in any other part of the country. New Democratic associations reported that only 5 percent of their 1988 volunteers were hold-overs from 1984. Obviously the NDP's 1988 Quebec campaigns were being staffed by rank beginners working out of paper associations. It is no wonder they did not make the electoral breakthrough in the province that many had predicted they might, though it is also obvious that a breakthrough will only come if they attract far more newcomers than they did in 1988.

Attracting Campaign Volunteers

Individuals come into politics for a wide variety of reasons. Some seek to pursue political ends but many others do it for more obviously social, psychological or economic reasons. The frequency with which local associations hold social events (see table 3.17) testifies to the parties' understanding of this. But at election time political work comes to dominate and individuals have to decide whether to volunteer and become active in the campaign. Given that "good help is hard to find" (Bell and Bolan 1991, 88), and the vast majority (84 percent) of local campaign organizations do not have enough volunteers to fill their needs, the constituency survey probed this apparent deficiency in the system by asking the riding presidents what attracted campaign volunteers. Table 7.13 recapitulates their responses.

The local party presidents ranked the importance of five factors in attracting volunteers: the local candidate, traditional party loyalty, party

Table 7.13
Most important factor in attracting volunteers to local campaign
(percentage associations ranking factor first)

	Candidate	Party loyalty	Policies	Leader	Opponent
All parties	46	25	22	14	6
Progressive Conservative	61*	28	11	7	4
Liberal	53	26	6	22	10
NDP	41	33	21	12	4
Reform	15	6	57	25	—
Christian Heritage	19	7	67	2	15
1988 winner	64	26	9	9	5
1988 loser	38	25	27	15	7

*Thus, 61% of Progressive Conservative associations rating candidates ranked it as most important factor.

policies, the national party leader and the local opponent. The latter was included on the grounds that some individuals may work to defeat a candidate they strongly oppose. The most striking finding is the importance given to candidates in building strong campaign organizations. In all three of the older established parties, the largest group of associations believe that the local candidate is the most important factor in attracting volunteers. Only in the two protest parties did the majority claim that their volunteers were principally attracted by policy concerns.

Policy did not rate second for Liberal, New Democratic or Conservative associations: traditional party loyalty did. The role of the party leader, which is given so much prominence in the national campaign, was rated the fourth most important for inducing local campaign effort. Significantly, among Reform associations, the second-largest group rated the leader first. That provides a measure of the appeal of Preston Manning, the party's founding leader, in developing a viable campaign organization. The CHP stands out as the party with the highest percentage (15) of associations that thought opposition to others was the most important factor attracting their campaign volunteers. Given the strong "right-to-life" position of the party, and the commitment of many who espouse that political philosophy, this is perhaps not too surprising. However, it does make for an essentially negative campaign orientation by many in that party.

Winning campaigns obviously feel that their candidate was central to their success in attracting volunteers, for they were almost twice as likely to rate it as the most important factor as were the losers. But in fact much of this difference can be accounted for by Tory responses: there was no such difference between winners and losers in either the Liberal or the New Democratic party on this. Why there should be such a sharp difference is not clear, though it is consistent with the Conservatives' campaign style of fostering more organizational autonomy at the constituency level.

If candidates are important in this way to the creation of an electoral machine in their ridings, the concomitant question is what would happen to a local association's campaign help if it had a different candidate? About two-thirds of the Conservative and Liberal ridings believe that they would end up with a basically different group of volunteers (table 7.14). A majority, though not a large one, of NDP (57 percent) and Reform (52 percent) riding parties disagree. They believe they would have essentially the same group of workers. CHP associations have little doubt: their policy commitment in opposition to modern secularizing Canada convinces them that their people will be there no matter who their candidate is. These patterns are quite consistent with the cadre–mass organizational distinction that has emerged throughout this analysis. The cadre parties recruit volunteers to elect their local notables, the mass parties attract volunteers to support the party.

Table 7.14
Impact of candidate on volunteer corps
(percentage associations)

	Different candidate would lead to	
	Different volunteers	Same volunteers
All parties	54	46
Progressive Conservative	67	33
Liberal	63	38
NDP	43	57
Reform	48	52
Christian Heritage	21	78
Region		
Atlantic	37	63
Quebec	77	23
Ontario	50	50
Prairies	54	46
British Columbia	53	47
1988 winner	61	39
1988 loser	51	49

Table 7.14 points to two other differences: the apparently greater candidate focus of campaign staffing in Quebec, and the close link between winners and their volunteers. The pattern in Quebec reflects the weakness of the NDP in the province, though that cannot be the whole story given the pattern in Atlantic Canada (where traditional party loyalties seem to persist in a way unlike the rest of the country). The complete overthrow of Liberal Quebec by the Conservatives in 1984 may have stimulated a greater candidate focus in constituency organizations. Whether it will persist is an open question. Less surprising is the attachment of volunteers to winners. A successful local political machine often takes on a family-like life of its own that cannot survive its leader's departure. This is what the (mainly Conservative) riding presidents with MPs are recognizing here.

This general line of argument suggests that discussions of the impact of local candidates on the vote (Ferejohn and Gaines 1991; Krashinsky and Milne 1991) need to recognize that one of the ways in which that impact manifests itself is in the creation of a local organization capable of mounting a local campaign and then mobilizing the vote.

The Local View of the Power of Incumbency

This brings us to a brief but relevant digression on the importance of incumbency to a local constituency campaign. There is no doubt local associations think incumbents have a "special advantage" in Canadian elections: 86 percent agreed they did. That view was widely shared, though Conservatives were somewhat less likely to agree (78 percent) while the New Democrats were virtually unanimous (98 percent) on the point. And as one might predict, associations with incumbents were not quite so sanguine. Three-quarters of them admitted that having an incumbent was an advantage, compared to 96 percent of those who finished third in 1988.

When asked to indicate what the most important advantage might be, half of the riding associations (in all three major parties) replied that it was the public recognition an incumbent enjoyed in the constituency. In this the party activists agree with national pollsters and strategists, who hold that name recognition is crucial to local electoral success (Laschinger and Stevens 1992, 7). Far fewer (about 20 percent) of the constituency presidents said more resources was the principal advantage, though substantial numbers in the Reform and Christian Heritage parties also thought that incumbents got better media treatment. This importance of local recognition takes on its real significance in the context of building a campaign organization when we remember that associations think the local candidate is the most important consideration in attracting volunteers. The formula is straightforward: incumbency means recognition, recognition attracts volunteers, volunteers contribute to a strong campaign organization and campaign organizations help win elections.

This process appears to account for one of the dynamics at work in constituency-level politics. As long as volunteers play a central role in riding electoral contests, the candidate's abilities and resources (the most potent of which may be incumbency) will likely be critical to building electoral machines in the ridings. We shall see, in the next chapter, how the impact of the candidate stretches beyond this to the very delicate task of campaign fund-raising to support the electoral organization.

What Do All These Volunteers Do, Anyway?

Having assembled the armies of volunteers, the campaign team must deploy them to maximum advantage. Large numbers of volunteers are used because most Canadian party organizations continue to believe that the most politically effective contact is the direct person-to-person link between campaign volunteer and voter. Table 7.15 lists the principal tasks that substantial numbers of constituency organizations reported using volunteer help for.

In the three major parties, more associations reported using volunteers for canvassing than any other job. The New Democrats stand out as being most keen on canvassing, but then they are widely regarded as the pioneers, and most successful practitioners of, the three-canvass method of working a constituency. This is consistent with their protest origins and mass structure: in its early decades the party depended on the volunteer canvass to get its message out, for it could afford no other means. The Conservatives appear to be the most committed to the modern technological equivalent of the door-to-door canvass, the telephone bank. Now almost as many Tory riding parties use volunteers on the phones (53 percent) as on the streets (55 percent).

Fund-raising (especially in NDP and Reform associations), sign and literature distribution, and election-day vote pulling are all tasks that occupy substantial numbers in many campaign organizations. Most organizations can readily list another dozen jobs done by volunteers, but most of those do not require the same armies of people. The big battalions are needed to reach the electorate, and when a campaign does not have them it faces an uphill battle. Sayers (1991, 29) describes the 1988 Vancouver Centre Liberal campaign as a media-focused "smoke and mirrors" effort to compensate for the lack of enough volunteers to engage in door-to-door canvassing. It failed.

Table 7.15
Principal volunteer tasks
(percentage associations)

	All parties	Progressive Conservative	Liberal	NDP	Reform	Christian Heritage
Canvassing	60	55	69	71	40	48
Telephone	43	53	41	39	34	31
Fund-raising	35	25	27	43	50	29
Literature/sign distribution	34	23	30	43	34	54
Election day	14	15	16	17	12	2

POLLS LOCAL AND NATIONAL

Public opinion polls are now inextricably linked to the practice of modern Canadian electoral politics. This is because the poll is one of the most important tools of modern mass communication and so politicians cannot and will not be separated from it. Most mass communication media principally involve flows of information from a small group of individuals to a mass population. That is what newspapers, radio and television do. Historically, politicians have used them to talk to the voters. Polls are fundamentally different. They are tools of mass communication in which the dominant information flows move from the masses of the citizenry to whoever is listening at the other end. In politics they allow politicians to listen to the voters. They also allow other voters to listen to their fellows as well as to the politicians.

Of course politicians have always had their own private means of listening to voters, and local party organizations were an important part of that process. The polls now allow them to do so in a systematic and disciplined fashion. Not surprisingly, successful democratic politicians pay attention to and learn from the conversations: they learn what argot voters speak and what jargon they understand, they learn what voters want to talk about and they learn what voters want. And when the poll results are made public others can listen in on the conversation which they are, by definition, already part of. All of this changes parties' and politicians' behaviours, and it seems reasonable to think it likely changes some voters' attitudes or behaviours.

Much has been written on the use and abuse of polling and poll results in Canadian politics (Lee 1989; Johnston et al. 1992). Here we are concerned with exploring their role and impact at the riding level. Does the seemingly endless publication of national poll results in the major media have an impact on the local campaigns? Has there been a replication of national trends so that constituency-level polling has become a vital tool of local campaign strategists? If polls are being used in local campaigns, who is using them and to what end? It is now possible to begin to answer such questions.

It has become something of a conventional wisdom that polls have more impact on the local campaign workers than they do on the voters. Leaving aside the latter issue, the impact of the publication of national poll results on local campaign volunteers is important, especially given the general difficulty most campaigns have in finding enough help. Three of the five constituency campaign studies done for the Royal Commission on Electoral Reform and Party Financing explicitly mention the adverse effect of published polls on local campaigns (Preyra 1991; Bernier 1991; Sayers 1991). Bernier reports that campaign organizers worry about national polls because they "do have a significant effect on the motivation of local organizers" (ibid, 127). Sayers elaborates on this thesis by suggesting that polls do more than drive the number and enthusiasm of volunteers. He claims their impact is more insidious and is destructive of the very essence of constituency politics: "Given that these polls nearly always [focus] on non-local issues and aggregate responses for provinces, they [accentuate] feelings of ineffectiveness among local campaigners" (1991, 32).

This is a plausible argument. These examples, and the many more that observers of contemporary Canadian politics could readily point to, appear to substantiate it. Together they suggest that national polling is leading to national political conversations and contests, but that this process is inherently dysfunctional in a system premised on, and structured by, the assumption that there will be something like 295 separate (but parallel) conversations and contests going on in an election. The curious thing is that the riding presidents, who ought to know, do not seem to agree with this new conventional wisdom. To be sure they believe the publication of polls "makes [a] difference to the local contest." Seventy-eight percent agreed with that proposition; the proportion was higher among New Democrats (88 percent) than Tories (72 percent), but still widely shared. Where they departed from the conventional wisdom was on the nature of the impact.

When asked to describe the major impact of the publication of polls on the local contest, just 9 percent mentioned worker morale. This response was more common from Conservative (17 percent) than Liberal (9 percent) or NDP (6 percent) associations, but it was well down on the list in all parties. Far more (41 percent) believed that polls induced a bandwagon effect, pushing voters to vote for the winner, or that they influenced the undecided (28 percent) in some other way. Taken all together, some three-quarters of the responses explicitly referred to some direct impact on the voters rather than on the parties or the system. Whatever the momentary disturbance they may create, most local party officials do not seem to think that making opinion polls public significantly affects their capacity to fight an election.

Despite the limited manoeuvring room available to local campaigns, and the cost of doing a good poll, local associations are now increasingly using them. About a third of the constituency parties in the country claimed to have done so in 1988 (table 7.16). But use of this tool varies considerably across both the political and regional spectrums. Large numbers of riding organizations in the two large cadre parties have embraced polling as a regular campaign tool: 48 percent of the Conservatives and 44 percent of the Liberal associations polled in 1988. In contrast, fewer than half that number of NDP, Reform or CHP constituency parties have done so. (This despite Fraser's report that NDP officials assumed polling would be a normal charge on a typical constituency campaign in their party: 1989, 169.) It is indicative of Reform's instinctively modern approach to communications that a higher proportion of their associations than the New Democrats' polled in 1988, an election that preceded Reform's real organizational take-off.

Quebec party associations engaged in a lot more polling in 1988 than did those in other regions. Whether this was an election-specific phenomenon, due to the electoral earthquake of 1984 which unsettled a political alignment of three generations' standing, or reflects a distinctive approach to campaign management is difficult to determine. Less problematic are the other two relationships documented in table 7.16. Winners were more likely to have used polling as a regular campaign tool than were losers in 1988, though that mirrors the party differences to some extent and it would be difficult to assign any causal link. More certain is the linkage between money and polling. Local constituency polls are relatively new and expensive tools (that often require professional help to use) so wealthy associations are much better positioned to do constituency polling than are poor ones. In 1988 over half (52 percent) of the rich associations did so, compared to less than a third (29 percent) of the poor.

Money spent on local polls often only confirms what an association and its campaign team already knew about the riding and its candidates. It serves as a pillar to reinforce campaign strategy and keep the organization focused on its basic plans. But as the politicians listen to the language and message of their local electorate they can also rethink what they have been saying, how they have been saying it, and

Table 7.16
Local polling by associations, 1988 general election
(percentage associations)

All parties	34
Progressive Conservative	48
Liberal	44
NDP	18
Reform	22
Christian Heritage	13
Region	
Atlantic	20
Quebec	57
Ontario	34
Prairies	26
British Columbia	33
1988 result	
Winner	43
Loser	30
Rich	52
Poor	29

Table 7.17
**Percentage of associations whose local polls led
to campaign changes**

All parties	33
Progressive Conservative	40
Liberal	39
NDP	22
Reform	17
Christian Heritage	11
Region	
Atlantic	42
Quebec	33
Ontario	34
Prairies	31
British Columbia	35
1988 result	
Winner	38
Loser	31

who they have been speaking to. Any or all of those lessons can lead
to a change in their local campaign. Table 7.17 shows that of the riding
associations that did a local poll in 1988 (one-third of them all), only a
third reported that the information they gathered led to changes in their

campaign. Not only did the Tories and Liberals poll more often (table 7.16), but they were about twice as likely as the local associatons of other parties to change their campaigns as a result of doing so. This difference is readily understandable given the entirely electoral preoccupations of many constituency organizations in cadre parties, compared to the more diverse orientations in the mass and protest parties. The data also indicate that winners were more likely to have altered campaign course than losers as a consequence of polling information. This implies that it can pay constituency politicians to listen to their voters.

To put this into perspective, it is necessary to bring the evidence of who are polling, and who are changing their campaigns as a result, together. Figure 7.5 does so for all five parties. It demonstrates vividly that polling is not having much impact on the campaigns of CHP, Reform or NDP riding parties, both because they do relatively little of it and because those who do don't often change their campaigns as a result. That is not so true in the Progressive Conservative and Liberal parties. Still, the overall proportion of PC or Liberal campaigns that were changed as a consequence of a local poll in 1988 was under 20 percent in each party. In terms of the impact of local polling on the wider Canadian political system, the data imply that 16.5 percent of the winners in 1988 changed their constituency campaigns in some way as a result of polling. That is equivalent to about 49 seats in the current House of Commons. In 1988 those seats were shared among the three major parties: the data suggest they probably divided about 34 to the Conservatives, 13 to the Liberals and 2 to the New Democrats.

Before making judgements on whether the growing use of constituency polls is a good thing for the health of constituency-level democracy, it is necessary to know something about the sorts of changes polling results lead to. It is also necessary to remember that whatever the modifications local campaign organizations make to their messages they know they "[can] not escape the electoral 'spins' shaped by their parent organizations" and so cannot hope to be "sovereign and autonomous in the conduct of their media campaigns" (Preyra 1991, 154). Table 7.18 indicates the principal ways in which local parties used local poll data to change their campaign. It suggests that relatively few changed their message, though such changes were reported relatively more frequently by NDP associations (25 percent) than by those in the Liberal (4 percent) or Conservative (19 percent) parties, which is the reverse of what one might expect of mass and cadre parties.

Most local associations use polls to help them identify the issues of particular concern to their electors, to identify the strengths and weak-

Figure 7.5
Use of constituency-level polling

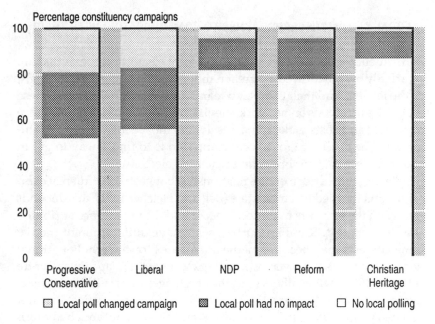

Percentage constituency campaigns

☐ Local poll changed campaign ▨ Local poll had no impact ☐ No local polling

Table 7.18
Campaign changes due to local polling
(percentage associations that reported changing campaign)

	Progressive Conservative	Liberal	NDP
Changed focus of campaign	31	39	25
Identified local issue	27	13	38
Knew strengths and weaknesses	12	26	—
Changed message	19	4	25
Motivated workers	8	9	12

ness they have in relation to the constituency and then to focus and target their campaign in ways that will maximize a positive response. It is their attempt to engage in a conversation with their electorate rather than simply talking at it. Local polls can also be used to motivate local volunteers but that is very much a secondary function. They are primarily an integral part of the communication activities of a modern campaign. They help set the stage for the campaign's attempts to talk to the local voters.

LOCAL CAMPAIGNS' APPROACHES TO COMMUNICATING WITH THEIR ELECTORATES

Constituency associations have to fight local electoral contests that are invariably overshadowed by great national media battles being fought by the leaders, and their campaign teams, of the national parties. These are battles that focus on network television, a medium whose audience structures and costs make it inaccessible to most constituency organizations. The challenge for a local campaign is to find a way to get in under this great TV umbrella and reach the electorate.

As the studies done on the relationship between constituency campaigns and the media demonstrate (Bell and Fletcher 1991), this depends greatly on the structure of the local media and the importance attributed to a local contest. Rural and urban seats have quite different media; some contests may become media surrogates for the whole national election (on this, see the very interesting discussion of Vancouver Centre in Sayers 1991); while others raise the challenges of a multilingual electorate. But for all that, constituency communication practice does not vary very much from riding to riding, and there is not much about it that would surprise constituency politicians of earlier generations.

Figure 7.6 summarizes the assessments local constituencies made of the relative importance of eight different communication tools to their riding campaigns. It is striking how closely the rank order matches those provided in the detailed accounts of a wide variety of different contests in Nova Scotia, Quebec and Ontario (Preyra 1991; Bernier 1991; and Bell and Bolan 1991). Personal canvassing is still the most important tool, although as we saw above more of it is now being done on the telephone. Local newspapers and literature drops are reported to be important methods for reaching a constituency electorate with a campaign message. As Sayers (1991) notes, the revival of community papers in the metropolitan areas (often distributed free of charge in a controlled circulation area) has been important in keeping the print media within the financial reach of many local campaigns.

At the other end of the spectrum are the electronic media, TV (regular and cable) and radio. The latter seems to be more widely used, presumably because it is both cheaper and easier to use for targeting audiences. In some instances local campaigns are able to tag a local message onto a national spot, although Sayers reports that the Kootenay West–Revelstoke Conservatives "complained that they could not even get a schedule of how much and when the national party would be

Figure 7.6
Importance of various communication methods to local campaigns

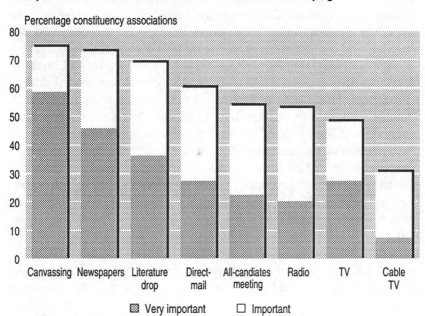

Percentage constituency associations

Legend: ▨ Very important   ☐ Important

advertising in the local constituency" (1991, 35). Despite a number of references in the constituency studies to the use of cable TV, often to broadcast all-candidates debates, relatively few local associations reported that its use had become an important part of their communication strategy. This may reflect a perception that nobody watches cable (Preyra 1991, 167), or perhaps means that the parties simply do not know who does, but it does represent a wasted opportunity. It may well be that as more MPs come to do regular constituency reports on cable TV it will assume a higher profile in future elections.

Direct mail and all-candidates meetings fall between the electronic media and the tried-and-true canvass techniques as important campaign communication tools for local riding parties. The former is a modern version of personal canvassing, and its use is likely to increase as more local associations develop the computer facility to do so. It does not have the advantage of face-to-face contact and two-way information flows that canvassing offers. But like canvassing (a private as opposed to public communication vehicle), it allows the campaign to tailor the message to the individual recipient. Its very important advantages are that it does not require the same army of volunteers to reach the electorate and it ensures the campaign leadership much greater control over what is actually communicated to the voter. However, it is not an unmitigated blessing for local campaigns. As Lee's (1989, 261–65) account of the Conservatives' Target '88 mail campaign indicates, it is also a tool by which national campaign organizations can reach around a constituency association to talk to voters directly.

All-candidates meetings are a time-honoured part of Canadian electioneering, though as early as 1906 Siegfried reported that they were more common in French-speaking than English-speaking Canada. This he attributed to the fact that "English political meetings [were] generally extremely dull," while a perfect debating combination of "heartiness and delicacy [were] the true characteristics of the French Canadian" (1966, 126) If Siegfried were to return he might be disappointed to discover that it is the Quebec associations, and French-speaking respondents, that are now less inclined to rate such encounters as an important aspect of their constituency campaign. The riding parties that stand out as particularly enthusiastic about all-candidates meetings are those in the protest parties, especially the CHP. Appearing with the representatives of the major parties no doubt gives their candidates enhanced credibility and helps draw a larger audience for their message.

SHARING THE STAGE: INTEREST GROUP INVOLVEMENT IN LOCAL CAMPAIGNS

Constituency party associations are no longer the only organizations involved in fighting elections. Increasingly, interest groups of various kinds are intervening to promote their political agendas and to try and influence the outcome. In a study for the Royal Commission on Electoral Reform and Party Financing, Tanguay and Kay (1991) developed a preliminary inventory of the types of groups now involved in constituency contests and examined their structure and practices. Their focus was on the groups themselves. In the constituency survey that focus was reversed, and two specific questions were asked about interest groups from the perspective of the local association's electoral self-interest.

Local parties were asked, "Did any single-issue interest groups play an active role in the local campaign in an attempt to support or oppose your candidate?" This question thus excluded interest activity designed to raise the salience of an issue or provoke conflict if it was not explicitly tied to the electoral fortunes of the local candidate. As table 7.19 reports, half the associations reported that their candidate was specifically supported or opposed by a single-issue group in the 1988 general election. The largest proportion were Conservative, which might be expected given that their party was in office, and that winners had to cope with group activity more often than losers. Across the coun-

Table 7.19
Interest group involvement to support or oppose candidate, 1988
(percentage associations)

All parties	50
Progressive Conservative	62
Liberal	45
NDP	54
Reform	24
Christian Heritage	41
Region	
Atlantic	49
Quebec	33
Ontario	57
Prairies	50
British Columbia	53
1988 result	
Winner	55
Loser	48

Figure 7.7
Constituency campaigns with active single-issue interest groups

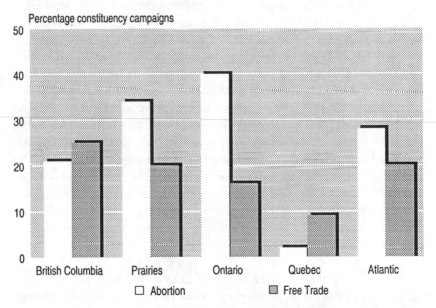

try Quebec stands out as the one region with a low rate of interest-group involvement. The reason for this is bound up with the politics of the issue that was provoking most of this constituency-level political warfare.

When asked what issue the groups were promoting or opposing, the associations faced with interest-group involvement overwhelmingly replied abortion (51 percent), or free trade (26 percent). Of course sometimes associations reported groups on both sides of the same issue, and a wide variety of other groups were identified, but these two issues dominated the responses. Free trade was itself the major issue of the national election, so those groups were simply replaying the national issue on a local stage. The big issue pushing its way into local campaigns was abortion, much as it did in the Liberal leadership contest in 1990 (see the discussion around figure 5.8). Bell and Bolan (1991) describe how the issue was used to capture a Liberal nomination in Perth–Wellington–Waterloo, and Bernier (1991) suggests it helped defeat an MP in Outremont. While CHP campaigns are themselves largely about this and related issues, about a third of the candidates of each of the major parties had to deal with active abortion-group electioneering.

But abortion politics did not seem to play in Quebec during the 1988 general election. Despite notable exceptions such as Madame Lucie Pépin's loss in Outremont (Bernier 1991), few Quebec campaigns reported active abortion-group involvement in their local campaign. The proportion in Quebec was just 2 percent, compared to the national average of 29 percent, and a high of near 40 percent in neighbouring Ontario (figure 7.7). With few abortion groups involved in the province's campaigns, Quebec ended up with a much lower incidence of direct group activity in constituency contests.

It turns out that single-issue interest group electoral politics, as least insofar as attempts to elect or defeat particular individuals in the constituencies are concerned, is currently largely about one single issue. Abortion is evidently an issue that draws people into politics to challenge their representative, and it is not one that is likely to be resolved in a fashion that will satisfy the combatants on both sides. Whether they like it or not, local parties are going to have to find some way to live with it as a part of the reality of contemporary constituency campaigns.

CADRE- AND MASS-PARTY ELECTIONEERING

Throughout the analysis in this chapter we have continually been drawn back to the distinction between cadre and mass parties. That distinction has considerable analytic utility for sorting out fundamental differences in the structure and organization of constituency association campaign activity. Despite the distance the parties have moved toward one another in terms of policy, or in their use of modern communication technologies, it is apparent that they continue to reflect their origins as very different kinds of political organizations. Liberal and Conservative associations on the one hand, and New Democratic associations on the other, do go about the business of electioneering differently. But perhaps that should not be too surprising, for the cadre–mass party distinction has its very roots in different orientations to candidates, politicians, elections and the essence of the democratic process itself.

These differences in the parties' electoral practices match, as they surely ought, some of the cadre–mass differences that we have observed in their interelection activities. It remains to be seen whether they extend to questions of electoral financing, for that is the area of party life most regulated by a common legal framework. It is the subject of the next chapter.

8

MONEY, RIDING PARTIES AND CONSTITUENCY ELECTIONS

T HE SEVEN WEEKS between the issuing of the writs of election and polling day is the period when the country's national political parties are most active. It is also the only period when parties and their local candidates have their expenditures carefully controlled and limited by the *Canada Elections Act*. But, ironically, the very mechanism the Act uses for regulating the election expenses of constituency-level contests deprives the parties' riding associations of direct control or responsibility for the financing of their local election campaigns. Each candidate must appoint an official agent as part of her or his formal nomination, and all the financial transactions of the campaign (income as well as expenditure), and all the reporting of them, must be controlled by that agent through specially established bank accounts. As we noted in the previous chapter, in the majority of cases it is the local candidate, and not the sponsoring party's constituency association, who appoints the agent (see figure 7.2, and Carty 1991). This means that the parties' riding associations have no direct control over, and sometimes even only limited knowledge of, the financial details of the constituency election campaign that they have planned for and that is run on their behalf.

This formal divorce of the riding party organization from its constituency election campaign's financial affairs challenges the sovereignty of constituency associations. Control of the campaign can become even more problematic when national parties insist on taking the reimbursements of electoral expenses made by the state to candidates receiving at least 15 percent of the vote. Thus, in 1988, the Liberals required all their candidates to sign over, at the beginning of the campaign, one-half of their reimbursement to the coffers of the national party. Some of the NDP's provincial sections applied a similar policy so that federal NDP constituency associations in those provinces were treated differently from others across the country. The result of such arrangements is that some constituency campaigns will have less income than others, or, without the same guarantees of a basic income, find their local decision making constrained and subject to very different pressures. These practices inevitably obscure the already complex, but substantial intraparty financial flows during elections, so that the parties are hard pressed to provide a coherent or comprehensive account of their election income and expenditures.

All this means that, to develop a detailed understanding of constituency-level election finances, it is necessary to examine the records of the individual candidates themselves, and to analyse how they go about financing their elections. By far the best study of that process is Stanbury's examination of the revenues and expenditures of candidates over the last four general elections (1979–1988) in his *Money and Politics: Financing Federal Parties and Candidates in Canada* (1991, especially chap. 12). Though he is the first to admit that there are great black holes in our knowledge, especially of the constituency parties' financial affairs, Stanbury's detailed analysis leads him to observe:

- "Candidates of federal parties, as a whole, have been able to become 'self-financing.' That is, even before reimbursement of half their 'election expenses,' candidates have been able to raise enough money to cover their 'election expenses' and 'personal expenses.'"
- With reimbursements, candidates are now ending up with a considerable surplus ($8.05 million in 1988), and "it appears that several million dollars of the surplus ended up in the accounts of riding associations."
- There are significant interparty differences in the financial strength of candidates: in 1988, Conservatives were, on average, able to raise and spend more than Liberals, who in turn raised and spent more than New Democrats. At the same time, however, there were also considerable regional differences in the financial strength of candidates of the same party.
- "The *number* of contributions from individuals to individual candidates rose steadily over the past four general elections," and such donations constitute the largest single source of candidate election income.

Donald Padget's (1991) analysis of large contributions to candidates in the 1988 election supplements Stanbury's observation about individual donations. He argues that individual candidates' fundraising ability may be the most significant factor governing local campaign income. It appears to be more important than even such variables as ministerial status, party or region. This is a very interesting finding and draws our attention to the importance and centrality of the candidate him- or herself in local election fund-raising. It is, of course, also consistent with the candidate-centred election expense regime provided for by the *Canada Elections Act*.

Any full account of constituency election campaign financing must, however, deal with the local party associations that stand behind the candidates. It is they that provide the institutional link to the wider national party; it is the parties that have access to the tax-credit system that has been such a powerful stimulus to individual giving; and it is the parties that define the context within which the campaign is fought. At the same time, no study of riding associations in Canadian political parties would be complete unless it considered the financing of constituency election campaigns. This chapter does so: it examines local campaign financing from the perspective of the riding associations, recognizing that the law does not acknowledge their existence until after the election is over.

The primary focus here, as in previous chapters, is on what a local party association does, and how it organizes and operates to do so. Several issues are of particular concern. The chapter begins by looking at two that involve associations' electoral spending independent of any done by their local candidate. The first is spending that occurs in the pre-writ period and therefore remains unregulated. The second is the extent to which associations themselves spend party money on the prenomination activities of potential candidates. Since money must be raised to be spent, the chapter then turns to the role of the local party organization in election fund-raising: how do constituency associations do it, and how does it differ from their regular fund-raising activities in interelection periods? This leads to a discussion of the role of individual candidates in this vital activity. The evidence suggests that individual candidates are critical to local fund-raising success, a conclusion that echoes Padget's (1991) in his study of large contributions.

Having considered both expenditure and income from the perspective of the constituency association, the chapter then examines intraparty financial flows. Notwithstanding Stanbury's observation that "it is impossible to properly sort out the flows of [election] funds within the parties" (1991, chap. 12, note 10), the constituency association survey does reveal something of the patterns within the parties and across the regions. It demonstrates that, in terms of their financial relationship with their parties, three principal types of riding association stand out amid a myriad of possibilities. The fourth section of the chapter examines constituency associations' experiences with local election expense reimbursements and surpluses. This is a particularly interesting issue because the *Canada Elections Act* requires that candidates' agents pay any election-fund surplus over to a local party association (alternatively, they are permitted to pay it to their national party's agent or the government), despite the fact that the law does not recognize or regulate any local associations. Finally, the chapter assesses riding-level satisfaction with the existing system and the degree to which local association presidents support proposals to reform the way reimbursements and surpluses are handled.

To make the questions in this part of the survey as concrete as possible, most of them referred explicitly to the association's experience in the 1988 general election. While there is no reason to expect that the general patterns described here differ significantly from those in other general elections, the discussion and tables ought to be read in the context of the constituency battles of that contest and the respective strengths of the parties going into and coming out of it.

LOCAL ASSOCIATIONS' PRE-WRIT ELECTION SPENDING

Spending in Anticipation

The provisions in the Act that regulate and limit what a candidate, or someone operating on her or his behalf, can spend in a constituency contest come into effect only after a writ of election has been issued. Associations are free to spend as they like, or are able, on what are essentially election-oriented activities, in advance of a writ. Indeed, the very existence of post-writ limitations logically provides them with an incentive to do so. In effect, the system may encourage aggressive local parties to push expenditures and activities back out of the official election period, thus extending campaigning time and ultimately increasing costs. And it would seem likely that the largest and strongest associations would be in the best position to capitalize on that opportunity.

To assess whether the election expense regime is being regularly or systematically circumvented in this way, and to measure the extent to which traditional electoral activity is drifting back into the weeks and months before an election is called, the constituency association survey asked riding parties whether the system now in place gave them "an incentive to shift certain expenditures and activities back into the pre-writ period." As we expected, associations that reported it did were significantly larger and had grown more in the year leading up to the election. They were the local associations of the cadre-style parties, whose primary orientation is electoral. As table 8.1 indicates, this difference manifests itself in partisan terms.

While 56 percent of all associations indicated that the system encouraged them to spend and act early, in anticipation of the election call, local Progressive Conservative parties were twice as likely as NDP associations (72 percent to 38) to feel such a pull. The Liberals fell between their two major opponents, though they were closer to the Tories. The minor parties differed from one another: Reform responded more like a typical cadre party, while the CHP's pattern looked more like that of the NDP. This does not appear to be simply a matter of having the money to spend for, at least across all the local parties, there is no significant variation between rich and poor associations on this. There is, however, a general difference between the most competitive parties (those finishing first or second in the riding) and those running further back: the former admitted incentives to "anticipation spending" more often than the latter. Of course there could be something of a chicken-and-egg situation here. Early spending might well contribute to greater electoral success, but partisan differences cloud the issue: Tories seeing an incentive were less likely to have finished first in 1988 (compared to other Tories), while the reverse was true among New Democratic associations.

Of the three major parties, it is the New Democrats that generally seem most resistant to the logic of the incentive system generated by the election expense regime. However, as table 8.2 indicates, this varies considerably within the party. There is a regional pattern, with Quebec and BC associations much more inclined toward anticipation spending than their counterparts in the other regions, but other local conditions also make a difference. Rich NDP associations and the party's winners are similarly much more inclined to shift expenditures into the pre-writ period. Naturally enough, these factors tend to reinforce one another so that, for example, three-quarters of the winning BC NDP associations confessed to having an incentive to change their behaviour in this fashion.

The data do not reveal if this sort of activity has increased in recent elections as the parties' constituency associations have become richer and their candidates more affluent. Certainly those local associations that reported an incentive to shift expenditures and activities back into the period before the election is called were divided on whether or not it was a good thing. Slightly over half of them (53 percent) thought that it was not. Despite the sharp partisan differences in the extent to which associations reported an incentive (table 8.1), there was very little difference among the major parties on the merits of such practices. Each

Table 8.1
**Constituency associations shifting expenses
to pre-writ period**
(percentage claiming incentive to shift expenditures and
activities back)

All parties	56
Progressive Conservative	72
Liberal	59
NDP	38
Reform	58
Christian Heritage	38
1988 finish	
First	65
Second	62
Third	48
Fourth	40

Table 8.2
**NDP constituency associations shifting expenses
to pre-writ period**
(percentage claiming incentive to shift expenditures and
activities back)

All associations	38
Region	
Atlantic	33
Quebec	50
Ontario	27
Prairies	35
British Columbia	60
Association characteristic	
Rich	67
Poor	39
1988 winner	63
Paid campaign manager	49

was divided about 50–50. More predictable is the fact that rich associations were more inclined to think early spending was a good thing than were poor ones.

Riding Party Spending to Aid a Nomination

In the analysis of internal party democracy in chapter 5, the issue of the cost of winning a nomination was discussed, largely in terms of the burden it placed on potential candidates and the competitiveness of the process. The general argument there was that money is not an issue in the great majority of nominations, in part because so many are not formally contested (see also Carty and Erickson 1991). At the same time we also noted that, in a substantial number (but still a minority) of riding parties, a core group of influential activists pretty well decides among themselves who should be the candidate and then works to get that individual nominated (see table 5.2). One way they might do that would be to commit riding association financial resources to assist a would-be candidate before he or she was formally chosen as the nominee by the local party membership.

There are two possible reactions to such constituency association spending. On the one hand, party members might well object to it on the grounds that the local élite should not use association funds in an attempt to predetermine the outcome of the local nomination contest, at least not unless the process is open and all party members who want to seek the nomination are treated equally. On the other hand, many might argue that local parties must be prepared to be aggressive and supportive in candidate recruitment activities, especially if they want to attract more women or members of visible minorities, who have traditionally found it harder to break into federal electoral politics. In either event, the public has a legitimate interest in knowing if, and how, local parties are using this money in internal party nomination contests, given that a significant proportion of party income is public money (a tax expenditure) generated through income tax credits.

Though the parties are now using the tax system to raise substantial sums, some of which are then used to cover the costs of their leadership contests (Archer 1991; Perlin 1991a), the same is not true of the nomination process. Constituency associations have generally been quite reluctant to assist candidates before their selection: only 6 percent of them did so in 1988. The decision to help potential candidates in this way appears to be a rather idiosyncratic one, reflecting local needs, for there is little pattern to the relatively small number of cases where it occurs. With the exception of the CHP, where no local party reported doing so, the proportion of riding associations offering potential candidates financial help before the nomination was about the same in each party. The only difference among the parties was the amount of such help. Given the small number of instances it is impossible to be confident about absolute amounts, but the median association reported spending $2,000, with the totals generally higher in Conservative associations than in Liberal ones, which in turn spent a bit more than those in the New Democratic Party.

The political context of the nomination does not help account for the practice. Constituency parties do not appear more likely to spend money to help would-be candidates in ridings they expect to win. In only one-fifth of the cases where they provided such support did they win in 1988. They actually finished third in more cases (33 percent), and were second in the others. But a counter-hypothesis, that associations are forced into such spending where it is particularly difficult to find a candidate, does not work any better. While half the financially assisted candidates were unopposed and acclaimed at the nomination meeting, this was less than the national acclamation rate (see table 5.1), and in 19 percent of the cases there were three or more individuals seeking the nomination at the meeting. Local sensitivity to the problem of money, as evidenced by the constituency association establishing spending rules for its nomination contests, also appears unrelated to such spending.

Associations with candidate search committees do, however, stand out as more likely to spend money to help their potential nominees. Where the local party provides financial help to candidates in the prenomination stage, it often appears to be a matter of active candidate recruitment: in 70 percent of the cases the association spent more than the potential nominee on prenomination politics. Though this does not show up as a distinctive factor among associations that nominated a woman candidate in 1988, local parties with visible-minority candidates were significantly more likely to have spent organizational funds in this way. Though relatively few of these individuals were nominated in 1988 (5 percent of the associations reported having a visible-minority candidate), this small piece of evidence suggests support for an argument that riding parties may have to use their resources more aggressively if they are to recruit increasing numbers of nontraditional candidates.

Most constituency associations do not have an active recruitment program, or system of controls on the nomination process (Carty and Erickson 1991), so it is not surprising that we discovered that only a few local associations are spending party money on candidates in the prenomination process. This situation will change only if riding party organizations take a stronger role in directing and managing that process. And that would require the riding parties to adopt a more proactive style than has characterized most of them to date.

ASSOCIATIONS' ELECTION FUND-RAISING ACTIVITY

Fund-raising is the most common activity reported by Canadian constituency associations between elections (table 3.17), and despite the fact that the law makes candidates' official agents accountable for it during the campaign, it remains a major preoccupation all during the election period as well. Most simply step up all their fund-raising activity at that time. As we noted in chapter 4 on association finances, the number of individuals and supporters giving to local party associations sharply increases in election years, even controlling for the dramatic membership increases experienced by the cadre parties' associations in an election year (table 4.6). Stanbury (1991) has documented the growth in candidates' incomes over the last four general elections. Here we look at the constituency associations' part in generating those funds.

Raising Money during Elections

The very large sums accumulated by candidates and local associations during elections indicate that it must be easier for them to raise money then than at any other time. The amounts also reflect the natural reality that associations work harder at it during election periods than at other times. They do so, not only because they require the money then, but also because Canadian voters see parties in cadre-style electoral terms and are more responsive to appeals for financial help when party and candidate needs seem so obvious. Individual constituency associations are clearly aware of these differences between election and non-election fund-raising: table 8.3 summarizes the differences as they are perceived at the grass roots.

Local associations provided a wide range of responses to a question about the differences between fund-raising in the two periods, but five dominated. Twenty-nine percent of the associations mentioned the fact that election periods brought in more individual donations, and a similar proportion noted that it was just easier to get people to respond and give. About one association in twelve pointed to a more explicit reason for those rather general characterizations. They said that elections stimulated more voter interest, so that fund-raising efforts took place in an inherently different setting. All three of these descriptions of the differences hang together as part of the same picture: the heightened interest that is inevitably generated by the election makes it easier for parties to ask for money and for voters to understand why they are being asked, and so leads to more people giving. The other two principal responses were of a somewhat different order. Seven percent of the associations claimed there really were no differences between the periods, while a smaller number (5 percent) thought that the big difference was that gifts were larger during election contests.

There is not a great deal of difference among the parties. The Conservatives and the two minor parties were somewhat more inclined to mention increased voter interest, though it was also the Tory and Reform associations that most frequently denied there was any

Table 8.3
DIfferences between election period and non-election period fund-raising
(percentages)

	"Main difference" in election period				
	More gifts	Ease	More voter interest	Size	None
All parties	29	30	8	5	7
Progressive Conservative	30	27	10	3	9
Liberal	21	39	6	1	6
NDP	39	27	2	9	4
Reform	26	23	16	7	13
Christian Heritage	19	30	13	8	3
Region					
Atlantic	21	44	15	6	3
Quebec	24	14	2	—	22
Ontario	27	31	9	8	3
Prairies	36	29	8	3	5
British Columbia	30	36	5	2	4
Association characteristic:					
Rich	19	35	5	3	19
Poor	36	32	2	8	6
Paper	42	29	3	11	6
1988 winner	30	33	5	1	9

Note: Rows may not add to 100 as only percentage of associations giving one of five principal reasons above are reported.

difference. This latter similarity may testify to those parties' associations having superior ongoing, interelection fund-raising programs. Counter to our expectations of the differences between cadre and mass parties, it was the NDP and CHP associations that were most likely to indicate that donations were bigger at election time. But none of these variations are significant, and they pale in comparison to some regional differences.

It is in the provinces east of the Ottawa River that responses differed most sharply from the national pattern. In Atlantic Canada, associations more often mentioned that election period fund-raising was easier (at a rate 50 percent higher than for all local parties), and that heightened voter interest stimulated giving. This is perhaps not too surprising for one might expect that the poorest part of the country would find money for riding parties only at election time. However, the pattern is quite different in Quebec, the other economically disadvantaged region. There, far fewer constituency associations were moved to claim it was any easier, and many more (three times the national figure) reported that there was no difference between election and inter-election fund-raising. This suggests that Quebec constituency associations have a very different experience of local political giving, perhaps in part a spillover from Quebec's distinctive system of provincial party finance, which is tied to regular giving by individuals (Massicotte 1991).

Rich associations less frequently reported that they received more gifts at election time, and were correspondingly far more inclined to see no difference in fund-raising between the two periods. But that must reflect their successful interelection fund-raising activities as much as anything, for, by definition, they have comparatively large interelection incomes. At the other end of the spectrum, paper associations stand out as receiving more and larger gifts at election time. But that too may reflect on their interelection activity, for they have little success at generating a significant income then. Finally, it is worth noting that associations whose candidates won in 1988 do not stand out from the others. Winners do not have some secret formula for election fund-raising.

Election Fund-raising in the Constituencies

In chapter 4 we saw that social events and association membership drives were the local parties' most important interelection fund-raising tools (table 4.8). During the election period their approach changes and they become, at once, more aggressive and more direct in their search for financial support. Table 8.4 documents those activities associations rated as "important" or "very important" to their fund-raising during the 1988 election campaign. By far the most highly rated were direct personal contacts by the fund-raiser. And, as one would expect given Stanbury's evidence that individuals are the source of the largest share of candidate income (1991, table 12.2), it is contacts with individuals that were most widely believed to be a critical fund-raising method. Ninety-seven percent of the associations appear to agree with NDP organizer Tom Brook's claim that "the most effective way of putting bucks in the bank is personal contact" (1991, 149). Approaches to businesses, unions and local organizations were the next most prized methods, though the two old established cadre parties were more likely to report them than were constituency associations in the other three parties. Of the various methods rated, the riding associations were least likely to indicate that support from other levels in the party apparatus was important. Where they did, the national organization was more often seen as an important source than were provincial or other riding parties.

About half the associations rated the very new fund-raising technology of direct mail as important to them. The CHP appears most

Table 8.4
Constituency associations' important election fund-raising methods, 1988
(percentage rating method "important" or "very important")

Fund-raising method	All parties	Progressive Conservative	Liberal	NDP	Reform	Christian Heritage
Personal contact						
Individuals	97	97	98	99	93	97
Businesses, unions,						
organizations	83	90	91	76	58	79
Direct mail	51	59	45	44	57	64
Special events (dinners, etc.)	50	45	59	36	73	60
Candidate's contribution	35	23	37	45	32	46
Walk-in (unsolicited) donations	32	30	24	37	50	35
National party contributions	20	22	23	16	14	24
Provincial party contributions	7	6	11	9	—	—
Other riding associations	5	5	7	5	—	4
Other	4	3	5	4	2	7

enthusiastic about election-time use of direct mail, which may reflect its special utility to them in reaching their more narrowly focused constituency. Their electoral mail targeting is noteworthy, for CHP associations were least likely among the five parties to rank it their most important interelection fund-raising method (table 4.8). A similar proportion of the constituency parties (50 percent) also rated highly the very old method of holding a special event for local partisans. These events symbolically replay Macdonald's famous tour of the picnic grounds of Ontario in the run-up to the 1878 election, whose legendary success continues to stimulate local organizations to emulate it. The evidence indicates that there was a considerable degree of interparty difference over the importance of this method in 1988. The two new parties, perhaps using this technique to interest and involve new supporters as well as simply raise money, appear to have used special events more widely than did their older opponents. Thus twice as many Reform associations rated it important to their election fund-raising in 1988 as did New Democratic riding parties.

Two further election fund-raising methods deserve mention. The first is what we might label "walk-in" donations. These are unsolicited gifts from interested members of the public who perceive a local need at election time and move, on their own, to fill it. That some Canadian voters respond this way is not unusual given that election-time financing is an essential part of the tradition of our cadre parties, and Canadian elections have always aroused the voters' combative instincts. However, that almost a third of the associations should rate these donations as an important part of their fund-raising indicates that many of them are curiously reliant on a rather *ad hoc* financial base. In the case of the Reform Party, the fact that half of its associations rated such gifts as important in 1988 testifies to the brush-fire growth it was beginning to undergo that year. One other aspect of the walk-in giving phenomenon is its geographic cast. There is a steady increase in the phenomenon as one moves west across the regions: only 20 percent of the associations in Atlantic Canada rated it important, but almost two-and-a-half times that many (48 percent) did so in British Columbia. The survey data cannot tell us why this difference exists, though it may reflect the populist traditions of spontaneous grassroots mobilization that have characterized much of western Canada's electoral history.

The other fund-raising method to note is the candidate's contribution. Over a third of the riding parties rated it as important or very important. It might be expected that in cadre parties, organized as they are around a candidate and his or her campaign organization, such contributions might be important, but it turns out that it is the constituency associations of the mass parties, the NDP and the CHP, that are most likely to rate it as an important fund-raising practice. Only in the governing Conservative party did fewer than a quarter of the associations think it was not important in 1988. In the last chapter we discovered that the local candidate can be a critical factor in a riding party's capacity to recruit volunteers for its campaign organization. This data supplements that perspective by pointing to the important role many candidates also play in helping to finance the local campaign. That was a practice long taken for granted in the first (pre–World War I) Canadian party system (Carty 1992). Its persistence in contemporary electoral politics is one of the unexpected findings of the survey.

In what seems a perverse twist of fortune, it is the candidates of the weakest and poorest constituency parties whose contribution is most important to their local election campaign fund. As these are the parties that are most likely to lose, local candidates are effectively being forced to pay for the privilege of being a sacrificial lamb: thus, a number of Liberal candidates in British Columbia ended up contributing several thousand dollars (some paid well into five figures) to hopeless causes. This general rule holds across all three national parties, though the pattern is strongest in the NDP (table 8.5). The impact of this meant that, for example, half of the losing NDP associations in 1988 counted

Figure 8.1
Where candidate's contribution counts

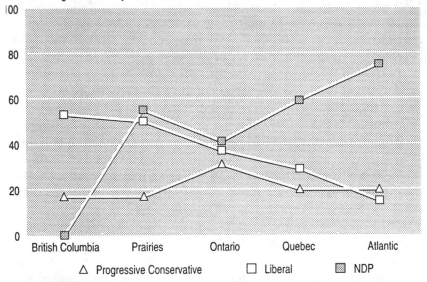

Note: Associations reporting candidate's contribution was "important" or "very important" to constituency's 1988 election fund-raising campaign.

Table 8.5
Candidate's contribution important to local campaign funds
(percentage associations deeming it "important" or "very important")

Association characteristic	Progressive Conservative	Liberal	NDP
Paper branch	66	40	67
Real branch	22	30	24
Poor	50	55	66
Rich	11	—	33
1988 loser	34	39	51
1988 winner	14	32	—

their candidate's contribution as important, but none of the winning ones did.

Within the three national parties, geographic differences in their organizational strength at the end of the 1980s meant that there was a pronounced regional cast to the importance of local candidates' contributions to constituency associations' election campaign funds. Given their success as a governing party which was in the process of being re-elected, there was little of that variation across the Conservative party in 1988. By contrast, the position of Liberal and NDP candidates was almost a mirror image of one another (figure 8.1). Among Liberals, the proportion of associations rating the candidate's contribution important grew from east to west. Within the NDP the opposite was true, with the extremes even more sharply drawn: in British Columbia no association claimed their candidate's contribution was important, in Atlantic Canada fully 75 percent did.

This burden on candidates is a local reality that the national parties need to recognize as they struggle to broaden the base of their candidate recruitment. One of the consequences of this problem can be seen in the parties' attempts to increase the number of women candidates they run. In any election, new (women) candidates are more likely to be adopted in less politically attractive ridings, available because some other party holds the seat. The general pattern described here leads us to assume that constituency associations with new women candidates may be among those forced to regard their candidate's contribution as important to their election campaign fund. But it is generally accepted that women are not as well connected to money, and so their ability to meet this expectation of their local associations will be more limited. If such potential candidates know that their national or provincial party will also go on to confiscate a portion of their expense reimbursement as a condition of the party endorsement, they may find the attraction of a nomination less than compelling.

Beyond this narrow question of any contribution a candidate makes to the constituency association's election fund, there is the wider issue of the role and importance of the candidate as a fund-raiser. The constituency association survey suggests that this is an important role, too often overlooked in accounts of candidates' principal campaign activities.

The Candidate as Constituency Party Fund-raiser

A simplistic view of election candidates sees their primary task as that of being the frontispiece of the constituency campaign, communicating with voters and asking for their support on election day. Successful candidates need to do more. They need to establish, build and nourish an organization that can mount and sustain an effective local campaign. As we saw in the previous chapter, that involves finding and appointing the right people for key positions, such as campaign manager and official agent, in the campaign team (figure 7.2), and then attracting the volunteers needed to staff their organization (table 7.14). But it also involves helping to find the financial resources necessary to mount the campaign. Though we readily recognize that American politicians must devote a good deal of time and effort to fund-raising, this aspect of a Canadian constituency candidate's role is often overlooked and not properly appreciated.

Most candidates get little financial help from the local party before they win the nomination and must therefore finance their bid for it. But once it has been won, they cannot always assume that the riding association will then take over, freeing them of any concern about questions of campaign finance. In the typical well-managed constituency party campaign, the candidate is a central figure in its financing. In extreme instances, where there has been a nasty struggle for the nomination, some may even find themselves forced to fend completely for themselves (Bell and Bolan 1991). Whatever the case, the candidate is always one of a campaign's prime assets (or liabilities) as it launches its election fund-raising campaign.

As Stanbury (1991, chap. 12) rightly notes, a candidate's ability to raise funds varies by both party and province. However it is also clear that some candidates are just better and more successful fund-raisers than others in their party or region (Padget 1991). There are two aspects to the importance of the candidate to a constituency association's efforts to generate election income. First, there is the question of who the candidate is – the "target" of the financial support. A good candidate will attract more support. Of course what makes a particular candidate attractive varies. For many, ministers may be especially desirable candidates on the assumption that they have the most power and influence to help the constituency or to effect some desired policy outcome. For others, candidates who share some common group characteristic or ideological perspective will be regarded as especially worthy of support. Second, beyond the idea of the candidate as a target of support, there is the role of the candidate him- or herself as an active fund-raiser. With personal contacts the most important method of raising election funds, the candidate is the person who is best placed to ask for help. Asking for money is a necessary prelude to asking for votes.

Table 8.6 (column 1) reports the constituency associations' views on the importance of the candidate to their local election fund-raising. Over half (58 percent) reported that they believed the local candidate was "very important" to the success of the fund-raising effort. This was particularly true of the associations of the old cadre parties, the Conservatives (68 percent) and the Liberals (61 percent). As one might expect in mass-style parties, the candidate was not so often seen as very important in the NDP (48 percent) or the CHP (44 percent). But few

Table 8.6
Importance of candidate to local election fund-raising
(percentage associations)

	Candidate "very important" to the success of election fundraising	Candidate's personal effort considered "vital" or "important" to local fundraising activities
All parties	58	44
Progressive Conservative	68	44
Liberal	61	52
NDP	48	43
Reform	56	56
Christian Heritage	44	34
Region		
Atlantic	69	42
Quebec	52	67
Ontario	58	39
Prairies	59	46
British Columbia	57	49
Association characteristic		
1988 winner	67	39
Rich	56	44
Poor	55	65
Paper	46	62
Male candidate	59	48
Female candidate	54	38

denigrated the role of the candidate in local election fund-raising: only 2 percent of all riding parties were prepared to say the candidate was "not important."

This perception of the importance of the candidate is widespread. It appears to be higher in Atlantic Canada, the region where a more personal, traditional political style endures, and where the cadre parties continue to dominate constituency-level contests. In general, paper associations are less reliant on their candidates than is the average association, though that relationship is reversed within the NDP, where paper associations more often see the candidate as very important than do its stronger, established riding parties.

Given that the majority of local party associations believe that their candidate is very important to election fund-raising success, it is important to ask if nontraditional candidates disadvantage them in this regard. If so, the parties will have to take this into account in their recruitment strategies; if not, then another shibboleth impeding the participation of women or members of visible minorities in federal electoral politics will have been exposed as simply another rationalization for the status quo. Constituency associations were asked if, in their experience, having a woman or visible-minority candidate hindered local election fund-raising. Most associations rightly noted they had no experience of either. Just 5 percent of those that had had a woman candidate said that it was a hindrance; rather more, but still just 17 percent, of those with experience of a visible-minority candidate claimed it had hindered their fund-raising. These are not large proportions and they indicate that nontraditional candidates do not often impose much of an extra burden on the finances of a constituency campaign. But some minority candidates may find it more difficult to raise funds. Knowing that, the national parties could easily make special arrangements for constituencies with such candidates, perhaps by channelling more national party money into such ridings, or by ensuring that those associations do not have their reimbursements confiscated by the national office.

The other face of the candidate's role in funding the local constituency contest is operating as one of the campaign's principal fund-raisers. Table 8.6 (column 2) indicates how the associations describe the attention or effort the local candidate must personally put into election fund-raising activities. It reports that 44 percent of the riding parties characterize it as either "vital – a major task of candidates" or as something that is "important – consumes considerable time." By contrast, just 16 percent say that "candidates must be kept out of it." There were some party differences on this in 1988: more Liberal and Reform candidates and fewer CHP candidates were considered central players in local fund-raising activity, but it was Quebec where candidates appear to have been most active in raising funds on their own behalf. Two-thirds of that province's federal party associations expected their candidate to be a very active fund-raiser.

Candidates selected by poor local associations more often have to work at raising money for their own campaign chest than do colleagues with richer riding parties standing behind them. Since candidates who win are less likely to be from poor riding parties, the majority of MPs do not come from ridings where they must spend much of their campaign personally engaged in fund-raising – but still, only 15 percent of them (in 1988) came from local parties where they had not been expected to do any.

Notwithstanding these differences, candidates are obviously devoting more time and energy to raising money than is generally acknowledged. This is the dark side of local election campaign financing, which has now become a self-financing process. Raising spending limits, as suggested by Heintzman (1991, 144) as an incumbency balancing factor, or reducing reimbursements to the local association (whether it be by the state or by a party itself) as suggested by Stanbury (1991, chap. 14), who sees them as now unnecessary, will only increase this pressure on candidates. If Canadians are to avoid burdening their constituency politicians with some of the financial strains visited upon their American counterparts, they ought to resist either of those courses of action.

We noted in table 8.4 that constituency campaigns derive some of their election income from other organizational levels in their parties. In the same way, all the money they raise does not stay at home: some finds its way to other parts of the party. Sorting those intraparty transactions is no easy task. The candidates' official election expense reports are little help. The constituency association survey does, however, provide another perspective on that financial maze. It indicates something of the structure of those flows and the place of constituency-level organizations in them.

WHERE THE MONEY FLOWS:
THE CHANNELS OF INTRAPARTY ELECTORAL FINANCE

At election time, money is raised and borrowed by party agents, candidates and the traditional fund-raisers, but then moved to where it can be most productively used. The amorphous and opaque quality of much of Canadian parties' internal affairs does not allow us to trace the amounts entailed in the many different intraparty financial flows that take place during an election. However, by focusing on the constituency associations that sit at one end of a particularly important set of organizational channels, it is possible to get a fix on the structures of the parties' electoral financing. Canadian parties have provincial and national-level organizations and campaign teams, but it is in the 295 individual constituencies that elections must ultimately be fought and won. This makes the local association a primary election unit, and draws our attention to the financial links that bind its campaign to others in the party.

The parties' constituency associations were asked if, during the 1988 general election, they (*a*) received financial support from, or (*b*) made financial donations to, their national party, the provincial (or territorial) party or other riding associations. As we shall see below large numbers reported they did one or the other, and sometimes both. A number of associations did not give any response, but unfortunately in a fashion that makes it difficult to differentiate those that chose not to answer from those that neither received nor made intraparty donations. As a result, the following analysis may underestimate the proportions of associations that are isolated and not part of an intraparty electoral financial channel. Note also that the data identify the channels through which electoral funds flowed into and out of constituency associations, but they tell us nothing about the dollar amounts involved in these intraparty money movements. (For an attempt at estimating the aggregate magnitudes of these transfers to candidates, not associations, see Stanbury 1991, tables 12.4 and 12.4a.) While some may have been large sums, others may well have been fairly modest transfers. With these two provisos in mind, let us consider the constituency-related patterns of money flows in Canadian parties during general elections.

Donations from other levels or units in the party are not rated by constituency associations as a particularly important source of funds (table 8.4). Nevertheless, a majority (53 percent) of the responding local parties claimed to have received financial support during the 1988 general election from some other party body. Table 8.7 summarizes these transfers into local associations by sources. The largest proportion (37 percent) of them received money from their national party organization, 6 percent from a provincial-level party, 5 percent from other constituency party associations and a further 5 percent from more than one other party unit.

The differences among the parties are modest, smaller than one would expect given the very different structures of the three major parties (Dyck 1991), and the quite different financial resources and internal allocation practices that have characterized them in recent years (Stanbury 1991; Morley 1991). This is particularly true of Conservative and NDP associations, which report an almost identical picture, while the Liberals stand out from their two national opponents in having more associations reporting the financial help of a provincial party. The two minor parties' associations have somewhat different patterns of intraparty support. There was simply less of it in the Reform Party in 1988, though associations which received help tended to get it from several sources. The CHP is distinctive in that more of its associations (11 percent) than in any other party claimed to have received a financial donation from another riding association.

Regional differences in the patterns of intraparty flows into constituency election funds are sharper than those between the parties. As with issues of election fund-raising discussed above, it is the economically weaker provinces east of the Ottawa River that stand out from the national picture. More riding party associations in Atlantic Canada received financial support from a more diverse set of sources than in other regions: 11 percent got help from other constituency parties, 18 percent got help from several elements of the party and only

Table 8.7
Intraparty financial flows into local election funds, 1988 election
(percentages)

	Financial support received from				
	National party	Provincial party	Other ridings	Multiple sources	None
All parties	37	6	5	5	47
Progressive Conservative	36	4	5	6	49
Liberal	41	12	3	—	44
NDP	37	5	5	8	45
Reform	32	—	—	10	58
Christian Heritage	38	—	11	4	46
Region					
Atlantic	36	7	11	18	29
Quebec	53	11	2	—	34
Ontario	32	4	3	6	55
Prairies	30	6	8	2	54
British Columbia	37	—	3	10	50
Association characteristic					
Rich	42	—	4	4	50
Poor	41	2	4	11	41
Paper	36	—	3	9	52
1988 winner	37	7	3	1	52

29 percent claimed to have received no help at all. In Quebec, associations were more likely to have had just national party support than those in other regions and, like their eastern counterparts, a smaller proportion (34 percent) claimed they had no intraparty financial help than was the case in the rest of the country.

Winning riding associations did not look very different from the typical association in 1988. Table 8.7 does indicate that more rich associations got help from their national party than did paper organizations, and also that more of the latter claimed to have had no party help than the former. Those differences are not large but they indicate that intraparty financial transfers are not part of any internal equalization scheme. Parties are far more likely to use resources where the probable returns are greater, and are not loath to let weak local associations take care of themselves.

Table 8.8 provides a measure of the other side of the intraparty electoral funds transfer process – the flow of donations from the constituency association to other elements of the party. Two preliminary points should be noted. First, more (7 percent) associations answered this question,

Table 8.8
Intraparty financial flows out of constituency associations, 1988 election
(percentages)

	Financial donations made to				
	National party	Provincial party	Other ridings	Multiple sources	None
All parties	57	4	3	12	25
Progressive Conservative	49	1	4	5	41
Liberal	42	8	7	14	30
NDP	58	6	—	23	13
Reform	57	—	9	—	35
Christian Heritage	97	—	—	—	3
Region					
Atlantic	44	13	4	17	22
Quebec	51	6	2	11	30
Ontario	68	3	3	5	21
Prairies	54	—	6	13	28
British Columbia	44	5	3	28	21
Association characteristic					
Rich	61	—	—	9	30
Poor	56	—	—	13	20
Paper	51	—	—	12	26
1988 winner	49	—	6	16	24

suggesting that transferring money out was a more common experience than receiving it. Second, of those who responded, a much smaller percentage (25 percent, compared to 47 percent) claimed not to have made an intraparty donation than not to have received one. This provides strong circumstantial evidence for an argument that the parties' constituency associations are less likely to be beneficiaries of financial support from other elements of their parties than they are to be part of an elaborate network of financial milch cows supporting the national organizations.

As table 8.8 indicates, the majority (57 percent) of the associations making intraparty electoral donations sent them to the national party. Few sent donations to the provincial level (4 percent) or to other ridings (3 percent), though 12 percent claim to have provided help to more than one party unit in 1988. The Conservatives stood out as having the largest proportion (41 percent) of associations not transferring money out, while the NDP (at 13 percent) had the smallest of the three nationwide parties. Given the Conservatives' greater emphasis on establishing local financial autonomy (Stanbury 1991, chap. 12, section 3.1), and the NDP's more integrated structure, these patterns are just what we would have expected. The CHP portrait reveals a national party that seems extraordinarily reliant on its grassroots organization: 97 percent of its associations made a financial donation to the national organization during the 1988 general election.

The regional variations apparent in the patterns of inward financial flows were not so obviously replicated in the outward movement of money. Fewer associations in the Atlantic region donated to the national party, but more of them there gave to their provincial wing. At the other end of the country, in British Columbia, associations were more likely to give financial help to several elements in the party than were their counterparts across the country. Rich associations contributed to their national party more often than poor ones, but they were also more likely to make no intraparty contributions at all.

These patterns of intraparty electoral transfers clearly indicate that constituency associations are part of an intricate web of intraparty

Figure 8.2
Constituency associations and election-period intraparty financial channels

Money flowing out of riding party to	Money flowing into riding party from				
	National party	Provincial party	Other ridings	Multiple sources	None
National party	Integrated				Taxed
Provincial party					
Other ridings					
Multiple sources					
None	Dependent				Autonomous

election financing. But having considered inflows and then outflows separately, we still have not come to grips with the full complexity of the system, for any one association may see funds move both in and out during an election campaign. If we take the five intraparty sources (counting "none" as one possibility for purposes of the analysis) identified in table 8.7, and cross them by the five destinations identified in table 8.8, we have a matrix of 25 possible intraparty financial channels that a constituency association might be a part of during an election. This matrix is illustrated in figure 8.2.

The data summarizing electoral money flows into (table 8.7) and out of (table 8.8) constituency associations made it evident that the principal intraparty channels either have the national party at the other end, or they are blocked (i.e., "none"). This makes the four corner positions in our schematic representation the principal types; they are the ones that are likely to encompass most local associations. They also can be said to define the ideal types of a fairly simple four-part typology. The first type of association is one that contributes to the national party with which it is affiliated, but also receives some contributions from it. Such a riding organization could be described as fully *integrated* into the wider political party. At the opposite extreme is the *autonomous* constituency association, which is financially on its own during elections. It neither makes contributions to other party units nor receives any. The third type of association could best be described as *taxed*. During elections it makes contributions (perhaps not always voluntarily) to the national party, but receives none in return. Such associations may still benefit from general party campaign expenditures, they just do not get national money to spend on their own local campaigns. One might assume that national parties would deal with their rich associations in this fashion. The fourth type of association is financially *dependent:* receiving money from its national body but able to contribute nothing in return. National parties, determined to run candidates in every constituency, might well find this the situation they face in areas where they have little electoral support. Thus, paper associations should be likely candidates for intraparty financial dependency.

Figure 8.3 uses this schema to classify the 1988 general election experience of all the constituency associations. It leads us to several important observations. First, although we identified 25 empirically possible channels, 10 of them were empty, with not a single case turning up. Second, 79 percent of all the associations fell into one of our four ideal types, identified by the corners of the matrix. Third, the distribution of associations within these four types was quite asymmetrical: there were very few (just 4 percent) dependent associations, with

Figure 8.3
Intraparty financial flows, 1988 general election
(Percentage associations)

	Money flowing into riding party from				
Money flowing out of riding party to	National party	Provincial party	Other ridings	Multiple sources	None
National party	23 *Integrated*	2	3	2	21 *Taxed*
Provincial party	1	1			1
Other ridings	2				2
Multiple sources	2				4
None	4 *Dependent*	1			31 *Autonomous*

three-quarters of them spread over the other three types. The largest single group (31 percent) were the autonomous associations.

The integrated, the taxed and the autonomous: most constituency associations find their intraparty financial relationships during election periods put them into one of these three types. On the basis of Dyck's (1991) analysis of party organization, Stanbury's (1991) of national party finances, and our discussion of interelection constituency association financing (see table 4.2), we would hypothesize that the Conservative party would have the highest proportion of autonomous associations, while the New Democrats would have more that are integrated. The Liberals, who operate two (provincially varied) models of national party–constituency organization linkage, are likely to have the most diverse pattern. We would also expect that fewer associations in the two eastern regions would be among the taxed, while more rich ones might be. Finally, though there are not many dependent

Table 8.9
Constituency association intraparty election finance types, 1988
(percentages)

Funds (to/from):	Integrated (national party/national party)	Taxed (national party/ none)	Autonomous (none/ none)	Dependent (none/ national party)	% of all in four ideal types
All parties	23	21	31	4	79
Progressive Conservative	19	14	49	2	84
Liberal	21	13	29	11	74
NDP	20	27	20	2	69
Region					
Atlantic	17	6	28	—	51
Quebec	34	9	34	6	83
Ontario	24	30	26	4	84
Prairies	15	21	38	2	76
British Columbia	29	21	29	4	83
Association characteristic					
Rich	28	16	32	8	84
Poor	20	21	27	—	68
Paper	19	23	35	—	77

associations, paper associations should dominate in that category. Table 8.9 provides a test of these propositions.

Our expectations about the parties' channels of intraparty electoral finance are only partially confirmed by the data. The Conservatives have structures and practices that encourage constituency autonomy and they have managed to achieve it to a considerably greater extent than the other parties. About one-half of the Conservative associations are autonomous, compared to only one-fifth of those in the NDP. On the other hand, the NDP does not appear to have greater levels of constituency association–national party integration than do the two cadre parties. Fewer of its constituency associations fall into one of the four principal types, evidence that the NDP has a more complex set of internal relationships than do the other parties. The Liberals have the most diverse network. They stand out from the other two national parties in having an unusually high proportion (11 percent) of dependent associations. Why that should be so is not clear, although it may just reflect the 1988 state of a once-great national cadre party fallen on hard times.

Few local parties east of the Ottawa River are in the group we have characterized as taxed, reflecting the reality that there is less money to be had for national politics and federal parties in those regions. But it is also true that there are not many dependent riding parties to be found in those five provinces. Instead, associations in those areas must be more adaptable, plugging into whatever channels are available. Thus, only half the local parties in Atlantic Canada fit one of the four dominant molds, a proportion lower than for any other group.

Rich riding parties are apparently less likely to be taxed, and more likely to be the beneficiary of unreciprocated national party support (making them a dependent) than are either poor associations or those that are paper branches. This seems to be a case of taking care of the healthy and strong while leaving the weak and the lame to fend for themselves. Though this is not a prescription for a homogeneous national campaign, it is undoubtedly the most appropriate strategy and use of limited financial resources given a plurality electoral system and geographically uneven electoral support. Paper associations are, almost by definition, to be found mainly in unwinnable seats (7 percent of them won their riding in 1988, 71 percent finished third or lower) and spending a bit more money is not likely to change that reality. That is why none of them were in the dependent category in the 1988 general election.

This picture of the channels of intraparty electoral finance suggests that constituency associations are part of distinctive party networks that are defined by the culture and resources of their party, but are also shaped by the imperatives of the electoral system and the economic disparities of the country. It demonstrates that to fully appreciate individual constituency campaigns they must be seen in terms of their party's own distinctive approach to intraparty finance, and the fundamental organizational assumptions that underlie it.

REIMBURSEMENTS AND SURPLUSES

Constituency Election Expense Reimbursements

One of the most ambitious reforms to Canadian election financing in the 1970s was the attempt to level the playing field of constituency contests by providing for partial reimbursement of the expenses of candidates who commanded 15 percent of the vote. This was done to ensure that serious candidates had the resources necessary to wage a minimally competitive campaign. Not only did the guarantee of public support supplement local resources, it also allowed a campaign organization to establish credit in the early period of an election when expenses were high but income remained somewhat uncertain. The general view is that this has been a successful reform, though Stanbury (1991, chap. 12) argues that local candidates no longer require the reimbursement to cover their election expenses.

National parties, hard-pressed to cover their election expenses, have begun to look at these candidate reimbursements in much the same light as Stanbury. That is, they see them as superfluous to most constituency needs and thus a potential source of national party income. The amounts are not small. They are a function of the amounts spent, so are largest in the biggest-spending parties: in 1988, candidate expense reimbursements totaled $6 million to Conservatives, $4.7 million to Liberals and $2.8 million to New Democrats. (See table 8.10, but note that reimbursements and surpluses are, strictly speaking, the concern of candidates, not constituency associations.) As we have noted, the Liberals had a policy, implemented through the national office's candidate endorsement power, of requiring candidates to hand one-half of their reimbursement over to the party, while the New Democrats applied a similar policy in some provinces.

The constituency survey investigated local understandings of how this practice worked on the ground by asking local association presidents whether their "candidate or constituency association [had] to turn over all or part of the government reimbursement of election expenses to the national party." Figure 8.4 demonstrates the striking interparty differences over this practice. Given the national parties' positions on their claim to local reimbursements the findings are not too surprising, but a small proportion (11 percent) of Conservative associations claimed they had to give up their reimbursement and about a quarter (27 percent) of the Liberals said they did not. This could betray some uncertainty about party practice by local presidents (which in itself would be worth noting given the amounts of money involved) but it may also reflect some unevenness in the ability of the national party organizations to apply their constituency policies uniformly.

Table 8.10
Major parties' election reimbursements and surpluses, 1988

	Progressive Conservative	Liberal	NDP
Reimbursements			
N	293	264	170
Percentage	99	89	58
Total ($000)	6 056	4 656	2 839
Average size ($)	20 669	17 636	16 700
Surpluses			
N	231	234	167
Percentage	78	79	57
Average size ($)	20 080	12 727	10 421

Source: Stanbury (1991), tables 12.32 and 12.33.

Figure 8.4
Constituency associations' election expense reimbursements, 1988

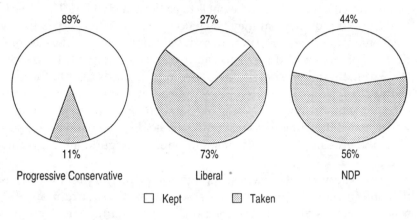

89%	27%	44%
11%	73%	56%
Progressive Conservative	Liberal	NDP

☐ Kept   ▨ Taken

It is the two national cadre parties, the Liberals and the Conservatives, who are most at odds over confiscating local reimbursements. Obviously the decision whether to do so is not related to organizational type. For the Conservatives it appears to be a philosophical question and reflects their commitment to making as many of their associations as autonomous as possible. In the case of the Liberals it was simply a consequence of the wretched state of their national finances and a recognition that there was a lot of easy money to be collected from their candidates. The New Democrats, whose practice in 1988 put them squarely between the Conservatives and Liberals, seemed to have left the question of how to treat federal reimbursements in the hands of provincial-level party decision makers. Thus all of the NDP associations (56 percent) that gave up reimbursement money in 1988 came from half the provinces: the survey found none in Atlantic Canada or Saskatchewan.

When the national parties take reimbursement money from their local candidates they are effectively depriving the associations of its use, because the *Canada Elections Act* directs that any final surplus be paid to the local association. For the most part the national parties use these reimbursement funds for their own purposes. Only 21 percent of the associations believe that some of the money is being held in trust for their future use. That percentage is highest (28 percent) among Liberals, lowest (11 percent) in the NDP.

Campaign Surpluses

Stanbury (1991, chap. 12) has demonstrated both how difficult it is to measure constituency election surpluses as they are currently defined and just how much money is involved (more than $13 million in 1988). Campaign surpluses are the responsibility of the candidates' official agents, and the law is clear on what is to be done with them. The *Canada Elections Act* requires that they "be paid by the official agent ... to any local organization or association of members of the party in the electoral district of the candidate or to the registered agent of the party" (s. 232(*h*)), though the possibility of paying the funds over to the government is also provided for. The implication is that the candidate's official agent, presumably acting in conjunction with the candidate in whose name the campaign was run, shall decide what to do with a surplus: the presumption is that it should normally go to a local riding party.

The reality is not always so straightforward. The first problem is that any surplus (for proportions of associations with a surplus in 1988, see table 8.10) will be determined only months after the election is over. Some (defeated) candidates will have little inclination or interest in tidying up after a losing campaign. Bernier (1991), for instance, reports that the NDP candidate rarely appeared in Frontenac during the election itself and one assumes had no interest in it once the campaign was over. In these cases the agent may receive little help in deciding what to do with a surplus. At the same time as the law directs the agent to pay the funds over to "any local organization or association of members of the party," it does not recognize or register such organizations, so the agent obviously has some discretion in doing so. (Recall, figure 7.2, that most agents are not appointed by these associations.) And with about 24 percent of the constituency associations in the three major parties being what we have called paper branches, the agent might conceivably have some difficulty finding the association or identifying its officers.

Table 8.11 reports who decided what was to be done with the candidates' surpluses after the 1988 general election. In practice only 2 percent of the associations reported that the official agent made the decision. A few more candidates (8 percent) took the decision, but it was left, in a large majority of cases (74 percent), to the constituency association itself to determine the disposition. This despite the fact that the associations did not have the funds under their control, were not responsible for them, did not legally exist and were the principal potential beneficiaries. Given that agents exist to provide for a legal control mechanism, this aspect of the system is obviously not functioning as the Act provides it should.

Liberal associations stand out as having less say over their constituency campaign's surplus than their counterparts in other parties.

Table 8.11
Who disposed of election fund surplus, 1988
(percentages)

	Constituency association executive	Candidate	Other*
All parties	74	8	18
Progressive Conservative	81	5	14
Liberal	58	15	27
NDP	80	2	18
Reform	84	16	—
Christian Heritage	74	11	15
Association characteristic			
Rich	83	3	14
Paper	58	17	25
1988 winner	81	4	15
1988 loser	71	11	18

*"Other" includes wide range of actors. More than half the instances are cases of joint decision making.

That is because more Liberal associations (19 percent of them) reported that some sort of joint decision was taken which involved several actors (e.g., party officials, agent, candidate, etc.). As we anticipated above, paper associations are less likely to have decided about the surplus than other riding parties, doubtless because some are so underorganized that they are virtually incapable of doing so. It is also noteworthy that newly elected MPs were not especially disposed to make the decision, but were content to leave it to their riding organization. Clearly they do not appear to view the surplus as some form of personal election fund which they have a right to control themselves.

Perhaps more important than who decides about the surplus is what they decide. This quickly comes down to who gets the money. As we have seen, the Act's presumption is that it ought to be the local party association and, as table 8.12 indicates, for the most part that is who does get it. Ninety-five percent of the constituency associations reported that it went into either their local general account or a special trust account. Among the parties, the Liberals appear to have a particular predilection for depositing it into a trust account, perhaps so that it cannot be too easily raided by those trying to solve the party's more general financial difficulties. The paper associations stand out on this issue. In 30 percent of them, the surplus goes elsewhere. That can only perpetuate their already organizationally and financially impoverished state, but it may represent a realistic decision by the parties as to where those funds can best be put to use.

Table 8.12
Who got the money: election fund surpluses, 1988
(percentages)

	Constituency association's general accounts	Constituency association's trust account	Given to provincial level of party	Given to national level of party	Other
All parties	67	28	2	1	1
Progressive Conservative	71	29	—	—	—
Liberal	49	42	4	4	2
NDP	69	19	3	3	6
Reform	79	21	—	—	—
Christian Heritage	94	—	6	—	—
Association characteristic					
Rich	66	34	—	—	—
Paper	50	20	10	10	10
1988 winner	67	32	—	—	1
Decision maker					
Candidate	71	21	7	—	—
Local association executive	73	25	1	—	1

Stanbury's estimate of the size of the average surplus (summarized above in table 8.10) led him to conclude that millions of dollars in election surplus funds ended up in local association accounts. By the associations' own reports they received most of that money. However our estimates of their financial resources in chapter 4 (see table 4.1) are somewhat at odds with this. While it is not possible to match reports (and the survey did not ask for or obtain local party financial statements), it would seem that some associations must have more money than they are admitting, or else in the two years after the election it was drawn away for other party use. Take, for example, the case of the NDP. Stanbury notes that 57 percent of their associations had a 1988 election surplus whose average size was over $10 000 (1991, table 12.33). Almost 90 percent of the party's riding associations claim to have kept their surpluses, but by the spring of 1991 only 15 percent (table 4.1) reported that they had more than $5 000 on hand. Given the complexities of NDP accounting and financing (e.g., Morley 1991), all this is quite possible. However it does caution us about assuming too much from the brief account here. What is necessary for a full accounting of constituency party election financing is to replicate Stanbury's analysis of the national parties' finances at the local level.

DOES THE SYSTEM WORK?

Constituency associations have now campaigned in several general elections under the current election expense and party financing regime. Earlier chapters have shown that they are generally satisfied with the basic system. Though local parties were divided over the potential merits of a more rigorous regulation of the financing of nomination and leadership contests (tables 5.8 and 5.9), there was only a limited amount of support for significant regulation of interelection financing (table 4.16). It seems that the constituency associations feel much the same way about the regulation of constituency election finances.

When reminded about the spending limits and the income and expenditure disclosure provisions of the present rules, 79 percent of all the riding parties said they thought them satisfactory or very satisfactory; only 4 percent called them unsatisfactory (table 8.13). When asked about the stringency of the rules, three-quarters (73 percent) thought the balance they struck was about right. Those who disagreed with that were evenly divided between those (15 percent – mostly New Democrats) who thought the rules too permissive, and those (11 percent – mostly Conservatives) who believed them too restrictive. By and large, however, the overall pattern is one of widespread partisan agreement and satisfaction with the current system. Though the rich are more approving than the poor, even the less affluent associations appear fairly content with the law as it stands.

Table 8.13
Local parties' views on election expense rules
(percentage associations agreeing)

	All parties	Progressive Conservative	Liberal	NDP	Rich	Poor
Current spending and expense rules						
Satisfactory/very satisfactory	79	77	85	74	84	62
About right	73	71	80	65	76	67
Most campaign workers can't understand system	44	44	47	41	43	43
Doesn't matter that system so complicated	59	65	57	57	58	54
Proposed changes						
Pay all campaign surplus over to local association	84	91	82	82	94	82
Forbid national party reimbursement seizures	63	78	62	55	70	68

This general satisfaction is all the more striking when we note that 44 percent of all the constituency association presidents report that, in their experience, "the current electoral expense system is so complex that most campaign volunteers and workers cannot understand it." But at the same time, 59 percent of them go on to say it does not matter "if most workers really can't follow the detailed rules." Apparently they believe rules and accounting can be left to strategists and managers in most cases. Those who believe that this ignorance does matter point to problems of avoiding mistakes and liability, or of ensuring compliance, as their principal concern, though some New Democrats and members of the two minor parties also mentioned the stress it placed on their workers.

What is missing here is any active concern for the health of a democratic system. It is difficult to accept as desirable an electoral system whose rules are admittedly too complicated for many of its most active participants to understand. Those rules, after all, are designed to promote electoral fairness and equality and so enhance the legitimacy of the system and the confidence of Canadians in it. If the local constituency association presidents are correct, even the most highly politicized Canadians are likely to have to accept that it does so on faith – their experience gives them little first-hand sense of this.

The constituency association presidents were asked for their reactions to two specific proposals for modest changes to the position of their local organizations in the current system. The first asked them if they supported a proposal that all campaign surpluses be paid over to the local constituency association. That, of course, appears to be the intention of the current Act, and is now the general practice. Eighty-four percent of the constituency associations think this should continue, though Conservative and rich associations were even more supportive of it than others (table 8.13). There was less support for the proposition that national parties should be forbidden to require local associations to turn over their candidates' expense reimbursements to some central fund. Just 63 percent agreed with that, though there was a partisan (right–left) difference in the responses: more Tories (78 percent) were supportive than New Democrats (55 percent). However, support for such a restriction is not rooted in the experience of actually having a local reimbursement taken. Only 56 percent of those associations that had had to give up part or all of their reimbursement in 1988 supported the proposal, as compared to 71 percent that had not lost any of their reimbursement.

Canadian constituency associations seem basically content with the electoral expense system as it affects them and their local campaigns. That being so there does not appear to be any widespread support for significant change, except perhaps for some modest regulation of the nomination process (see chapter 5). The evidence does suggest that the current system is already too complex for many participants; a more complex regulatory system would risk making the system comprehensible only to an even smaller élite.

NATIONAL NETWORKS OF LOCAL ASSOCIATIONS

This analysis of constituency associations' election financing issues, like those in earlier chapters, again forces us to reflect on the nature of Canadian political parties and the character of the differences across the party system. Some of the apparently clear differences we thought had been pinned down seem to slip away when forced under the lens of electoral party finance.

In the analysis of constituency association election-campaign organization and activity, the cadre–mass party distinction was central to an explanation of the differences among Canadian political parties. Yet cadre–mass party differences are not a dominant theme in this discussion of how the parties finance that same electoral activity. Party structure seems to have a relatively limited impact on local riding associations' fund-raising activities. The hard realities of the country's economic geography, with the Ottawa River marking a powerful boundary, more often intrude as the salient and dominant forces. Regional differences clearly mark the interelection financial affairs of constituency associations, so it is not surprising that they again appear important when we come to the issue of election money. This is to say that organizational structure may give shape to much party activity, but that when money is at issue these structural differences give way to the economic realities of the environment within which the constituency associations operate.

Throughout this discussion of riding parties and election finance we discovered a number of issues on which there is limited partisan or regional difference. Constituency election financing may even be the subject on which there is most interassociation consensus on appropriate and effective practice, and the area in which the demand for reform is least sharp. It is not what one might have expected given the economic and financial inequalities that abound. What is particularly interesting is that this is perhaps the most comprehensively regulated aspect of Canadian party life. It suggests that working under a common regulatory framework has led the diverse set of constituency associations that make up the Canadian party system to operate in much the same way, and to recognize and accept the virtues of those common standards.

In earlier chapters, Canadian parties' individual constituency associations have been described as the units of a national franchise system, in which the local franchises are controlled and staffed by shifting sets of volunteers over whom the central office has limited influence and less authority. The national centre is further handicapped in its relationship with riding-level activity by being forced to have a local franchise in every constituency regardless of the support or demand for it. Thus, from this perspective, strong associations are relatively free to do as they wish, weak associations must be put up with. This is a powerful image. It provides a useful way of thinking about parties as groups of organized volunteers, and it helps shed light on how and why the parties operate as they do. It is, however, a model that emphasizes the particularistic character of a party's riding-level organizations and suggests that Canadian parties are, in the abstract, essentially little more than loosely linked groups of unevenly mobilized partisans.

The analysis of the channels of intraparty finance in this chapter takes us behind that image to reveal something of the golden threads that bind these constituency associations together at election time, arguably the one critical moment when an extraparliamentary party organization must come together and work effectively as a coherent unit. It emphasizes the common position but divergent interests of constituency associations in the matrix of financial relationships that supports the essential electoral activities of the parties.

Using this conceptualization, the Conservatives stand out as having the most distinctive national party. The other parties have a network of associations marked by something of a balance between the major types of associations, but the Conservative party comes closest to being a pure type. It has done so by establishing a party organization which prizes and maximizes local independence and so has a disproportionate number of its constituency associations in the autonomous mould. But, by its very nature, that structure minimizes the bonds between its constituency associations and other elements of the party. Rather ironically, that leads us back to the franchise model in which a party is defined by the sum of a set of individual local associations.

The national parties cannot be understood separately from their constituency associations. It is time to turn back and focus on the national parties, and consider what the analysis of their constituency associations has taught us about them.

9

A CONSTITUENCY-BASED PORTRAIT OF CANADIAN PARTIES

THE PORTRAIT of Canada's political parties that has emerged in the previous chapters indicates just how diverse they are as national organizations. Trying to describe them in terms of their constituency associations reminds one of the old fable of the blind people asked to describe the elephant. After touching only the tail, the tusk, the trunk, the legs or the ears, no one was able to provide much of an account of the beast. And so it is in our case. If we were to try and base a description of a Canadian party on this or that constituency association the result would not be a very satisfactory portrait. This is why party activists often provide contradictory accounts of the same party; many really only have first-hand experience of a small number of party associations.

Each of the national political parties has up to 295 constituency associations and, despite the fact that all of them are part of a common organization and subscribe to common principles and rules of operation, they vary enormously. Much of the analysis above has concerned itself with the range and nature of that variation, and what it tells us about the organization and operation of party politics in the constituencies. Some of that variation is purely local, reflecting the idiosyncrasies of history, personality or chance. Thus, a Liberal association suddenly invaded by a Frank Stronach, or the Quebec NDP one embraced by Paul "The Butcher" Vachon (Lee 1989, chaps. 6 and 7) is unlikely to be much like those in neighbouring ridings. Another part of the variation, however, reflects significant and enduring differences (often regional) engendered by the socio-economic and cultural cleavages that mark the Canadian electorate. The number of times the Ottawa River intruded as a significant boundary in our accounts of the parties is a powerful reminder of that. Of course institutional factors also generate and sustain some of the variation among local riding parties. Associations with incumbent MPs are an obvious example. This was particularly obvious in our analysis of NDP constituency organizations, though few could doubt that being in office as the governing party has transformed virtually all Conservative riding associations in Quebec over the past decade.

It is well to keep in mind that much of the organizational diversity within the major parties stems from their attempts to maintain local associations, and their practice of running candidates, in every constituency of the country whether or not they command much real support there. As we saw in chapter 2, none of the three principal parties was able to identify a local association in every riding in early 1991, and in the 1988 general election all of them had some riding parties that were so weak that their candidate failed to recover his or her deposit and obtain an election expense reimbursement. But Canadian parties persist in what appear to be often rather futile efforts, putting up with paper branches, because they define a serious national political party as one that offers itself (at least for election purposes) to the voters in all parts of the nation.

For all their diversity, constituency associations remain the basic organizational units of the extraparliamentary parties. Like jigsaw-puzzle pieces of many different shapes and colours, it is only when sorted out and put together that they reveal their pictures, in this case of Canada's national political parties. Our interest is not so much in any one of the hundreds of individual associations, despite the enormous amount that they disclose about grassroots political life in Canada, as in what they contribute to the overall picture we are able to assemble of the parties. Each of the parties structures itself in its own way, and each organizes its activity as it is able, but all reflect the sum of their many parts. This last chapter turns to these larger reflections to provide a constituency-based portrait of Canadian political parties.

THE CHANGING WORLD OF CANADIAN PARTIES

The organizational world that the parties and their constituency associations occupy has changed dramatically in the past two decades. It is not possible, or necessary, to describe all those changes here, but it is important to note some that are impinging on the local associations in major ways and in so doing are changing the nature, structure and behaviour of the parties.

The first is the election and party financing system established in the 1970s that has brought so much money into Canadian parties. They have gone from being poor to being relatively rich. As Stanbury

(1991, chap. 12) observes, over three-quarters of the Conservative and Liberal candidates, and almost 60 percent of the New Democrats, came out of the 1988 general election with a financial surplus. This suggests that money need not often be a significant obstacle for a competitively minded association or a viable party organization, though it must be admitted that for much of the 1980s the national Liberal party made it one by persistently spending more than it raised. Local associations, and the national parties they support, now have (or can raise) the money necessary to maintain much more active interelection organizations and to engage their members in an ongoing way. Ironically, however, that same money can also free a local party élite from dependence upon an active membership, for most of the tools of modern electoral organization and campaigning can now be purchased on the open market. Where that happens local organizations may be disparaged and could easily decay. At a minimum, the new financial world, and the communications technologies it can buy (see Axworthy 1991), may reduce the premium traditionally placed on large and active grassroots party memberships.

Paltiel's (1989) analysis of these developments in party financing led him to conclude that they have tightened the grip of the three big parties on the national party system, by strengthening their central organizations to the point of making them virtually unchallengeable. But the experience of the Reform and Christian Heritage parties in recent years casts some doubt on that proposition. Those two parties have been able to generate substantial resources (and, in Reform's case, a membership as well), using new fund raising technologies. With those resources they have become viable and lively organizations, able to reach big audiences through the electronic media of television and computer-driven personal mailings. Though the CHP's narrow appeal seems unlikely to win it many seats under the system's plurality electoral rules, Canadian electoral politics now seems more open to new participants than it has been for a generation.

Demands for greater participation in both electoral and party politics are also shifting the parties' world in significant and perhaps permanent ways. Canadian history is full of periods when social movements and/or interest groups have become especially politicized, and the recent decade seems another high point in that cyclical pattern. The pressure has come from a host of different directions and is being applied to the parties on several fronts simultaneously. At one level there is a call for parties that, with their candidates, will better reflect the diversity of the population they seek to represent. Groups such as women and visible minorities, whose politicization has been escalated by the country's new Charter politics, demand the opportunity to play a role in party politics that is commensurate with their numbers in the electorate. They do so irrespective of party or policy issues, calling on all the parties to transform themselves in ways that will ensure the full involvement of members of their group. Other groups, however, dedicated to a particular issue or cause, are content to penetrate individual units of a specific party in order to turn them to whatever short-term use suits their interests. Clear examples of that are to be seen in the 1990 Wappel national Liberal leadership campaign (described in chapter 5), or the anti-abortionists' local victory in the Perth–Wellington–Waterloo Liberal nomination contest described by Bell and Bolan (1991) in their study of electioneering in Ontario during 1988.

In still another fashion, interest groups, able to buy into the media of mass (public and private) communication, are now entering the electoral fray at both national and constituency levels as actors in their own right. In doing so they are invading the traditional turf of the parties and threatening the entire system of expense limitation designed to provide a level playing field for electoral competition. As table 7.19 demonstrated, half the constituency associations in the country reported that their campaign had had to cope with a single-issue group intervening actively in their local riding contest, for or against their local candidate. Coupled with popular cries for referendums and recall, these developments challenge the parties' long-standing dominance of electoral politics.

Traditional Responses

The principal responses to these changes have been the traditional ones of trying to interest and involve currently excluded groups, but only in order to co-opt them into the existing parties, and on the parties' own terms. That, for example, was the point of the controversial 1983 amendment to section 70.1 of the *Canada Elections Act* (subsequently ruled unconstitutional by the Court of Queen's Bench of Alberta in the midst of the 1984 general election) that sought to force any individual or group interested in engaging in electoral debate into doing so through one of the registered political parties or their candidates. Riding associations report that one of their most common interelection activities is an annual membership drive, and many claim they are now making special efforts to increase the participation of particular groups, such as women or visible minorities, in the central affairs of their party. But judging by the results described in earlier chapters, the parties have been slow to change the face they show the electorate.

Like most organizations, parties are more likely to commit themselves to a special effort to change their existing practice when they perceive some direct and immediate reason for doing so. Given that a large majority of Conservative (88 percent) and Liberal (81 percent) constituency association presidents agreed with the assertion that "Complaints about a lack of opportunities for women are exaggerated. They could easily get ahead in our riding if they just got more involved," one ought not to be too surprised if little change is occurring in the part played by women in those two parties. By contrast, only 27 percent of NDP association presidents supported that proposition. The majority of them believed instead that it was "harder for women in politics" and so the parties had to adopt special provisions "to ensure fair and equal opportunity." In light of this sharp difference one might predict that the NDP will be more successful than its two larger opponents in increasing the participation of women, though to date this has been truer of their candidates than of their riding party office holders.

Part of the difficulty Canadian parties have in changing in response to wider societal pressures stems from their decentralized, constituency-based character. Until local partisans are convinced that there is a problem it is difficult to get them to change, and the constituency-based character of the organization means that each constituency is often relatively free to decide the extent of the problem in its own area and how best to respond to it. Of course the national party officials can enforce rules on issues such as nominations (e.g., the NDP has moved toward gender quotas for its candidates in some units of the party), but local political realities are often more compelling in stimulating change. That is inherent in the imperatives of a territorially organized electoral system.

Figure 9.1 indicates that special efforts to increase the participation of previously excluded groups in local party affairs are driven by cold electoral calculation. Taking visible minorities as a case, it reveals the proportions of constituency associations that are making special efforts to involve them in their central activities. That number is greater where such groups "exist in significant numbers," and even greater again where such groups are perceived as having "become a factor in [the] constituency's politics." The figure also reveals that, of the three major parties, the Liberals are currently making the fewest special efforts to attract members of visible-minority communities. But if that is so, it must also be noted that the Liberals now have more such individuals holding executive positions in their riding parties than do either the Tories or the New Democrats. With more members of visible-minority communities making their way in Liberal associations, the party may simply feel under less pressure to make special efforts to woo those groups than do its principal opponents. That is consistent with an

Figure 9.1
Mobilizing and involving new participants: the case of visible minorities

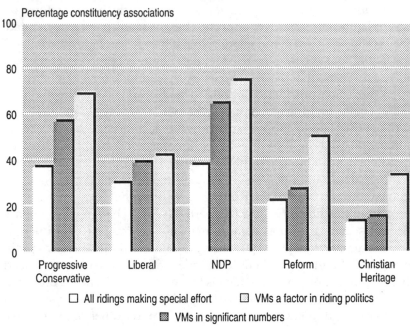

Percentage constituency associations

☐ All ridings making special effort   ▨ VMs a factor in riding politics

▨ VMs in significant numbers

VM = Visible minority

argument that perceived need and electoral self-interest remain the most powerful forces pushing parties to increase their attractiveness and openness to groups they do not now represent.

The Changing Parties

All these developments have taken their toll on the parties and the party system. Their vulnerability to penetration by interest groups has led to calls for more internal party regulation in an attempt to defend the parties against being used and manipulated by groups seeking to promote some special agenda. In some ways this has led to an opening up of the parties to increased membership participation, but in others the result has been a tightening of the rules and some closing of party processes.

The most dramatic, and potentially far-reaching, of the changes now opening up Canadian parties is the adoption of a leadership selection process in which every party member will have a direct vote for a leadership candidate. As we noted in chapter 5, a number of such systems have been used in various provincial parties (the Parti québécois in 1985 and 1988; the Prince Edward Island and Ontario Conservatives in 1990; the Ontario and Nova Scotia Liberals and the Alberta Conservatives in 1992), and the national Liberal party adopted one in early 1992 that will be used to choose future leaders. Not all of these systems have done away with conventions of constituency delegates completely, but they are bound to weaken traditional constituency-shaped strategies of party leadership and support management in favour of ones that focus on membership numbers. No matter what provisions parties may try to use to protect small constituencies (see Woolstencroft 1992, 220), those with large memberships will come to dominate. At the same time, however, those large memberships are no longer going to be forced to speak with one voice if there are no longer any winner-take-all constituency delegate selection battles.

Increased openness, which in this case means giving all members a leadership vote, is likely to lead to party contests assuming the qualities of mass politics, in which the salience of constituency organization and constituency-level activity is sharply reduced in favour of centralized professional machines. The danger to the national parties is that such a degradation of the local stage may leave individual party members feeling that they have less opportunity to make a difference, and that there is less point than ever to joining, building and participating in vibrant constituency association activity. Certainly the experience of the Ontario Conservative party points in this direction (Woolstencroft 1992), and similar pressures are likely to be even stronger in the more heterogeneous and less intimate setting of a national party. Given that the national parties' memberships are already low, and in the two major parties quite dependent upon local internal party competition, the growth of party-wide, unmediated contests poses a major challenge to the riding associations and to local participation in constituency party affairs.

Opening leadership contests to all members is one response to special interest penetration. The aim is to defeat it by diluting the impact of such groups and so giving them little incentive to move into or capture a party's constituency associations. But if the openness strategy can work for leadership contests, it obviously will not for nominations, where the local association has to name one individual as its electoral standard-bearer. Thus the parties are moving to close or limit the nomination process, either to protect their party from some external insurgency, or to push their local associations into some decision they might not otherwise take, or perhaps for both reasons. Both the Reform and Liberal parties have begun to institute stronger candidate-screening procedures, giving the central party more say in who the candidate may be. In the Liberal case, the application of these rules during nominations held in 1992 was partially directed toward protecting incumbent MPs. The New Democrats, on the other hand, are moving toward mechanisms that will promote a greater gender balance among their candidates. That involves central party strategists pushing riding associations to take decisions that the party must assume they would not otherwise make. What seems common to these changes is that they all appear to constrain local decision making, and in some cases to stifle local competition. Thus, like changes designed to open the parties, they too may threaten the vitality of constituency organizational life.

The parties are only just beginning to experiment with these changes to their structures and rules, so the question of what impact they will have on constituency associations is still an open one. But internal party changes have not been the only response to the changing environment. The party system itself is under challenge, and for the first time since the 1960s the three large parties find themselves facing a number of smaller parties all seeking to crowd onto the political stage.

Multiparty politics is not new to Canadians, though its incidence and impact have varied over our history. The most significant periods were in the years after World War I, and then again in the 1960s when five parties jockeyed in three successive minority Parliaments. As the party system enters the 1990s, Canadians may again be facing another period in which a number of new parties seek to play a significant part in the system. As in earlier periods, these new parties take distinct forms and approaches to politics, but they are also replaying some familiar Canadian party themes. Thus, among others, the Bloc québécois appears to be a classic example of a French-Canadian nationalist party, the Christian Heritage party a typical mass party pursuing a relatively narrow ideological agenda (reminiscent of early socialist or social credit parties), while the Reform Party, with its conservative socio-economic agenda coupled with a demand for political reform, echoes the western Progressive movement of the 1920s.

Having said all this, it is time to turn to the parties themselves, and to pull our data together, assembling our constituency-based portraits of the parties into a picture of the national political organizations they are.

CANADA'S POLITICAL PARTIES

Two New Parties

Both the Christian Heritage party and the Reform Party first contested a national general election in 1988. Both were relatively minor players in that election: the CHP won 0.8 percent of the national vote

(3.6 percent in the ridings where it ran), while Reform did better only by comparison, with 2.1 percent of the national vote (but 8.5 percent in the ridings it contested). Of the 135 candidates nominated by these two parties, only 11 Reformers (15 percent of their 72 nominees), and none of the CHP candidates, crossed the 15 percent vote-share threshold entitling them to an election expense reimbursement. This very newness means that both parties were still learning and developing a distinctive electoral style and set of practices which will undoubtedly change as the lessons of that campaign are assimilated. Thus our sketch of both these parties is necessarily more tentative, more time-bound than those of the established parties.

These two new parties are national organizations in the sense that they operate in the national party system and have no significant organizational entanglements with provincial-level parties. However, neither are nationwide parties. At the time of the 1988 general election, and even when this study was conducted in the spring of 1991, Reform was confining itself to the four western provinces. Though it has since begun to expand eastward, the party has no presence in Quebec and has made very little impact anywhere east of the Ottawa River. Similarly, the Christian Heritage party has made little impact in the eastern half of the country. In 1988 it was largely confined to Ontario and the two westernmost provinces, which together provided it with 90 percent of its support.

As new parties they are principally driven by ideas. In both cases their associations report that the persona of the local candidate has little impact on riding organization or party activity. And in both cases the absence of a set of incumbent MPs undoubtedly enhances the status and role of the extraparliamentary organization and the party members who operate it. The parties do differ in the breadth of their appeal: in the case of the CHP it is deliberately focused on the issues of traditional family values, while Reform has launched a broadside attack on the very operating norms and structure of the Canadian political system. The other significant difference here is that Reform's leader, Preston Manning, dominates his party like no other contemporary Canadian political leader, while the CHP's leader has no public visibility whatsoever. And Manning's appeal seems to have been an important factor in Reform Party growth. As Siegfried (1906, 136) said of Canadian party leaders four generations ago, his "mere name is a programme in itself."

For all their newness, there is one sense in which these two parties reflect old, long-established patterns in Canadian party life. Neither appears particularly responsive to the claims of groups, such as women or visible minorities, traditionally underrepresented in Canadian politics. Both parties are largely dominated by white males. This puts them at odds with one of the powerful pressures for increased inclusion and participation in modern Canadian society. Whatever their claims to a new politics, these parties' organizations suggest that one of the impulses driving them appears to be a reactionary response to new and changing political norms.

The Christian Heritage Party

The Christian Heritage party, rooted in a few pockets of English-speaking, Protestant Canada, is a small, stable, simple party. It is small not only in the sense that it has local associations in only about a fifth of the constituencies in the country, but also in that its associations typically have a smaller membership than those of any other national party. Since the kick-start provided by the 1988 general election, party membership has remained fairly stable and independent of the electoral cycle. Individual local associations appear to have a rather more volatile membership pattern, though their (comparative) rate of change is somewhat exaggerated by their small size. It is a simple party in that its associations are almost exclusively federal, independent of a provincial party and largely concerned with federal politics. They have comparatively few auxiliary organizations (and those only for youth), preferring to focus all their activity through the main constituency association. Despite this very modest organization, a large proportion of the party seems satisfied with the status quo. Forty percent of its associations report that they are making no special efforts to increase the participation of any identifiable group in their local riding party. That is hardly the sign of a party with a strong electoral vocation.

The party must have considerable difficulty getting its message out, for it has a relatively small income and possesses few financial or material assets. Not only does it have a comparatively high proportion (31 percent) of poor constituency associations, but it is the only party with no rich ones. Some of its organization is essentially a paper structure, though more often than not even its small, poor branches exhibit quite high levels of activity.

As one might expect of any new organization, Christian Heritage associations and members are busy with party affairs, reporting activity levels that are higher than for the three established parties. But despite its preoccupation with public policy, there appears to be less policy study in the CHP than in the other parties. Perhaps that is because the party is clear on where it stands, and is more concerned with propagating its views by holding public meetings and publishing newsletters than with debating the fine points of its policies. The party seems especially enamoured of direct mail, both as a fund-raising and an electioneering device. This is a technique it may well have picked up from the interest groups whose focus, and views, on abortion the CHP shares.

The party is policy-driven. Its campaigns attract volunteers and contributors because of its policy commitments, not because of the candidates who are espousing them, and the campaigns themselves are largely defined in terms of the CHP's policy orientation. In an important sense one might describe the party as an interest group that has decided to enter the world of party politics, making only as many concessions to the form of a political party as are necessary to do so. This may be why comparatively few CHP candidates (in 1988) found their campaigns attacked or supported by single-issue interests. Right-to-life groups knew they did not need to intervene in constituencies where the CHP was effectively doing their job for them.

Whether an interest group can long sustain its own political party in the Canadian system remains to be seen. Our constituency-based portrait suggests that the CHP is little more than that, and there is little to its organization or operation that indicates it will, or even wants to, grow into something larger.

The Reform Party

Of all the parties whose portraits we have been assembling in this study, that of the Reform Party of Canada seems the most unsatisfactory, or at least the most incomplete. It is as if they keep creating new pieces for the puzzle while we are attempting to piece it together. This is because Reform appears to be a classic flash party, and was still in its take-off stage when the data were collected. How large the party will grow, and what will become of it when its growth stops, are questions yet to be answered. It seems likely that these answers will emerge only after the party has gone through another general election. Our account of Reform must be seen as a portrait of a flash party during its initial critical period of explosive membership growth and organizational expansion.

By the spring of 1991 the Reform Party was mobilizing large numbers in the four western provinces where it was organizing. No other national party was growing at anything like the same overall rate as Reform, though, to put its success in perspective, it must be noted that both Liberal and NDP 1990 memberships were higher in that region. The (temporary) Liberal boom was driven by its leadership contest that year, while the NDP's membership was underpinned by strong provincial parties preparing for provincial elections. The Reform Party's organization is far simpler than those of its opponents: it eschews any connection to provincial-level organizations and few local associations have any associated branches into which its members' activity or resources might get diverted.

By all our measures, the Reform Party is the most active one in the country. Its associations do more things, and do them more often, than those of any other political party. Reform's membership is fully occupied with politics and party, working more at organizational maintenance, policy discussion, communication and campaign planning than anyone else. It obviously has an involved and committed membership: there is more internal party competition for (less subsidized) delegate positions at party meetings than in any of the other Canadian parties. This is the portrait of a party with an active, involved mass membership concerned with changing the nation's policy agenda, and is reminiscent of accounts of the early CCF (Young 1969) or some of the farmers' movements that rose and fell in the 1920s (Morton 1950). It is not typical of the long-serving established Canadian parties, and one wonders how long Reform can sustain this atypically high level of activity.

These large, active memberships have also provided the party with money. Its organizations have high incomes and comparatively large financial resources at their disposal, but it is also true that they work hardest at fund-raising. And its policy orientation pervades its fund-raising, for Reform ties policy-focused events to fund-raising activities far more frequently than do other parties. The result is that the party has the highest proportion of rich constituency associations, and the lowest of poor ones, of any of the five parties in this study. Well known for its scolding admonitions on the state of public finances, the party appears to practice what it preaches: more of its local associations live within their means than is true of any other party. It is also the only party that is not maintaining some paper branches in order to sustain a nominal presence in some constituencies.

The election campaign the party fought in 1988 gave every evidence of being a rather traditional grassroots protest effort. It was constituency-driven, with campaign teams made up of local volunteers and amateurs attracted principally by the party's policies rather than its candidates. Though the party's campaign organizations reported large shortages of volunteers in 1988, that actually reflects their more ambitious definition of what is needed to run an effective local campaign. The party seems to have mobilized a larger proportion of its members to work in that election than was true of its opponents. If it can maintain that pattern, its now much larger membership ought to give it a particularly strong constituency campaign apparatus. However, it is also true that Reform's capacity to draw volunteers to its campaign depended far more on the appeal of its leader than was true of the other parties. This suggests that the party organization has yet to establish whether its electoral machine is truly independent of Mr. Manning's appeal and has an institutional capacity in its own right.

This puzzle of the Reform Party reminds us that if the CHP is an interest group in party politics, then it is also true that Reform remains a protest movement struggling to transform itself into a political party. Canada has a fair amount of experience with just such politics, and it is clear that there is no simple or single outcome. Some western movements (e.g., the Progressives) peaked and then quickly declined, others (e.g., Social Credit) turned themselves into quite traditional cadre-style parties with a limited, regional electoral base, while still others (e.g., the CCF) ended as "a protest movement becalmed" (Zakuta 1964). Of course it is also possible that Reform might end up as either a major cadre or mass party playing a principal part in the national party system. Unfortunately, this study's data cannot tell us to which of these ends the Reform Party is in the process of moving.

The Three Established National Parties

Since the emergence of the third Canadian party system in the early 1960s, the Liberal, Progressive Conservative and New Democratic parties have all had to struggle to maintain national party organizations amidst uneven and uncertain competitive pressures. At least until the mid-1980s, none of them could really be said to have a genuinely national organization and membership, and until then none was able to win two majority victories in succession. The Liberals dominated the system for two decades, but nothing like in the previous period when they could rightly be described as "the Government Party" (Whitaker 1977). After 1984, the Conservatives reasserted their claim to national status in the most unexpected way: they won consecutive majorities in Quebec for the first time since Sir John A. Macdonald's 1882 and 1887 victories there a century earlier. During this same period the New Democrats oscillated between fearing they faced annihilation (Morley 1988) and thinking they were about to replace the Liberals and emerge as Canada's second party (Fraser 1989, 224–26).

These turbulent years have seen all three parties build and rebuild their organizations. For all the change that this has entailed, and the competitive incentives leading each to develop an "electoral-professional" structure (Panebianco 1988, 262–67), there remain some basic organizational differences between the New Democratic Party, with its mass-party origins and norms, and the Conservatives and Liberals, who continue to reflect their origins as cadre-style parties.

The New Democratic Party

The New Democrats have created a complex party organization in which both federal and provincial structures are intertwined in all provinces except Quebec. This interpenetration of their organizational units reaches down to the constituency level, so that only a minority of its local associations consider themselves concerned solely with federal politics. Morley (1991) and Stanbury (1991) have described something of the Byzantine complexity of the party's internal financing, and it is clear from the data in this study that few of its associations are financially autonomous, either between or during election periods. This increases the interdependency of all parts of the party, but probably also makes it easier to insist on a stricter adherence to nationally defined procedures and rules, even in matters traditionally thought the business of local members and constituency associations.

As a party with a mass membership tradition, the NDP has a very stable membership base that appears relatively impervious to the impulses of the electoral cycle. This is true whether the impulse is provided by internal party competition or by a general election. The party has little experience of the membership disruptions, common to its two larger opponents, that are caused by campaigns to mobilize new groups of supporters around nomination or leadership contests. Given that NDP memberships are, by and large, smaller than those in either the Liberal or Conservative parties, this means that the party is effectively forgoing opportunities to expand its organizational base in the interest of maintaining a coherent definition of membership and a stable core of local activists.

Despite the NDP's oft-declared dedication to the norms and forms of internal party democracy, rather little of it (at least as indicated by an electoral contest) characterizes the party's organizational life. Morley (1992) describes NDP national leadership politics in terms of a coronation, and our portrait reveals that contests are also the exception, rather than the norm, at most other levels of the party. There is little competition for party nominations, and even less for delegate positions at national policy and leadership conventions. But then the party does not make it easy for its members to get involved in partywide activity, for it provides less financial support for such activity than do the other two national parties. As we have noted, this is ultimately a conservative force. It works to maintain party membership at a low, steady level, which in turn helps to perpetuate the party's oligarchic ruling élite.

Mass parties are generally distinguished not only by more formal, structured membership requirements and obligations, but also by higher levels of involvement and activity by their members. On this score, like that of internal party competition, the NDP departs from the model, and from the popular image it has promoted of itself. Its local associations are generally less busy and, in their ongoing operations, they have a less diversified round of activities than do those of the other parties. The NDP has always believed that its political activity is particularly important and must be distinguished from that of its opponents by the special emphasis it gives to the serious discussion and development of public policy positions. But this too seems to be contradicted by the constituency-based portrait of the party. The NDP's membership does not regularly engage in more policy study than other parties, and it appears to do less than both the Conservative and the Reform organizations.

The NDP's small, stable memberships and comparatively low levels of activity mean that a good deal of its organization is poor. And despite the high levels of organizational integration, there is little top-down subsidization of weak branches. The result is that the party does not really possess a genuinely national working organization: about half of the party's formal constituency structure has little presence in the real world of political life in the ridings. The party maintains this essentially nominal organization so that it has at least some framework in which to run candidates in every riding of the country during a general election. That is, however, largely a grandiose gesture designed to persuade Canadians that the party is a national actor. In fact, without a real organization for support in many constituencies, over two-fifths (43 percent) of all the NDP candidates in 1988 did not even reach the 15-percent vote threshold required to save their election deposit.

This organizational weakness, along with the party's general predilection for state regulation, provides some of the explanation for its enthusiasm for increased public funding of political parties and their election campaigns, and for tighter limitations on party and election spending. Both would help overcome the disadvantages resulting from the party's comparative organizational weakness. It might also be noted that the party's integrated structure, when coupled with the limited capacity for local resistance implicit in weak riding associations, leaves the NDP better able to push change throughout its organization when it is determined to do so. The best example of that is to be seen in the party's openness to increasing the participation of women, and particularly in getting more of them nominated as election candidates.

NDP campaign organization stands out from that in the two large cadre parties. A significant number of the constituency parties resist having campaign teams dominated by their candidates, and so retain some organizational ties to, and responsibility for, the local campaign machine. The NDP is more prone to use professional campaign organizers and managers, often brought from outside the riding, in areas that it has targeted for success. But at the same time, the party's standard campaign practice continues to rely heavily on traditional approaches such as a volunteer canvass. Campaign volunteers appear to be attracted more to serve the party than to support a local candidate, and a significant proportion are regular financial contributors to their constituency association.

Any simple sketch of the New Democratic Party, like the one we have been drawing here, is ultimately unsatisfactory and in some respects may be misleading. The very fact that we need to refer to the real and paper parts of its organization implies as much. Throughout the study we have continually noted that there are dramatic regional variations in the party's organizational character (which help mark the boundaries of the paper NDP), and that the presence of an incumbent MP makes a significant difference to the vitality of NDP constituency organization. Taking region and incumbency as defining characteristics, there are, in an important and very real sense, three distinctly different NDPs.

East of the Ottawa River, in Quebec and the four Atlantic provinces, the national party can hardly be said to exist. As table 9.1 indicates, in the eastern end of the country the party has a tiny membership, inactive associations, no money and little clout in national decision-

Table 9.1
Three faces of the NDP
(constituency associations)

	West of Ottawa River		East of Ottawa River
	Incumbent	No incumbent	
1990 membership (median)	1 600	331	50
Convention delegate allotment (median)	18	5	1
Activity level (%)			
Very active	25	14	5
Inactive	—	12	45
Contributor:member ratio (median)	1.0	0.25	0.19
1990 association income (%)			
< $1 000	8	38	91
> $10 000	33	7	—
Funds currently available (%)			
< $1 000	14	43	87
> $10 000	14	4	—
Paper branches (%)	12	39	95

making. This is where 95 percent of the constituency-level organization can best be classified as a paper structure. This organizational feebleness mirrors, and presumably helps perpetuate, the party's electoral weakness in the area. In the 1988 general election it did not win one of the 107 seats in the five provinces, and in two of them (New Brunswick and Prince Edward Island) did not manage to save its deposit in a single constituency.

At the other end of the party spectrum are the NDP organizations west of the Ottawa River headed by incumbent MPs. This part of the party is particularly rooted in Saskatchewan and British Columbia, the two provinces where it won over half its seats in 1988, and where it is built upon strong provincial party machines. This is clearly a radically different organizational world. The associations are thirty times larger, far more active and relatively affluent. These are the associations that bring the big battalions of delegates to party conventions and are able to dominate policy making and leadership choice (Archer 1991).

In between these two organizational faces of the party lies a middle ground where the NDP is a relevant part of the party system but has not been able to use the advantages of incumbency to build a significant organization. Memberships are modest, local activity is still quite low for a party that prides itself on involving its supporters, and party income is correspondingly limited. Though other parties are also often weaker in areas where they do not hold a seat, this gap is abnormally large in the NDP. The party's significant weakness in these ridings, where it must advance if it is ever to remodel the party system, is revealed by the fact that fully 39 percent of its organization there is made up of paper associations.

Other Canadian political parties have a good deal of internal organizational variation, but these very large differences in the NDP, tied as they are to sociogeographic cleavages and institutional imperatives, make it impossible for the party to operate as a genuinely national party. Its capacity to campaign in the constituencies and to engage all Canadians at election time is limited, and thus fundamentally different from that of the two old cadre parties. Our constituency portrait makes clear that the New Democratic Party, like the CCF before it, does not have a nationwide organization: it remains, in many ways, a profoundly regional party dressed up in national clothing.

The Two Traditional Governing Parties

Only the Liberal and Progressive Conservative parties have ever had enough support to form a Canadian government. Their origins can be traced to the parliamentary coalitions of 19th-century British North America (Stewart 1986), when their local organizations were shaped by the parochial demands of a constituency-focused politics fuelled by patronage. The early national parties, centred on the parliamentary caucuses, were the very model of cadre parties – transient (but recurring) electoral machines tied to constituency notables. And a century later, though now attired in the formal membership structures and internal democratic accountability of mass parties, the Liberal and Conservative organizations continue to bear witness to their cadre-style heritage.

The parties have unstable membership patterns that are defined by, and driven by, the electoral cycle. Party memberships atrophy between elections, when local associations are primarily concerned with basic organizational maintenance and social activities, but then grow rapidly when the pressures of an electoral contest give candidates an incentive to mobilize their followers. These bursts of membership growth and activity centre on contests for both public office and party positions such as nominee or leadership convention delegate. The timing, frequency and intensity of internal party contests varies considerably between the parties, and from riding to riding, which adds to the irregular and volatile character of their memberships.

There is another important sense in which these parties' memberships and organizations are fluid and volatile. Given that contests in cadre parties are heavily defined in terms of the candidates involved, this means that the membership waves stimulated by successive contests often contain a large proportion of individuals who were not part of the previous wave, and may not be part of the next. Thus about two-thirds of the Liberal and Conservative organizations believed that if they ran a different candidate they would have a different set of volunteers to work with.

The two cadre parties have a wider array of affiliated branches for groups such as youth, women or ethnic communities than do the other parties in the system. While some of these organizations may be a hangover from an earlier period when they served to keep those individuals out of the main affairs of the local and national party, they are also a logical response to the challenge of attracting, involving and holding more people in a system characterized by fairly high levels of membership instability. It may be this very uncertainty that contributes to the relatively high (compared to the NDP) levels of activity in a typical Liberal or Conservative constituency association.

This more casual, or open, approach to membership is coupled with lower membership fees so that Conservative and Liberal associations cannot live on their membership fee income and are dependent upon other local fund-raising activities. Few get regular financial help from their national parties, and many of them make regular contributions to national party funds.

The parties' organizational bases are clearly tied to the parochial and immediate electoral interests of the constituencies' political notables; they depend upon drawing in local short-term volunteers in order to operate; and they are largely financially independent of the party centres. Thus it is not surprising that a good deal of organizational decision making on issues such as candidate selection or local campaign management is very decentralized. Where one of these parties is able to convince itself that it has an overriding interest in establishing some national rules or standards, it has generally been able to establish them. That has obviously been the case in the area of leadership selection, though even there the parties have been more successful in regulating delegate selection than candidate spending. But where the local associations are not convinced of the need for a partywide rule, they seem resistant to change. This has been most obvious with nominations: the clearest example being their failure to increase the numbers of women candidates. Though both the Progressive Conservative and Liberal national party leaderships have publicly called for it, the message is either not being received, or not being taken seriously, in the constituencies. Local partisans do not want to surrender control of that process. As far as they are concerned it is about far more than the identity of a particular candidate: as one of the central mechanisms for attracting activists and building a local organization, it regulates the very lifeblood of their constituency party.

At election time, the formal party apparatus tends to fade into the background as the candidate-centred imperatives of these cadre parties assert themselves. Local campaign organizations are set up by the candidate and left to run the local party campaign pretty much as they choose. This means that responsibility for the tasks of building a campaign team, attracting volunteers and raising money to finance the campaign falls heavily on the shoulders of the candidate. To succeed in these parties, candidates need to be independent political entrepreneurs who know and understand their constituencies and their support base. And their success ultimately works to perpetuate the cadre-style cast of the two old parties.

Some of the differences we have observed between the Liberal and Progressive Conservative parties in this study simply reflect their differing positions in terms of the electoral cycles that are so critical to their organizations. For instance, the Liberals lost office in 1984 and so inevitably had fewer incumbents for the 1988 cycle. But fewer incumbents meant more open nominations to contest, and more move-ment into, and out of, the party around those contests. That, plus the party's 1990 leadership contest, itself stimulated by the results of the 1988 general election, left the party with a large but quite unstable mem-bership in recent years. And as we noted in chapter 5, in cases where this membership volatility was too large it sometimes became dys-functional for constituency associations unable to manage it. On the other hand, Conservative success has also changed that party. The median Conservative association was bigger in Quebec than in any of the other regions over the four years around the 1988 general election. It was also bigger than the typical Liberal organization in that province during the same period. This is surely the first time in this century for which this has been true, and it flows from the Conservative party's 1983 leadership contest (Graham 1986, 157–58 reports that Quebec Conservative membership jumped from 5 to 30 thousand then) and the subsequent electoral mobilization for the 1984 election. Had the Conservatives lost the election, many of those instant members would have disappeared as quickly as they had appeared.

Not all the differences between the two parties are a result of their current electoral position. Within their common tradition of a broad, electorally oriented cadre organization, the Conservatives and Liberals have taken distinctive approaches to building and maintaining a national political party.

The Liberal Party

The Liberal Party of Canada is now a complex semifederal organiza-tion whose basic structure varies across the country. In four provinces (British Columbia, Alberta, Ontario and Quebec) the party has severed its formal links to the provincial Liberal party, so that members and constituency associations there are tied directly to the national party. In the other six provinces, members join the Liberal Party of Canada only by becoming a member of the provincial Liberal party and so inevitably local organizational fortunes are tied much more directly to provincial politics in those provinces. Thus, about half the federal Liberal con-stituency associations report that their membership is held jointly with a provincial party and a good proportion of their time and effort is spent on provincial political affairs.

This intermingling of the federal and provincial parties undoubt-edly affects party memberships. It is probably no accident that Liberal memberships were extraordinarily high in Atlantic Canada at the time of the study, for the party was particularly strong and in office in three of the provinces in the region. But this means that the party's organization is subject to the vagaries of two electoral cycles (the national and the provincial) in provinces where the old federated structure persists. Though the national constituency associations may have benefited from this in recent years, they can also suffer when those provincial parties are at the low points of their cycle, or when federal-provincial tensions aggravate party members' divided loyalties (Black 1965).

From the top of the party right down into the constituency associations, money continues to be a problem for the Liberal party. It has twice as many poor associations as rich ones. A low proportion of its members appear to be regular contributors and, as a result, its associations have limited financial resources and are often not able to support their members' participation in the wider affairs and meetings of the party.

The combination of these two factors, a more intertwined structure and penury, has produced a party organization that is more interdependent than that of the Conservative party. Between elections, Liberal local associations are more likely (than PC ones) to be involved in a network of intraparty transfers, and at election time a far smaller proportion of their campaign teams are financially autonomous. More Liberal associations report that they share their direct mail list with their national office, and the central party plays a greater role in decisions about campaign surplus disposal as well, confiscating a portion of the expense reimbursement that the state provides to local candidates.

Finally, it might be noted that the Liberal party appears more willing to change. They are more prepared than the Tories to admit more state regulation of party activity, and they have moved far more aggressively to regulate the excesses of their decentralized, open nomination process and to transform the leadership selection process. But it is easier for the Liberal party to make these changes, whose general thrust (standardizing party processes and increasing central control) is to reduce local association autonomy, for that autonomy is not as important an element of their organizational style as it is in the Conservative party. It is also true that being in opposition both provides a cadre party with greater incentive to change, and makes it easier to do so.

The Progressive Conservative Party

The Conservatives have a simple, classic cadre-party structure. Their constituency associations are tied directly to the national party centre and are more sharply focused on national political activity than are those of either the New Democrats or Liberals. Activity levels in the party are high, and most associations provide financial support to members who are representing their riding at party meetings and conventions outside the constituency.

At the same time the Conservatives expect their local associations to be as autonomous, independent and self-sufficient as possible. Between elections, the national party leaves them to manage their own finances, neither providing help to, nor extracting resources from, most constituency parties. The riding associations have responded by developing strong systematic fund-raising programs of their own and resist sharing their mailing lists even with the central party. By the end of the 1980s this emphasis on local autarky had left most of the party organization comparatively well off: rich associations outnumbered poor ones by three to one.

The same pattern persists during elections. During the 1988 general election about half the party's associations reported that they ran a financially autonomous campaign, and few reported giving up their local expense reimbursement to the national party. As one might expect of such a decentralized approach to constituency election financing, this makes the persona of the local candidate an important factor in fund-raising, and strengthens the candidate-centred dynamic that animates the party organization.

But Tories are not simply preoccupied with winning elections. Their associations are typically busier, with more kinds of activities, than those of the other two major parties. And of the three large parties it is the Conservatives that report engaging in the most policy study, both for its own sake but also as part of its regular fund-raising projects.

Aside from all their deliberate efforts to build a stable, self-sufficient party, it is important also to recognize that the Conservatives have had the benefit of being in government since 1984. For a cadre party that is a distinct advantage. It attracts supporters and money around a core of established incumbents, while minimizing the amount of internal party conflict associated with efforts to mobilize new members and nominate candidates. As the example of the Liberal party (particularly in its traditional fortress of Quebec, where almost half its branches are now paper) reveals, however, this can prove a feeble foundation; cadre party structures can quickly atrophy. And the history of the party would suggest that in defeat it could quickly turn on itself in a bout of destructive internecine conflict (Perlin 1980). Thus the next change of government will prove an important test of the Conservative's model of party building and reveal whether it can withstand the winds of electoral adversity when they inevitably blow.

THE SUCCESS OF CONSTITUENCY-BASED PARTIES

Canadian parties have always been deeply embedded in the constituencies. National parties and their local associations have what might be best described as a symbiotic relationship, and any important changes in the electoral system will quickly work their logic out through the parties. In the absence of such developments, the parties naturally resist structural or organizational changes that threaten, or promise, to alter their character. Despite the centralizing and nationalizing pressures of contemporary Canadian society and its politics, which are putting considerable strain on the parties, the very decentralized and relatively autonomous character of their basic constituency-level organizations has proved an anchor against easy or rapid change.

This local independence has been the great strength of Canadian parties which, after all, predate the state and have been a central agent in its transformation from an uncertain federation of four small rural colonies into a modern urban society of ten provinces and two territories stretched across a continent. The constituency-structured parties are among the oldest and most successful institutions of our society. The differences within parties testify to their capacity to respond to the enormous variation across Canadian society. The differences among them testify to the creative ways in which Canadians have adapted them to distinctive political visions. Their capacity to modernize themselves over time testifies to their inherent organizational flexibility. Their endurance testifies to their capacity to meet the needs of the political class that manages the political system as well as serve the political interests of ordinary Canadians.

No one forces Canadians to join national political parties or can keep them active when their interest wanes. But it is the local constituency associations that provide most Canadians with the options of "exit, voice or loyalty" in their world of democratic electoral politics. Canadian constituency associations are therefore only as varied as the people and communities that they serve, and Canadian political parties only as varied as the constituency associations they build and sustain.

APPENDIX

CONSTITUENCY PARTY ASSOCIATION ORGANIZATION AND ACTIVITY
A Survey on Practice and Reform

SECTION A: THE ORGANIZATION OF THE ELECTORAL PROCESS

This first set of questions is about enumeration and election organization at the constituency level.

Enumeration Practice
The Royal Commission has heard complaints about the current enumeration system. It would like to know what the experience in your constituency was in the 1988 general election. (Please check the appropriate response.)

1. How would you characterize the enumeration process in your riding?

   a) ☐ Worked well, no significant problems
   b) ☐ Some minor problems we could deal with
   c) ☐ Major problems that need to be addressed
   d) ☐ A real mess, the system needs a complete overhaul

   If you answered (a) please skip to question 8.
   If (b), (c) or (d) please answer questions 2 through 7.

2. There were problems with the enumeration in

   ☐ Only a few polls
   ☐ 10 to 25% of the polls
   ☐ 25 to 50% of the polls
   ☐ More than half the polls

3. What proportion of electors appear to have been left off the preliminary voters list?

   ☐ Less than 5%
   ☐ 5% to 10%
   ☐ More than 10%
   ☐ Don't know

4. After revision, what proportion of potential electors appear to have been on the final voters list?

   ☐ 98% or more
   ☐ 95% to 98%
   ☐ 90% to 95%
   ☐ Less than 90%
   ☐ Don't know

5. How many complaints would you say your local campaign received about enumeration during the 1988 election?

   ☐ A few
   ☐ Between 25 and 100
   ☐ 100 to 300
   ☐ We were swamped

6. Did complaints generally relate to individuals left off the voters list or to groups/areas in which numbers of people were left off?

   ☐ Mostly individuals
   ☐ Mainly groups or areas omitted
   ☐ Both

7. To what extent could the problems have been solved if voters had been allowed to get on the list up to a day or two before election day? Could you have solved:

   ☐ All enumeration problems
   ☐ Most of them
   ☐ Some of them
   ☐ A few of them

8. Was your local association responsible for providing lists of enumerators to the returning officer in 1988?

   ☐ Yes ☐ No

   If no, please skip to question 13.
   If yes, were you able to:

   ☐ Provide enough names easily
   ☐ Barely managed to name required number
   ☐ Not able to find enough enumerators

9. If finding enough enumerators was difficult, why was that? (Please check as many as applicable.)

    ❏ They are not paid enough
    ❏ People won't go door-to-door in parts of the constituency
    ❏ People won't go out at night
    ❏ Usual enumerators now have full-time jobs
    ❏ Other _____(please specify)

10. What proportion of the individuals you recommended as enumerators later worked in the local party campaign?

    ❏ Most
    ❏ Some
    ❏ A few
    ❏ None

11. How important were these people to the local campaign?

    ❏ Very important
    ❏ Somewhat important
    ❏ Not too important
    ❏ Unimportant

    What proportion of your volunteers would they have made up? _____ %

12. How many of the individuals you recommended contributed some of their enumeration income to the local campaign?

    ❏ Most
    ❏ Some
    ❏ A few
    ❏ None

13. The two largest parties in a riding now have the right to name enumerators. Do you think that privilege is:

    ❏ An advantage for their campaigns
    ❏ More hassle than it is worth
    ❏ A disadvantage because it ties up people who would otherwise work in the campaign
    ❏ Don't know

14.   In 1987, how was your constituency altered by the boundary
         revisions of that year?

    ❏   Major disruption, virtually a new riding
    ❏   Large changes
    ❏   Limited change
    ❏   No significant alteration

Options for Reform

The Royal Commission heard many proposals for reform. Please tell us what
you think of these proposals by indicating one of the following opinions:

    1. Strongly favour
    2. Somewhat favour
    3. Somewhat oppose
    4. Strongly oppose

Enumeration: The Voters List

1.   Allow unenumerated electors to register to vote at the
        polls on election day if they produce adequate ID.   _____
2.   Returning officers should be given full control of
        recruiting enumerators, independently of the parties.   _____
3.   *All* registered parties in a riding should be allowed
        to submit names of enumerators.   _____
4.   Enumerators should not have to live in the riding,
        though priority should be given to riding residents.   _____
5.   Young people, aged 16 and 17, should be allowed to
        work as enumerators.   _____
6.   Adopt a permanent voters list system (which may
        cost more but allow for a shorter campaign).   _____

Election Officials

7.   Allow Elections Canada to appoint returning officers
        without requiring nomination by the local MP or the
        party in power.   _____
8.   Returning officers should work on a paid, part-time basis
        between elections to promote the electoral process and
        maintain contact with different groups and areas within
        the constituency.   _____
9.   Returning officers should not be allowed to recruit
        deputy returning officers and poll clerks for election
        day without nominations from the parties.   _____
10.   Young people, aged 16 and 17, should be allowed to
        work as poll clerks.   _____

Advance and Absentee Voting

11.   Replace proxy votes with a mail ballot for those
        who need it.   _____

Voting Process and Voting Hours

12.   Move election day from Monday to Sunday.   _____
13.   How do you think *most voters* in your constituency
        would react to moving election day to a Sunday?   _____

Voters with Special Needs

14.   Elections Canada should carry out special programs to
        assist the homeless in being enumerated and in exer-
        cising their vote.   _____
15.   To assist people with reading or language difficulties,
        the ballot should include a party logo with each
        candidate's name.   _____
16.   In a polling district where a significant number of
        people frequently use a language other than English or
        French, posters and other election material should be
        in that language in addition to English and French.   _____
17.   People who are too sick to get out to vote should be
        able to request a mobile poll come to their home in the
        week before the election.   _____

SECTION B: CONSTITUENCY ASSOCIATION ORGANIZATION AND ACTIVITY

Your Constituency Association

1.   How would you describe the level of activity of your association?

        ❏   Very active, something happening every month
        ❏   Moderately active, at least several events a year
        ❏   Quiet, meets only for annual meetings, nominations, etc.
        ❏   Inactive, meets very infrequently between elections

2.   How many individuals are on the executive? _____

3.   How often does the executive meet?

        ❏   At least once a month
        ❏   At least four times a year
        ❏   At least once a year
        ❏   Irregularly, as necessary
        ❏   Other_____ (please specify)

4.   How often does the full membership meet?

        _____

5. Would you say there is a "core group" in your riding that does most of the work between elections?

    ☐ Yes   ☐ No

    If yes, how big is it? _____

6. How long has the current local association president held that office?

    _____ years

7. Could you tell us what the size of your constituency party membership was in the following years?

    1990 _____   1988 _____
    1989 _____   1987 _____

    If there were any sudden changes in these years, how would you explain them?

    _____

8. Of your current membership what proportion are:

    _____ % Women
    _____ % Visible minorities

9. Please indicate which, if any, of the following have separate branches attached to the constituency association. (Please check all applicable groups.)

    ☐   Women
    ☐   Youth
    ☐   Ethnic groups
    ☐   Other_____ (please specify)

10. How many individuals contributed financially to your local association in:

    1990   _____
    1989   _____
    1988   _____

11.   Does your constituency association have any paid staff (separate from an MP's constituency office)?

☐   Yes   ☐   No

12.   If your party holds the riding, does the constituency association use the MP's office for association business?

☐   Regularly
☐   Often
☐   Occasionally
☐   Never
☐   Not applicable

13.   Is your local association executive concerned with:

☐   Federal politics exclusively
☐   Mainly federal politics but sometimes provincial affairs
☐   Federal and provincial politics equally
☐   Mainly provincial politics but sometimes federal affairs

14.   Is your local association involved in municipal politics?

☐ Yes   ☐ No

15.   Is the association's membership:

☐   Exclusively federal
☐   Joint with the provincial party
☐   Our association has no "formal" membership

16.   What is your local association's annual membership fee?

$ _____

17.   Between elections, which of the following activities are carried out, at least once a year, by the local association? (Please check as many as applicable.)

☐   Support work for MP or local candidate
☐   Social events
☐   Fund-raising
☐   Policy study and development
☐   Campaign planning
☐   Publishing newsletters
☐   Conduct local polling

❑ Arrange public meetings
❑ Appear on local or cable television
❑ Membership campaign
❑ Other _____ (please specify)

Which of the above would you rank as the three most important?

1. _____
2. _____
3. _____

18. In recent experience in your constituency association, how would you characterize:

Federal candidate nominations

❑ Source of local conflict
❑ Competitive
❑ No competition
❑ A chore to find a candidate

Delegate selection to leadership convention

❑ Source of local conflict
❑ Competitive
❑ No competition
❑ A chore to find delegates
❑ No recent experience

Delegate selection to regular party convention

❑ Source of local conflict
❑ Competitive
❑ No competition
❑ A chore to find delegates
❑ No recent experience

Options for Reform
Which of the statements in the following pairs comes closest to representing your opinion? (Please check the appropriate response.)

1. ❑ Political parties should be free to regulate their internal affairs by their own rules, as they think best.
OR
❑ Political parties have important public responsibilities and their internal affairs should be subject to at least partial regulation by public law.

2.   ❐   Constituency associations should have the right to issue tax receipts for financial contributions.

OR

       ❐   The right to issue tax receipts must remain with the national party to prevent abuses.

3.   ❐   Constituency associations should register with Elections Canada and be obliged to provide an annual report of their financial activities.

OR

       ❐   Constituency associations should remain unregistered and governed only by their party's constitution.

SECTION C: NOMINATIONS AND LEADERSHIP SELECTION

Current Local Practice

1.   Does your constituency association have a regular candidate search committee?

    ❐ Yes   ❐ No

2.   Does the core group of the association pretty well decide among themselves on who the candidate ought to be, then work to get that individual nominated?

    ❐ Yes   ❐ No

3.   Have any special efforts been made to recruit women candidates by your association?

    ❐ Yes   ❐ No

4.   How long do supporters need to be party members to vote in your constituency association's nomination meetings?

    ❐   A week or less
    ❐   One–two weeks
    ❐   Two weeks–one month
    ❐   A month or more

5.   Does your association have formal rules governing spending on nomination campaigns?

    ❐ Yes   ❐ No

6.   Would you say that excessive nomination spending in your riding association has been:

❑   A major problem
❑   Something that needs to be watched
❑   Not an issue

7.   What has been the experience with recruiting "instant members" in your association for *nominations?*

❑   Positive, it increases our membership
❑   Negative, it is very disruptive of the association
❑   It has not happened in our constituency association

8.   What has been the experience with recruiting "instant members" in your association for *leadership convention delegate selection meetings?*

❑   Positive, it increases our membership
❑   Negative, it is very disruptive of the association
❑   It has not happened in our constituency association

9.   How many individuals sought the nomination in your constituency association for the 1988 general election?

❑   One, it was an acclamation
❑   Two
❑   Three
❑   More than three

10.   How much would you estimate was spent on the nomination campaign by

The eventual nominee $ _____
The runner up (if any) $ _____

Options for Reform

Which of the statements in the following pairs best represents your opinion? (Please check the appropriate response.)

1.   ❑   Party leaders should be chosen by delegate conventions as now.

OR

❑   Party leaders should be chosen not by convention but by a direct vote of all party members.

2. ☐ Election law should establish some common standards and principles to govern the *selection of leaders* in all parties which are officially registered under the law.

OR

☐ The parties should be left entirely on their own to decide by what standards and principles they will *select their leaders*.

3. ☐ Only those eligible to vote should be entitled to participate in meetings to elect delegates to leadership conventions.

OR

☐ All party members (including those under 18 years of age or non-Canadian citizens) should be entitled to participate in meetings to elect delegates to leadership conventions.

4. ☐ Election law should establish some common standards and principles to govern the *nomination of candidates* in all parties which are officially registered under the law.

OR

☐ The parties should be left entirely on their own to decide by what standards and principles they will *nominate their candidates*.

5. ☐ Only those eligible to vote should be entitled to participate in nomination meetings.

OR

☐ All party members (including those under 18 years of age or non-Canadian citizens) should be entitled to participate in nomination meetings.

6. Should there be legal spending limits for nomination contests in the way there are spending limits for election campaigns?

☐ Yes   ☐ No

If yes, what would be a reasonable limit? $ _____

7. Should there be legal spending limits for candidates in party leadership campaigns?

☐ Yes   ☐ No

8. Should leadership candidates be required to file detailed statements on how they spend their campaign funds?

☐ Yes   ☐ No

9. Should there be government reimbursements of certain eligible expenses (similar to those for general elections) for individuals running for a *party nomination?*

    ❏ Yes ❏ No

10. Should there be government reimbursements of certain eligible expenses (similar to those for general elections) for individuals running for *party leadership?*

    ❏ Yes ❏ No

11. Do you think that the tax credit arrangement now used for donations to political parties should be used to cover fund-raising for:

    Party leadership candidates

    ❏ Yes ❏ No

    Individuals running for a nomination

    ❏ Yes ❏ No

SECTION D: CONSTITUENCY ASSOCIATION CAMPAIGN ACTIVITY

Campaign Organization and Activity

1. How many volunteers do you require to run an effective local campaign in your constituency? _____

2. How many volunteers did you have in 1988? _____

3. Did your local campaign in the 1988 election have any paid staff?

    ❏ Yes ❏ No

    If yes,

    a) How many? _____

    b) Were they:

        ❏ Locals
        ❏ Some locals, some outsiders

❑ Outsiders

c)   What positions/activities were performed by the paid staff?

_____

_____

4.   Did your local campaign team have any individuals come in to help you from outside the constituency in 1988?

❑ Yes   ❑ No

If yes,

a)   How many? _____

b)   Were these outsiders (please check as many as appropriate):

         ❑   Volunteer workers
         ❑   Strategists/managers
         ❑   Paid organizers
         ❑   Other _____ (please specify)

c)   If the outsiders were paid, who paid them?

         ❑   Our constituency association
         ❑   The candidate
         ❑   The national/provincial party organization
         ❑   Private business
         ❑   Trade unions
         ❑   Interest groups
         ❑   Don't know
         ❑   Other _____ (please specify)

5.   Who appointed the local campaign manager?

         ❑   Local constituency party executive
         ❑   The candidate
         ❑   Provincial or national party official
         ❑   Other _____ (please specify)

6.   Was the campaign manager a regular member of your local constituency association?

❑ Yes   ❑ No

7. How would you describe the relationship between the local association executive and the local campaign team?

   ☐ Association executive maintains control
   ☐ Control completely delegated to the campaign team
   ☐ A balance between these two positions

8. Of the volunteers you had in your campaign team in 1988, what proportion would you say:

   _____ % are regular party members
   _____ % are regular financial contributors to your association
   _____ % worked in the 1984 general election
   _____ % were women

9. How would you rank in importance the following factors in attracting volunteers to your campaign? (Please rank 1 to 5.)

   _____ Local candidate
   _____ Opposition candidate
   _____ Party leader
   _____ Party policies
   _____ Traditional party loyalty

10. Why do you think people volunteer to work in election campaigns?

   _____

11. Please list in order of importance the most important tasks performed by volunteers in your campaign organization.

   1. _____
   2. _____
   3. _____

12. If you had a different candidate would you expect to have:

   ☐ Almost completely different group of volunteers
   ☐ Somewhat different group of volunteers
   ☐ Largely the same group of volunteers
   ☐ The very same group of volunteers

13. Do you think incumbents have any special advantages in local campaigns under our current system?

   ☐ Yes   ☐ No

If yes, what are the most important ones?

_____

_____

14. Did your riding association do any public opinion polling on its own in 1988?

◻ Yes   ◻ No

If yes, did the information change your local campaign?

◻ Yes   ◻ No

If yes, how?

_____

15. Do you think the publication of public opinion poll results makes any difference to the local contest?

◻ Yes   ◻ No

If yes, what is the major impact?

_____

16. Was your campaign organization:

◻ In place before the candidate was nominated
◻ Only set up after the candidate was nominated

17. Do the principal media in your area:

◻ Focus on the national campaign and ignore local contests
◻ Give balanced coverage of both local and national campaigns
◻ Focus mainly on the local candidates and campaign

18. How would you rate the following methods of communication in terms of their importance to your <u>local</u> constituency campaign? (Please check the appropriate box.)

	Very important	Somewhat important	Not too important	Important
Television	◻	◻	◻	◻
Radio	◻	◻	◻	◻
Newspapers	◻	◻	◻	◻

Cable television	❏	❏	❏	❏
Direct mail	❏	❏	❏	❏
All candidates meetings	❏	❏	❏	❏
Literature drops	❏	❏	❏	❏
Canvassing	❏	❏	❏	❏

19.   How satisfied were you with the media coverage of the local
       campaign in 1988?

   ❏   Very satisfied
   ❏   Satisfied
   ❏   Somewhat satisfied
   ❏   Not very satisfied

20.   How satisfied were you with the media coverage of your local *candi-
       date* in 1988?

   ❏   Very satisfied
   ❏   Satisfied
   ❏   Somewhat satisfied
   ❏   Not very satisfied

21.   Did any single-issue interest groups play an active role in the local
       campaign in an attempt to support or oppose your candidate?

   ❏ Yes   ❏ No

   If yes, what issue were they promoting or opposing?

   _____

Options for Reform
Please indicate what you think of the following proposals by indicating
opinions:

   1. Strongly favour
   2. Somewhat favour
   3. Somewhat oppose
   4. Strongly oppose

1.   The minimum share of the vote required to obtain an
      election expense reimbursement should be lowered
      from the current 15%.   _____
2.   Local election expense reports should list all paid
      staff with the amount of their remuneration.   _____

3.   Candidate deposits should be increased to at least $1,000
(from the current $200) to discourage nuisance candidates. _____

4.   Constituency parties should be required to alternate their
candidates between men and women so that if they run   _____
a man in one election, the next (new) candidate they
nominate would have to be a woman, and vice versa.   _____

5.   The party leader's right to veto a locally selected candidate
by refusing to approve the nomination (for ballot label
purposes) should be abolished.   _____

6.   Local expense limits restrict our ability to campaign
effectively and should be increased.   _____

SECTION E: CONSTITUENCY ASSOCIATION FINANCE AND FUND-RAISING

Here we have questions about associations' finances in the years between
elections. Please be as specific as possible.

Association Financing

1.   Please indicate which of the following methods of fund-raising your
local association regularly uses in nonelection years (Please check as
many as applicable.)

         ❏   Annual membership drive
         ❏   Personal canvassing
         ❏   Direct mail
         ❏   Social events
         ❏   Women's group activities
         ❏   Youth group activities
         ❏   Seminars; special events with a policy focus
         ❏   Other _____ (please specify)

2.   Which would you rate as the three most important for your association?

         1. _____
         2. _____
         3. _____

3.   Using 1989 and 1990 as recent nonelection year examples, what was
the total *income* of your local association?

1989		*1990*	
❏	Under $1,000	❏	Under $1,000
❏	$1,000–$4,999	❏	$1,000–$4,999

❏	$5,000–$9,999	❏	$5,000–$9,999
❏	$10,000–$19,999	❏	$10,000–$19,999
❏	$20,000–$39,999	❏	$20,000–$39,999
❏	$40,000+	❏	$40,000+

4. Please indicate which (if any) of the following are important costs for your association between elections. (Please check as many as relevant.)

   ❏ Office rental expenses
   ❏ Paid staff
   ❏ Printing and postage
   ❏ Organizing membership events
   ❏ Policy work
   ❏ Local PR activities
   ❏ Other _____ (please specify)

5. Which would you rate as the three most important for your association?

   1. _____
   2. _____
   3. _____

6. Using 1989 and 1990 as recent nonelection year examples, what were the total *expenses* of your local association?

   1989   *1990*

   ❏ Under $1,000   ❏ Under $1,000
   ❏ $1,000–$4,999   ❏ $1,000–$4,999
   ❏ $5,000–$9,999   ❏ $5,000–$9,999
   ❏ $10,000–$19,999   ❏ $10,000–$19,999
   ❏ $20,000–$39,999   ❏ $20,000–$39,999
   ❏ $40,000+   ❏ $40,000+

7. Did your association have an operating surplus or deficit in 1989 and 1990?

   1989 ❏ Surplus ❏ Deficit   Size $ _____
   1990 ❏ Surplus ❏ Deficit   Size $ _____

8. Please indicate what assets your local association owns in its own right.

   ❏ Office furnishings
   ❏ Computer

❏   Photocopying equipment
❏   Postage meter
❏   Telephone/answering machine
❏   Building/real estate
❏   Other _____ (please specify)

9.   What is the value of the funds your association currently has available to it?

     ❏   Under $1,000
     ❏ $1,000–$4,999
     ❏ $5,000–$9,999
     ❏ $10,000–$24,999
     ❏ $25,000–$49,999
     ❏ $50,000–$99,999
     ❏ $100,000–$249,999
     ❏   Over $250,000

     Are these funds:

     ❏   Held in local association accounts
     ❏   Held in trust by provincial or national party offices
     ❏   Some held locally, some by other party offices
     ❏   Held in accounts by local trustees

10.   Does your association generally help subsidize delegates to attend (please check as many as appropriate):

     ❏   Party meetings outside the riding
     ❏   Provincial-level conventions
     ❏   National-level conventions
     ❏   National leadership selection conventions
     ❏   None of these are supported with local association funds.

11.   During nonelection years is there:

     ❏   A net flow of funds from your local association to higher party levels
     ❏   A net flow of funds into your local association from higher party levels
     ❏   No significant flow of funds between the association and other party levels

12.   Has the growing use of national direct mail fund-raising campaigns by the parties:

     ❏   Hindered your local association's ability to raise money

❏   Helped local fund-raising by increasing awareness and interest

❏   Had no impact on your local fund-raising

13.   Does your local association:

      ❏   Freely share its mailing lists with central party offices

      ❏   Guard its own lists to protect its local fund-raising ability

14.   Do local party members complain about the number of appeals for party funds they now get?

      ❏ Yes   ❏ No

Options for Reform

Please indicate if you *agree* or *disagree* with the following proposals.

		Agree	Disagree
1.	Registered associations of political parties should be provided with office space and furnishings in government buildings.	❏	❏
2.	The government should provide matching funds up to some amount (for example, $5,000) raised locally to help local associations maintain a presence in the riding between elections.	❏	❏
3.	Limits should be set on the amount an individual could give to a constituency association in a given year.	❏	❏
4.	Only residents who are eligible to vote in a constituency should be allowed to donate to a local constituency party association.	❏	❏
5.	The national parties should not be allowed to use the tax credit arrangements to require associations to remit some proportion of locally raised funds to provincial and/or national offices.	❏	❏

SECTION F: CONSTITUENCY-LEVEL ELECTION EXPENSES

This section is primarily concerned with the operation of the current election expense system and your experience with it in 1988.

Election Expenses

1.   The election spending of federal candidates and parties is now limited by law, and detailed reporting on spending and contributions is required. In your view, are these rules:

      ❏   Very satisfactory

      ❏   Satisfactory

❏   Somewhat unsatisfactory
❏   Unsatisfactory

2.   Are these rules:

❏   Too permissive
❏   Too restrictive
❏   About right

3.   Some have complained that the current electoral expenses system is so complex that most campaign volunteers and workers cannot understand it. Has that been your experience?

❏ Yes   ❏ No

Does it really matter if most workers really can't follow the detailed rules?

❏ Yes   ❏ No

If yes, please indicate why.

_____

4.   Does the election expenses system now in place give your constituency association an incentive to shift certain expenditures and activities back into the pre-writ period?

❏ Yes   ❏ No

If yes, is this a good thing?

❏ Yes   ❏ No

What activities/expenditures occur earlier than they might otherwise?

1. _____
2. _____

5.   During the 1988 election year how much did your constituency association spend on all its activities from the beginning of the year (January 1) *until* the election was called (October 1)?

$ _____

6. During the 1988 general election what was the amount of spending (sometimes called "campaign expenses") incurred by the candidate on items that are not "election expenses" subject to limits under the *Canada Elections Act?*

    $_____

7. Please indicate what the main "campaign expenses" were used for.

    _____

8. During the 1988 general election, did your association receive financial support from:

    ❏   The national party
    ❏   The provincial (or territorial) party
    ❏   Other riding associations

9. During the 1988 general election did your association make financial donations to:

    ❏   The national party
    ❏   The provincial (or territorial) party
    ❏   Other riding associations

10. Please indicate the importance of each of the following methods of raising funds in your constituency *during* the 1988 election campaign.

    1. Very important
    2. Important
    3. Somewhat important
    4. Unimportant

    _____ Direct mail
    _____ Personal contact with individuals
    _____ Personal contact with businesses, unions, organizations
    _____ Fund-raising events (dinners, etc.)
    _____ Walk-in (unsolicited) donations
    _____ National party contributions
    _____ Provincial party contributions
    _____ Other riding associations
    _____ Candidate's contribution
    _____ Other _____ (please specify)

11. How important is the local candidate to the success of election fund-raising?

   ❏   Very important
   ❏   Important
   ❏   Somewhat important
   ❏   Not important

12. Does having a woman candidate hinder local election fund-raising?

   ❏ Yes ❏ No   ❏ No experience

13. Does having a visible-minority candidate hinder local election fund-raising?

   ❏ Yes ❏ No   ❏ No experience

14. How would you describe the attention or effort the local candidate must personally put into election fund-raising activities?

   ❏   Vital – a major task of candidates
   ❏   Important – consumes considerable time
   ❏   Intermittent – occasional role for candidates
   ❏   None – candidates must be kept out of it

15. Did your candidate or constituency association have to turn over all or part of the government reimbursement of election expenses to the national party?

   ❏ Yes   ❏ No

   If yes, what percentage? _____ %

   If yes, is any of it being held in trust for your association's use?

   ❏ Yes   ❏ No

16. Did your candidate's campaign have a financial surplus at the end of the 1988 election campaign?

   ❏ Yes   ❏ No

   If yes, how large was it? $_____

If yes, what was done with the surplus?

☐   Put into the constituency association's general accounts
☐   Put into the constituency association's trust account
☐   Turned over to the provincial level of the party
☐   Turned over to the national level of the party
☐   Other _____ (please specify)

17.   Who decided how the campaign surplus was to be disposed of?

☐   Candidate
☐   Constituency association's executive
☐   Party officials _____ (please specify)
☐   Other _____ (please specify)

18.   Did the local association spend more in 1988 in the period before the writ than it did in the election period itself?

☐ Yes   ☐ No

19.   How would you describe the main differences between election period fund-raising and nonelection year fund-raising for your constituency association?

_____

20.   Were association funds used to assist candidates for the nomination before they were nominated?

☐ Yes   ☐ No

If yes, how much was spent on this activity? $ _____

Options for Reform

Please indicate whether you *agree* or *disagree* with the following proposals to alter the current system.

		Agree	Disagree
1.	Abolish the distinction between election and campaign expenses and regulate total spending of all sorts.	☐	☐
2.	Forbid parties from requiring that government reimbursements of local expenditures be turned over to the national organization.	☐	☐
3.	Require all campaign surplus funds to be paid over to the local constituency association.	☐	☐

4.   Income and expenditure for nominations contests
should be regulated in the way those in elections are. ❐   ❐

5.   Income and expenditures of leadership campaigns
should be regulated in the way those in elections are. ❐   ❐

6.   Regulate party spending between elections as well
as during the campaign.   ❐   ❐

SECTION G: CONSTITUENCY ASSOCIATION PARTICIPATION

Many submissions to the Royal Commission spoke of the need to broaden
the base of participation in political parties. Could you please tell us about
your constituency association?

1.   Has your constituency association made a *special effort* to involve
any of the following groups in an attempt to increase their participation in the central affairs of the local party? (Please check as many as
appropriate.)

    ❐   Women
    ❐   Youth
    ❐   Visible minorities
    ❐   Aboriginal peoples
    ❐   Other _____ (please specify)
    ❐   No special efforts made

2.   Do groups of visible minorities exist in significant numbers in your
constituency?

    ❐ Yes   ❐ No

    If yes, have they become a factor in your constituency's politics?

    ❐ Yes   ❐ No

3.   Please indicate the gender of those holding the following positions
in your constituency association and whether they are a member of
a visible minority or not.

	Male	Female	Visible minority (please check if yes)
Constituency Assoc. President	❐	❐	❐
Constituency Assoc. Treasurer	❐	❐	❐
Constituency Assoc. Secretary	❐	❐	❐
1988 election candidate	❐	❐	❐
1988 election campaign manager	❐	❐	❐
1988 election candidate's agent	❐	❐	❐

Which statement in the following pairs best expresses your opinion?

4. ☐ The national parties talk a lot about increasing the participation of women but do little about it.

OR

☐ There is real pressure on our constituency association from the national office to increase the involvement of women in the party.

5. ☐ Complaints about a lack of opportunities for women are exaggerated. They could easily get ahead in our riding if they just got more involved.

OR

☐ It is harder for women in politics. Special provisions must be adopted by the parties to ensure fair and equal opportunity.

6. Do you think a woman would have a harder time being a candidate in your riding than a man?

☐ Yes   ☐ No

If yes, why? _____

DIFFERENCES IN THE ENGLISH AND FRENCH INSTRUMENTS

Some last-minute changes in the questionnaire got missed in the final translation of the questionnaire into French from the English original. They involve eight questions – four have slight variations in the response sets offered the respondent; two are matters where the translation is not as parallel as it might be; one question was simply omitted from the French version, and in the last case different questions were asked.

All of these differences are minor, and none involved questions that are important to the analysis in this study. It might be noted that, though respondents in bilingual and French-speaking constituencies received the questionnaire in both languages, 87.3 percent of all the respondents chose to answer the English version, so that these differences between the instruments are even less significant.

Full details of the coding protocol on the questions involved have been deposited with the data in the Royal Commission's archives, and can also be obtained from the author.

BIBLIOGRAPHY

ABBREVIATIONS

am.	amended
c.	chapter
en.	enacted
R.S.C.	Revised Statutes of Canada
S.C.	Statutes of Canada
s(s).	section(s)

Ames, H.B. 1905. "Electoral Management." *The Canadian Magazine* 25:26–31.

Archer, Keith. 1991. "Leadership Selection in the New Democratic Party." In *Canadian Political Parties: Leaders, Candidates and Organization,* ed. Herman Bakvis. Vol. 13 of the research studies of the Royal Commission on Electoral Reform and Party Financing. Ottawa and Toronto: RCERPF/Dundurn.

Axworthy, Thomas S. 1991. "Capital-Intensive Politics: Money, Media and Mores in the United States and Canada." In *Issues in Party and Election Finance in Canada,* ed. F. Leslie Seidle. Vol. 5 of the research studies of the Royal Commission on Electoral Reform and Party Financing. Ottawa and Toronto: RCERPF/Dundurn.

Bashevkin, Sylvia B. 1985. *Toeing the Lines: Women and Party Politics in English Canada.* Toronto: University of Toronto Press.

Bell, David V.J., and Catherine M. Bolan. 1991. "The Mass Media and Federal Election Campaigning at the Local Level: A Case Study of Two Ontario Constituencies." In *Reaching the Voter: Constituency Campaigning in Canada,* ed. David V.J. Bell and Frederick J. Fletcher. Vol. 20 of the research studies of the Royal Commission on Electoral Reform and Party Financing. Ottawa and Toronto: RCERPF/Dundurn.

Bell, David V.J., and Frederick J. Fletcher, eds. 1991. *Reaching the Voter: Constituency Campaigning in Canada.* Vol. 20 of the research studies of the Royal Commission on Electoral Reform and Party Financing. Ottawa and Toronto: RCERPF/Dundurn.

Bernier, Luc. 1991. "Media Coverage of Local Campaigns: The 1988 Election in Outremont and Frontenac." In *Reaching the Voter: Constituency Campaigning in Canada,* ed. David V.J. Bell and Frederick J. Fletcher. Vol. 20 of the research studies of the Royal Commission on Electoral Reform and Party Financing. Ottawa and Toronto: RCERPF/Dundurn.

Black, Edwin R. 1965. "Federal Strains Within A Canadian Party." *Dalhousie Review* 45 (3): 307–23.

Blake, Donald E. 1991. "Party Competition and Electoral Volatility: Canada in Comparative Perspective." In *Representation, Integration and Political Parties in Canada*, ed. Herman Bakvis. Vol. 14 of the research studies of the Royal Commission on Electoral Reform and Party Financing. Ottawa and Toronto: RCERPF/Dundurn.

Blake, Donald, R.K. Carty and Lynda Erickson. 1988. "Ratification or Repudiation: Social Credit Leadership Selection in British Columbia." *Canadian Journal of Political Science* 2:513–37.

———. 1991. *Grassroots Politicians: Party Activists in British Columbia.* Vancouver: University of British Columbia Press.

Brodie, Janine, with the assistance of Celia Chandler. 1991. "Women and the Electoral Process in Canada." In *Women in Canadian Politics: Toward Equity in Representation*, ed. Kathy Megyery. Vol. 6 of the research studies of the Royal Commission on Electoral Reform and Party Financing. Ottawa and Toronto: RCERPF/Dundurn.

Brook, Tom. 1991. *Getting Elected in Canada.* Stratford, Ont.: Mercury Press.

Canada. *Canada Elections Act*, S.C. 1969–70, c. 49, ss. 23(2)(*h*), 31(1)(*b*).

———. *Canada Elections Act*, R.S.C. 1970, c. 14 (1st Supp.), s. 70.1, en. 1973–74, c. 51, s. 12; am. 1980–81–82–83, c. 164, s. 14.

———. *Canada Elections Act*, R.S.C. 1985, c. E-2, ss. 24, 232, 310.

———. *Canadian Charter of Rights and Freedoms*, Part I of the *Constitution Act, 1982*, being Schedule B of the *Canada Act 1982 (U.K.)*, 1982, c. 11.

———. *Dominion Elections Act*, S.C. 1938, c. 46.

———. *Election Expenses Act*, S.C. 1973–74, c. 51.

Canada. Elections Canada. 1989. *Report of the Chief Electoral Officer of Canada as per Subsection 195(1) of the Canada Elections Act.* Ottawa: Minister of Supply and Services Canada.

Carty, R.K. 1988a. "Campaigning in the Trenches: The Transformation of Constituency Politics." In *Party Democracy in Canada: The Politics of National Party Conventions*, ed. George Perlin. Scarborough: Prentice-Hall.

———. 1988b. "Three Canadian Party Systems: An Interpretation of the Development of National Politics." In *Party Democracy in Canada: The Politics of National Party Conventions*, ed. George Perlin. Scarborough: Prentice-Hall.

———. 1991. "Official Agents in Canadian Elections: The Case of the 1988 General Election." In *Issues in Party and Election Finance in Canada*, ed. F. Leslie Seidle. Vol. 5 of the research studies of the Royal Commission on

Electoral Reform and Party Financing. Ottawa and Toronto: RCERPF/Dundurn.

Carty R.K., ed. 1992. *Canadian Political Party Systems: A Reader*. Peterborough, Ont.: Broadview Press.

Carty, R.K., and Lynda Erickson. 1991. "Candidate Nomination in Canada's National Political Parties." In *Canadian Political Parties: Leaders, Candidates and Organization*, ed. Herman Bakvis. Vol. 13 of the research studies of the Royal Commission on Electoral Reform and Party Financing. Ottawa and Toronto: RCERPF/Dundurn.

Carty, R.K., Lynda Erickson and Donald Blake. 1992. *Leaders and Parties in Canadian Politics*. Toronto: Harcourt Brace Jovanovich.

Christian, William, and Colin Campbell. 1990. *Political Parties and Ideologies in Canada*, 3d ed. Toronto: McGraw-Hill Ryerson.

Clarkson, Stephen. 1979. "Democracy in the Liberal Party: The Experiment with Citizen Participation Under Pierre Trudeau." In *Party Politics in Canada*, 4th ed., ed. Hugh G. Thorburn. Scarborough: Prentice-Hall.

Converse, Philip E., and Georges Depeux. 1966. "Politicization of the Electorate in France and the United States." In *Elections and the Political Order*, ed. A. Campbell, P. Converse, W. Miller and D. Stokes. New York: Wiley.

Courtney, John C. 1973. *The Selection of National Party Leaders in Canada*. Toronto: Macmillan of Canada.

———. 1978. "Recognition of Canadian Political Parties in Parliament and in Law." *Canadian Journal of Political Science* 11:33–60.

Duverger, Maurice. 1954. *Political Parties: Their Organization and Activity in the Modern State*. London: Methuen.

Dyck, Rand. 1989. "Relations between Federal and Provincial Parties." In *Canadian Parties in Transition: Discourse, Organization, and Representation*, ed. A.-G. Gagnon and A. Brian Tanguay. Scarborough: Nelson.

———. 1991. "Links between Federal and Provincial Parties and Party Systems." In *Representation, Integration and Political Parties in Canada*, ed. Herman Bakvis. Vol. 14 of the research studies of the Royal Commission on Electoral Reform and Party Financing. Ottawa and Toronto: RCERPF/Dundurn.

Eagles, M., J. Bickerton, A. Gagnon, and P. Smith. 1991. *The Almanac of Canadian Politics*. Peterborough, Ont.: Broadview Press.

English, John. 1977. *The Decline of Politics: The Conservatives and the Party System 1901–20*. Toronto: University of Toronto Press.

Epstein, Leon D. 1986. *Political Parties in the American Mold.* Madison, WI: University of Wisconsin Press.

Erickson, Lynda. 1991. "Women and Candidacies for the House of Commons." In *Women in Canadian Politics: Toward Equity in Representation,* ed. Kathy Megyery. Vol. 6 of the research studies of the Royal Commission on Electoral Reform and Party Financing. Ottawa and Toronto: RCERPF/Dundurn.

Ferejohn, John, and Brian Gaines. 1991. "The Personal Vote in Canada." In *Representation, Integration and Political Parties in Canada,* ed. Herman Bakvis. Vol. 14 of the research studies of the Royal Commission on Electoral Reform and Party Financing. Ottawa and Toronto: RCERPF/Dundurn.

Fraser, Graham. 1989. *Playing for Keeps: The Making of the Prime Minister, 1988.* Toronto: McClelland and Stewart.

Globe. 1887. "West Toronto Tories." 27 January, 5.

―――. 1926. "Dean of Parliament Beaten in Convention for South York Seat." 18 August, 1.

Globe and Mail. 1993. "Tories Shut Down Riding Association." 24 March.

Graham, Ron. 1986. *One-Eyed Kings: Promise and Illusion in Canadian Politics.* Toronto: Collins.

Hanson, Lawrence. 1992. Contesting the Leadership at the Grassroots: The Liberals 1990. In *Canadian Political Party Systems: A Reader.* ed. R.K. Carty. Peterborough, Ont.: Broadview Press.

Heintzman, D. Keith. 1991. "Electoral Competition, Campaign Expenditure and Incumbency Advantage." In *Issues in Party and Election Finance in Canada,* ed. F. Leslie Seidle. Vol. 5 of the research studies of the Royal Commission on Electoral Reform and Party Financing. Ottawa and Toronto: RCERPF/Dundurn.

Hirschman, Albert, 1970. *Exit, Voice, and Loyalty: Responses to Decline in Firms, Organizations, and States.* Cambridge, MA: Harvard University Press.

Johnston, Richard. 1980. "Federal and Provincial Voting: Contemporary Patterns and Historical Evolution." In *Small Worlds: Provinces and Parties in Canadian Political Life,* ed. David J. Elkins and Richard Simeon. Toronto: Methuen.

Johnston, Richard, André Blais, Henry Brady and Jean Crête. 1992. *Letting the People Decide: History, Contingency and the Dynamics of Canadian Elections.* Montreal and Kingston: McGill-Queen's University Press.

Katz, R.S., and P. Mair. 1992. "The Membership of Political Parties in European Democracies, 1960–1990." *European Journal of Political Research* 22:329–45.

Kirchheimer, Otto. 1966. "The Transformation of Western European Party Systems." In *Political Parties and Political Development,* ed. Joseph LaPalombara and Myron Weiner. Princeton: Princeton University Press.

Krashinsky, Michael, and William J. Milne. 1991. "Some Evidence on the Effects of Incumbency in the 1988 Canadian Federal Election." In *Issues in Party and Election Finance in Canada,* ed. F. Leslie Seidle. Vol. 5 of the research studies of the Royal Commission on Electoral Reform and Party Financing. Ottawa and Toronto: RCERPF/Dundurn.

Land, Brian. 1965. *Eglinton: The Election Study of a Federal Constituency.* Toronto: Peter Martin.

Laschinger, John, and Geoffrey Stevens. 1992. *Leaders and Lesser Mortals: Backroom Politics in Canada.* Toronto: Key Porter.

Latouche, Daniel. 1992. "Universal Democracy and Effective Leadership: Lessons from the Parti Québécois Experience." In *Leaders and Parties in Canadian Politics: Experiences of the Provinces,* ed. R.K. Carty, Lynda Erickson and Donald E. Blake. Toronto: Harcourt Brace Jovanovich.

Lee, Robert Mason. 1989. *One Hundred Monkeys: The Triumph of Popular Wisdom in Canadian Politics.* Toronto: Macfarlane Walter and Ross.

Massicotte, Louis. 1991. "Party Financing in Quebec: An Analysis of the Financial Reports of Parties, 1977–89." In *Provincial Party and Election Finance in Canada,* ed. F. Leslie Seidle. Vol. 3 of the research studies of the Royal Commission on Electoral Reform and Party Financing. Ottawa and Toronto: RCERPF/Dundurn.

Meisel, John. 1962. *The Canadian General Election of 1957.* Toronto: University of Toronto Press.

———. 1963. "The Stalled Omnibus: Canadian Parties in the 1960s." *Social Research* 30 (3): 367–90.

———. 1975. "Howe, Hubris and '72: An Essay on Political Elitism." In *Working Papers on Canadian Politics,* 2d enlarged ed. Montreal and Kingston: McGill-Queen's University Press.

———. 1979. "The Decline of Party in Canada." In *Party Politics in Canada,* 4th ed., ed. Hugh G. Thorburn. Scarborough: Prentice-Hall.

———. 1991. "Dysfunctions of Canadian Parties: An Exploratory Mapping." In *Party Politics in Canada,* 6th ed., ed. Hugh G. Thorburn. Scarborough: Prentice-Hall.

Meisel, John, ed. 1964. *Papers on the 1962 Election.* Toronto: University of Toronto Press.

Morley, J. Terence. 1988. "Annihilation Avoided: The New Democratic Party in the 1984 Federal General Election." In *Canada at the Polls,* 1984, ed. Howard Penniman. Durham, NC: Duke University Press.

Morley, Terry. 1991. "Paying for the Politics of British Columbia." In *Provincial Party and Election Finance in Canada*, ed. F. Leslie Seidle. Vol. 3 of the research studies of the Royal Commission on Electoral Reform and Party Financing. Ottawa and Toronto: RCERPF/Dundurn.

———. 1992. "Leadership Change in the CCF/NDP." In *Leaders and Parties in Canadian Politics: Experiences of the Provinces*, ed. R.K. Carty, Lynda Erickson and Donald E. Blake. Toronto: Harcourt Brace Jovanovich.

Morton, W.L. 1950. *The Progressive Party in Canada*. Toronto: University of Toronto Press.

Noel, S.J.R. 1987. "Dividing the Spoils: The Old and New Rules of Patronage in Canadian Politics." *Journal of Canadian Studies* 22 (2): 72–95.

Padget, Donald. 1991. "Large Contributions to Candidates in the 1988 Federal Election and the Issue of Undue Influence." In *Issues in Party and Election Finance in Canada*, ed. F. Leslie Seidle. Vol. 5 of the research studies of the Royal Commission on Electoral Reform and Party Financing. Ottawa and Toronto: RCERPF/Dundurn.

Paltiel, Khayyam Z. 1989. "Political Marketing, Party Finance and the Decline of Canadian Parties." In *Canadian Parties in Transition: Discourse, Organization, and Representation*, ed. A.-G. Gagnon and A. Brian Tanguay. Scarborough: Nelson.

Panebianco, Angelo. 1988. *Political Parties: Organization and Power*. Cambridge: Cambridge University Press.

Pelletier, Réjean. 1991. "The Structures of Canadian Political Parties: How They Operate" In *Canadian Political Parties: Leaders, Candidates and Organization*, ed. Herman Bakvis. Vol. 13 of the research studies of the Royal Commission on Electoral Reform and Party Financing. Ottawa and Toronto: RCERPF/Dundurn.

Perlin, George. 1980. *The Tory Syndrome: Leadership Politics in the Progressive Conservative Party*. Montreal and Kingston: McGill-Queen's University Press.

———. 1991a. "Attitudes of Liberal Convention Delegates Toward Proposals for Reform of the Process of Leadership Selection." In *Canadian Political Parties: Leaders, Candidates and Organization*, ed. Herman Bakvis. Vol. 13 of the research studies of the Royal Commission on Electoral Reform and Party Financing. Ottawa and Toronto: RCERPF/Dundurn.

———. 1991b. "Leadership Selection in the PC and Liberal Parties: Assessing the Need for Reform." In *Party Politics in Canada*, 6th ed., ed. Hugh G. Thorburn. Scarborough: Prentice-Hall.

Perlin, George, ed. 1988. *Party Democracy in Canada: The Politics of National Party Conventions*. Scarborough: Prentice-Hall Canada.

Power, C.G. 1966. *A Party Politician: The Memoirs of Chubby Power*, ed. Norman Ward. Toronto: Macmillan.

Preyra, Leonard. 1991. "Riding the Waves: Parties, the Media and the 1988 Federal Election in Nova Scotia." In *Reaching the Voter: Constituency Campaigning in Canada*, ed. David V.J. Bell and Frederick J. Fletcher. Vol. 20 of the research studies of the Royal Commission on Electoral Reform and Party Financing. Ottawa and Toronto: RCERPF/Dundurn.

Reid, Escott. 1936. "The Saskatchewan Liberal Machine before 1929." *Canadian Journal of Economics and Political Science* 2:27–40.

Sabato, Larry J. 1981. *The Rise of Political Consultants: New Ways of Winning Elections*. New York: Basic Books.

Sayers, Anthony M. 1991. "Local Issue Space in National Elections: Kootenay West–Revelstoke and Vancouver Centre." In *Reaching the Voter: Constituency Campaigning in Canada*, ed. David V.J. Bell and Frederick J. Fletcher. Vol. 20 of the research studies of the Royal Commission on Electoral Reform and Party Financing. Ottawa and Toronto: RCERPF/Dundurn.

Selle, Per, and Lars Svasand. 1991. "Membership in Party Organizations and the Problem of Decline of Parties." *Comparative Political Studies* 23:459–77.

Siegfried, André. [1906] 1966. *The Race Question in Canada*. Carleton Library Series, no. 29. Toronto: McClelland and Stewart.

Simpson, Jeffrey. 1980. *Discipline of Power: The Conservative Interlude and the Liberal Restoration*. Toronto: Personal Library.

——. 1988. *Spoils of Power: The Politics of Patronage*. Toronto: Collins.

Smith, David E. 1981. *The Regional Decline of a National Party: Liberals on the Prairies*. Toronto: University of Toronto Press.

Smith, David. 1985. "Party Government, Representation and National Integration in Canada." In *Party Government and Regional Representation in Canada*, ed. Peter Aucoin. Vol. 36 of the research studies of the Royal Commission on the Economic Union and Development Prospects for Canada. Toronto: University of Toronto Press.

Stanbury, W.T. 1991. *Money in Politics: Financing Federal Parties and Candidates in Canada*. Vol. 1 of the research studies of the Royal Commission on Electoral Reform and Party Financing. Ottawa and Toronto: RCERPF/Dundurn.

Stewart, Gordon. 1980. "Political Patronage Under Macdonald and Laurier 1878–1911." *American Review of Canadian Studies* 10 (1): 3–12.

Stewart, Gordon. 1982. "John A. Macdonald's Greatest Triumph." *Canadian Historical Review* 63 (1): 3–33.

———. 1986. *The Origins of Canadian Politics: A Comparative Approach.* Vancouver: University of British Columbia Press.

Tanguay, A. Brian, and Barry J. Kay. 1991. "Political Activity of Local Interest Groups." In *Interest Groups and Elections in Canada,* ed. F. Leslie Seidle. Vol. 2 of the research studies of the Royal Commission on Electoral Reform and Party Financing. Ottawa and Toronto: RCERPF/Dundurn.

Ward, Ian. 1991. "The Changing Organizational Nature of Australia's Political Parties." *Journal of Commonwealth and Comparative Politics* 29 (2): 153–74.

Warwick, M. 1990. *Revolution in the Mailbox.* Berkeley: Strathmoor Press.

Wearing, Joseph. 1981. *The L-Shaped Party: The Liberal Party of Canada 1958–1980.* Toronto: McGraw-Hill Ryerson.

———. 1988. *Strained Relations: Canadian Parties and Voters.* Toronto: McClelland and Stewart.

Whitaker, Reginald. 1977. *The Government Party: Organizing and Financing the Liberal Party of Canada, 1930–58.* Toronto: University of Toronto Press.

Williams, J. 1956. *The Conservative Party of Canada.* Durham, NC: Duke University Press.

Woolstencroft, Peter. 1992. " 'Tories Kick Machine to Bits': Leadership Selection and the Ontario Progressive Conservative Party." In *Leaders and Parties in Canadian Politics: Experiences of the Provinces,* ed. R.K. Carty, Lynda Erickson and Donald E. Blake. Toronto: Harcourt Brace Jovanovich.

Young, Walter D. 1969. *The Anatomy of a Party: The National CCF, 1932–1961.* Toronto: University of Toronto Press.

Zakuta, Leo. 1964. *A Protest Movement Becalmed: A Study of Change in the CCF.* Toronto: University of Toronto Press.

ACKNOWLEDGEMENTS

Care has been taken to trace the ownership of copyright material used in the text, including the tables and figures. The authors and publishers welcome any information enabling them to rectify any reference or credit in subsequent editions.

~

Consistent with the Commission's objective of promoting full participation in the electoral system by all segments of Canadian society, gender neutrality has been used wherever possible in the editing of the research studies.

THE COLLECTED RESEARCH STUDIES

VOLUME 1
Money in Politics: Financing Federal Parties and Candidates in Canada

W.T. STANBURY

Money in Politics: Financing Federal Parties and Candidates in Canada

VOLUME 2
Interest Groups and Elections in Canada
F. Leslie Seidle, Editor

JANET HIEBERT

Interest Groups and Canadian Federal Elections

A. BRIAN TANGUAY AND
BARRY J. KAY

Political Activity of Local Interest Groups

VOLUME 3
Provincial Party and Election Finance in Canada
F. Leslie Seidle, Editor

LOUIS MASSICOTTE

Party Financing in Quebec: An Analysis of the Financial Reports of Parties, 1977–89

DAVID JOHNSON

The Ontario Party and Campaign Finance System: Initiative and Challenge

TERRY MORLEY

Paying for the Politics of British Columbia

HUGH MELLON

The Evolution of Political Financing Regulation in New Brunswick

DOREEN P. BARRIE

Party Financing in Alberta: Low-Impact Legislation

VOLUME 4
Comparative Issues in Party and Election Finance
F. Leslie Seidle, Editor

HERBERT E. ALEXANDER

The Regulation of Election Finance in the United States and Proposals for Reform

CÉCILE BOUCHER   Administration and Enforcement of the
                                         Elections Act in Canada

VOLUME 11
*Drawing the Map: Equality and Efficacy of the Vote
in Canadian Electoral Boundary Reform*
   David Small, Editor

KENT ROACH   One Person, One Vote?
                                         Canadian Constitutional
                                         Standards for Electoral Distribution
                                         and Districting

HOWARD A. SCARROW   Apportionment, Districting and
                                         Representation in the United States

ALAN STEWART   Community of Interest in Redistricting

MUNROE EAGLES   Enhancing Relative Vote Equality
                                         in Canada: The Role of Electors in
                                         Boundary Adjustment

DOUG MACDONALD   Ecological Communities and
                                         Constituency Districting

ALAN FRIZZELL   In the Public Service: Representation in
                                         Modern Canada

DAVID SMALL   Enhancing Aboriginal Representation
                                         within the Existing System of
                                         Redistricting

VOLUME 12
Political Ethics: A Canadian Perspective
   Janet Hiebert, Editor

PIERRE FORTIN   Ethical Issues in the Debate on
                                         Reform of the *Canada Elections Act:*
                                         An Ethicological Analysis

VINCENT LEMIEUX   Public Sector Ethics

IAN GREENE   Allegations of Undue Influence in
                                         Canadian Politics

WALTER I. ROMANOW,   Negative Political Advertising:
WALTER C. SODERLUND   An Analysis of Research Findings
AND RICHARD G. PRICE   in Light of Canadian Practice

JANE JENSON   Citizenship and Equity: Variations
                                         across Time and in Space

COMMISSION ORGANIZATION

CHAIRMAN
Pierre Lortie

COMMISSIONERS
Pierre Fortier
Robert Gabor
William Knight
Lucie Pépin

SENIOR OFFICERS

Executive Director
Guy Goulard

Director of Research
Peter Aucoin

Special Adviser to the Chairman
Jean-Marc Hamel

Research
F. Leslie Seidle,
  Senior Research Coordinator

Legislation
Jules Brière, Senior Adviser
Gérard Bertrand
Patrick Orr

Coordinators
Herman Bakvis
Michael Cassidy
Frederick J. Fletcher
Janet Hiebert
Kathy Megyery
Robert A. Milen
David Small

Communications and Publishing
Richard Rochefort, Director
Hélène Papineau, Assistant
  Director
Paul Morisset, Editor
Kathryn Randle, Editor

Assistant Coordinators
David Mac Donald
Cheryl D. Mitchell

Finance and Administration
Maurice R. Lacasse, Director

Contracts and Personnel
Thérèse Lacasse, Chief

Editorial, Design and Production Services